Use It All

THE CORNERSMITH GUIDE TO A MORE SUSTAINABLE KITCHEN

Alex Elliott-Howery
& Jaimee Edwards

murdoch books

Sydney | London

SHOPPING BASKET 5

PAGE 149

- MUSHROOMS
- RICE
- KALE
- GREEN BEANS
- GRAPES
- DRIED FRUITS

SHOPPING BASKET 6

PAGE 179

- SILVERBEET
- BEEF BONES
- A BUNCH OF CELERY
- FROZEN PEAS
- CHICKPEAS
- CITRUS

SHOPPING BASKET 7

PAGE 211

- A WHOLE PUMPKIN
- BACON
- A BUNCH OF BEETROOT
- CARROTS
- WOODY HERBS
- DRIED BEANS
- PEARS
- BANANAS
- GINGER

SHOPPING BASKET 8

PAGE 243

- TOMATOES
- EGGPLANT, ZUCCHINI & CAPSICUM
- CHILLI
- BASIL
- MINCE
- STONE FRUITS

INTRODUCTION

We are living in complex and challenging times. Many of us fear for the future of our planet, and yearn for ways to make life simpler. We find ourselves drawn to long-lost skills and practices to ground and connect us in ways that are more ethical and sustainable. Because it is increasingly clear that the personal choices we make are political: amidst our busy lives, how and what we feed ourselves and our loved ones can make a difference.

Many of us are looking to reduce the amount of food waste that ends up in the bin each week, make better choices at the supermarket, save money and cut down on the ever-increasing volume of plastic and packaging that comes into our homes. We don't have time to cook every night, but we want mostly home-cooked food rather than takeaway or highly processed options. After years of experimenting and trying to find this balance, we can boil it down to this: buy less, buy whole, use it all.

We have been friends since our twenties and, back when our kids were small, we quickly realised that the question of 'what's for dinner' had bigger implications. We noticed that kitchen knowledge was increasingly being displaced by lots of packaging and so-called 'convenience'. Troubled by the state of the food system, we set to figure out how to feed our families efficiently, affordably and sustainably. We taught ourselves how to preserve, ferment and bake; and make pasta and butter. We learned how to shop and eat seasonally; which meat, eggs and milk to buy; which supermarket products to avoid and what to do with all the left-over half-eaten apples. As the kids got older and our work lives became busier, we now use this knowledge to run our kitchens at home in the most sustainable ways we can. Don't worry – there are still plenty of takeaway pizzas and the occasional fish finger in the freezer when life gets too busy. But, ultimately, we have learned that the only way to feed our families and friends quickly, economically and sustainably is to use it all.

When Alex and her husband James opened the first Cornersmith cafe in 2012, they wanted to show their customers how to eat seasonally; that a few well-chosen, simple ingredients could make the most memorable meal; and what preserving was all about and why it's still important. To take this idea further, the Cornersmith Cooking School opened in 2013, with the aim of teaching people just how relevant traditional skills are in modern, urban kitchens. We, along with a team of incredible teachers, have since taught thousands of people how to pickle and ferment; how to make jam, tofu and cheese; how to preserve tomatoes; and how to turn vegetable scraps into something delicious.

We talk endlessly with our students about how knowing your way around a kitchen saves money, reduces packaging, avoids food waste, is healthier and tastes better. Once you know how to use up a whole pumpkin or chicken, for instance, you'll be free from a dependency on expensive pre-cut and packaged portions. We want to equip people with the skills they need to get back into the kitchen and use whole ingredients for less wasteful and more sustainable and nutritious cooking.

But for all our love of cooking from scratch, we know that people are time poor and on a budget. The ability to pull a meal together quickly comes with knowledge of ingredients and flavours, and in our classes we spend as much time focusing on these things as we do the recipes. So, we start from there – ingredients and flavours – to show that every part of a vegetable, fruit or animal has value.

This book is the result of us trying to figure out how to eat sustainably, work full time and keep our sanity. It's the kitchen guide to modern food wisdom that we wish we had when we first started out. We hope it helps.

HOW TO USE THIS BOOK

Most cookbooks present one recipe after another, and – delicious and inspiring as they might be – each dish stands alone. To cook out of most cookbooks is to buy an enormous amount of ingredients, put a lot of time and energy into cooking a meal, eat it and then start all over again. While both of us have shelves that heave with cookbooks we love, we wanted to do something a bit different. We wanted to write recipes that were interrelated, driven by produce and totally focused on teaching readers how to make the most of what they buy. Not just for one recipe, but for many recipes. Not just for many recipes, but for a better way to shop and eat altogether.

The logic of this book is simple. Each chapter features a shopping basket of seasonal produce – an example of a weekly shop that contains a selection of well-chosen complementary ingredients. Vegetables and fruits are always central, with an emphasis on buying whole produce where possible. In addition, each basket features a different protein, such as fish, cheese, chicken or pulses, to create complete and nutritious meals. From there, you add your pantry staples. The idea is that a small shop should stretch far if you know what to buy and how to use it well.

Each basket features recipes that show you how to prepare and cook these ingredients, so you can plan the week's meals with flexibility and variety. Plus we've included plenty of tips and techniques that will extend your knowledge much further. Suggestions and creative ideas for pairing flavours mean that you aren't reproducing the same dinner over and over. We show you how to transform leftovers and cook in bulk so you don't have to start from scratch every night: look for ideas on how to use things up under the 'What to do with…' headings. We've also included hundreds of waste hacks to show you how to use every last bit of produce.

Throughout the book we feature 'foundation recipes': flexible recipes designed to make use of whatever you have in the cupboard or fridge. Think of these recipes as a general set of instructions that you can use as a framework to swap ingredients in and out. They've been devised so that like-for-like ingredients can be substituted for each other, subtly changing the flavour and texture of the meal, but not the end result. Not only does this mean you can use what you already have, but it also provides countless variations on a favourite dish.

Neither of us has the aspirational pantries you see on social media – in fact, our shelves would probably look bare to a lot of people. Our approach to the pantry is to keep it minimally stocked to avoid wastage, save money and space. This doesn't mean there is a scarcity of good food, but instead that we're stocked up with one version of each important staple, and not a whole lot of forgotten packets incubating moths. You don't need four different types of beans, six different flours or three types of cream in the house at one time. If you've got white beans one week, buy chickpeas the next and lentils the week after, and alter recipes to use what you already have rather than buying more to check off every ingredient. We encourage you to think of a recipe as a guided set of suggestions. If you are making something that calls for smoked paprika and you don't have it, don't go to the shops and buy it. Sweet paprika will do, or you could ditch it all together and add some more pepper.

Use the ideas in this book to help you run a more sustainable kitchen, from shopping to cooking and eating. Our hope is that the information here will enable you to look at a kilo of carrots, a dozen eggs or a bag of beef bones and five meal ideas will spring to mind. Using it all will change the way you shop, cook and eat.

*Storing vegetables well
makes them last longer*

HOW TO SHOP

Where possible, choose to shop small and local. If you can only buy at the big supermarkets, buy seasonally and buy Australian.

SEASONAL FRUIT AND VEGETABLES

Seasonal eating has always been at the very heart of Cornersmith's approach. Geographical differences affect seasonal availability and as our planet's weather changes, many crops are growing at different times of the year. For a guide to what's in season when, we recommend asking your grocer or getting online. As a rule of thumb, whatever is most plentiful and affordable at the market will be in season.

Throughout this book we provide suggestions for swapping out fruit and veg. We keep it simple: starchy vegetables are often cooked in the same way and can, therefore, be swapped in and out; you can usually substitute one member of the allium family (garlic, leeks, chives, etc.) for another; and most leafy greens can cover for each other. So make do with what is in season and what you already have in the house.

'UGLY' FRUIT AND VEG

So called 'ugly' fruit and vegetables are gaining in popularity. There is nothing actually wrong with this produce; they just tend to be a bit misshapen or wonky. Supermarkets choose produce that can be stored well for long periods of time and stacked uniformly. At Cornersmith, we have rescued many kilos of fruit and vegetables that have been rejected by supermarkets just because they didn't fit this criteria. In the past, this kind of produce went to landfill, but look out for these 'ugly' beauties where you shop as retailers are increasingly selling them off cheaper than the 'premium' product.

PACKAGING

We love bulk-food suppliers where we can take our own bags and containers and get all our basic goods. Make an effort to support these retailers, but if there isn't one near you there is plenty you can do to reduce packaging. Bring your own bags to the supermarket and stop using plastic bags. Choose pasta that comes in boxes, and buy bigger quantities of butter and yoghurt so you aren't doubling up on packaging. Buy whole vegetables, such as cabbage and pumpkin, whenever possible. Try not to buy pre-packed salads and herbs – they are often washed with all kinds of chemicals. And if you only have the big supermarket chains to choose from, make a noise and tell them you disapprove of their attitude towards plastic. It worked for shopping bags, so it can work for all single-use plastics.

ETHICAL MEAT AND ANIMAL PRODUCTS

Meat and dairy take huge amounts of resources to produce, so our approach is to only buy from trusted suppliers who take into account animal welfare and sustainable farming practices with minimal environmental impact. We advocate eating meat less frequently and in smaller amounts – making it the garnish rather than the hero of the meal. Our take on using dairy is to cut back; think of them as special ingredients and never waste a drop. Buy the best-quality dairy products you can afford, with the least amount of ingredients, and only buy what you need. Learn how easy it is to salt excess ricotta to make your own crumbly hard cheese, and save your parmesan rinds and use them to extract as much flavour as you can. Moving towards a diet with minimal animal products is probably the most sustainable choice we can make.

*Green sauces for using up
tired herbs (see pages 32–33)*

BROCCOLI

LEAFY GREENS

EGGS

SOFT HERBS

SHOPPING BASKET 1

We use this spring shopping list when we want to mostly eat vegetarian meals. It ticks all the boxes for easy and nutritious breakfasts, lunches, dinners and snacks. We love this selection because it's simple and economical, and all the ingredients can be stretched to the limit to feed many mouths. Remember that it's often the humblest of ingredients – well chosen and simply prepared – that bring the most pleasure at meal times.

PARMESAN

RHUBARB

RICOTTA

FROM THIS BASKET ...

MEALS

Baked eggs (page 21)

The best vegetable slice (page 23)

Tired broccoli toasties (page 25)

Green pockets (page 28)

Spinach and ricotta dumplings in lemon butter sauce (page 39)

SIDES

Charred broccoli (page 25)

Whole broccoli pesto (page 25)

The best green sauce (page 27)

What's-in-the-fridge tabbouleh-style salad (page 27)

Baked ricotta (page 37)

Rhubarb compote (page 41)

SNACKS, SWEETS & DRINKS

Whiskey sours (page 18)

Spicy nuts and seeds (page 18)

Coconut macaroons (page 18)

Strawberry curd (page 19)

Coral's parmesan biscuits (page 35)

Rhubarb compote (page 41)

Rhubarb and ricotta tea cake (page 42)

QUICK PRESERVING IDEAS

Cured egg yolks (page 19)

Salted left-over ricotta (page 37)

Roasted rhubarb cheat's relish (page 41)

Rhubarb ketchup (page 41)

NOTHING GOES TO WASTE

Mayonnaise (page 19)

Green sauces for using up tired herbs (page 32–33)

Parmesan rind broth (page 35)

Parmesan and cracker crumbs (page 35)

EGGS

Eggs get us from breakfast to dinner. We love them because they are economical, nutritious and simple to prepare. Some eggs are really cheap, while others are more expensive. In short, the price of an egg often reflects the quality of life of the chicken that laid it. Free range means that chickens have access to the outdoors during daylight hours and live on a farm with a low density of chickens per hectare. Sadly, the life of a factory-farmed chicken bears no resemblance to this. Even at the pricier end of the scale, a free-range egg is still often the least expensive source of good-quality protein you can eat.

Free-range eggs are widely available. Supermarkets will always carry a selection and at farmers' markets you can often buy eggs from the farmers themselves. There are great apps you can download that will tell you exactly how free range your eggs are, so being informed has never been easier.

Despite many years of having a reputation for being bad for your health, eggs (with their ability to elevate our levels of 'good' cholesterol) are now recommended as part of a healthy diet once more. And so they should be! Eggs are incredibly nutritious. They are high in vitamins A, B and folate, as well as phosphorous and amino acids. One egg provides 20 per cent of our daily recommended protein intake. They are true powerhouses.

Temperature fluctuations are not good for eggs. If you leave a cold egg out of the fridge, it will begin to sweat, which can encourage bacteria growth leading to egg contamination. As a rule of thumb, you should store eggs at the temperature you bought them, unless you live in a warm climate in which case it's recommended to store them in the fridge.

Keep your eggs in the cardboard container they came in, as this prevents them from losing moisture and absorbing the flavours of other foods in the fridge. Eggs will stay fresh for up to 6 weeks after laying, so check the use-by date on the carton.

USE IT ALL

Some recipes call for only whites or yolks to be used. Most of the time the remaining part of the egg gets stored in the fridge with the best of intentions, only to be forgotten. See overleaf for our guide on how to use up the whites and yolks.

WHAT TO DO WITH EGG WHITES

WHISKEY SOURS

Make these classic whiskey sours using two left-over egg whites.

Make a sugar syrup by dissolving 1½ tablespoons caster (superfine) sugar in 1½ tablespoons warm water. Pour 120 ml (4 fl oz) whiskey (or use bourbon or brandy) into a cocktail shaker along with 45 ml (1½ fl oz) lemon or lime juice, 2 egg whites and the sugar syrup. Fill with ice and shake vigorously, then strain and serve in fancy glasses, with a pickled grape (page 171) if you have it!

Makes 2

SPICY NUTS AND SEEDS

Coating nuts and seeds in egg whites help spices stick and make them crunchy when toasted. Toss through salads or enjoy them as a snack with a drink. They'll last for up to 1 week in an airtight container.

Preheat the oven to 160°C (315°F/Gas mark 2–3). Whisk an egg white until foamy, add 1½ teaspoons salt, 2 teaspoons caster (superfine) sugar and 3–4 teaspoons ground spices of your choice. Add 1 cup (140 g) mixed nuts and seeds and mix until they are well coated. Spread out on a baking tray lined with baking paper and roast for 15–20 minutes, until golden brown. Shake the tray every 3–4 minutes for even cooking.

Makes about 1 cup (140 g)

SPICE MIXES WE LIKE

- 2 teaspoons ground cumin, 1 teaspoon smoked paprika, pinch of cayenne pepper
- 1 teaspoon ground fennel seeds, 2 teaspoons lemon zest or powder (page 204), 1 teaspoon chilli flakes
- 2 teaspoons chopped fresh or dried rosemary, 1 teaspoon smoked paprika, 1 teaspoon freshly cracked black pepper

TOASTED MUESLI

Coat your muesli mix in egg white and spices then bake following the instructions in the previous recipe. We like ground cinnamon, nutmeg, allspice and orange zest or powder (page 204).

COCONUT MACAROONS

Make these in next to no time. They are light and chewy and perfect for afternoon tea.

Preheat the oven to 170°C (345°F/Gas mark 5) and lightly grease a baking tray. In a stand mixer or using electric beaters, beat 2 egg whites (80 g/2¾ oz) until soft peaks form. Little by little, add ½ cup (110 g) caster (superfine) sugar while continuing to beat the eggs until stiff peaks form. Beat until satiny, then fold through 1½ cups (90 g) shredded coconut. Drop teaspoons of the mixture onto the baking tray, and bake for 15–20 minutes. The longer they cook the chewier they will be.

Makes 16

WHAT TO DO WITH EGG YOLKS

CURED EGG YOLKS

This really simple preserving process turns left-over egg yolks into a flavour and texture similar to a hard cheese. Cured eggs yolks can be grated over salads, pasta, risotto, baked potatoes, and avocado or tomatoes on toast for an extra hit of nutty umami.

Combine 2 cups (560 g) pure salt and 2 cups (440 g) caster (superfine) sugar in a bowl and whisk well. Pour half the salt and sugar into a shallow dish. Make four egg yolk–sized indents in the salt and sugar and carefully place a yolk into each one (don't freak out if they break, it will still work!). Cover with the remaining salt and sugar, then cover the tray with plastic wrap and store in the fridge for 1 week.

Remove the yolks from the salt and sugar, rinse and pat dry with paper towel, then transfer to an oven rack. Pop into a preheated 60°C (140°F/Gas mark ¼) oven for 30 minutes or until the yolks are dry to touch (you want the yolks to be firm but not rock hard). Allow to cool and store in an airtight container in the fridge for up to 4 weeks. Grate as needed.

STRAWBERRY CURD

This tastes like old-fashioned strawberry ice cream and is amazing on pavlova, waffles and sponge cake.

Hull 125 g (4½ oz) strawberries and roughly chop. Using a stick blender or food processor, blitz the strawberries and 3 egg yolks to make a purée. Transfer to a small saucepan and add ⅔ cup (150 g) caster (superfine) sugar and the zest and juice of 1 lemon. Whisk over medium heat for 3–4 minutes, until the mixture thickens. Pour into a non-reactive bowl and whisk in 70 g (2½ oz) room-temperature butter until well combined. Allow to cool, then pour into a jar or airtight container and place in the fridge to set for a few hours or overnight. The curd should last 2 weeks and can be frozen, too!

Makes 1 x 300 ml (10½ fl oz) jar

MAYONNAISE

If you like, you can flavour your mayonnaise with a tablespoon of chopped preserved lemon rind, finely chopped dried chilli or fresh herbs – just add to the food processor with the egg yolks.

Place 2 room-temperature egg yolks, 1½ teaspoons white wine vinegar, ½ teaspoon Dijon mustard and a good pinch of salt in a food processor. With the motor running, very gradually pour in 1 cup (250 ml) good-quality vegetable oil in a thin, steady stream until you have a thick mayonnaise. Add a minced garlic clove to make aioli or flavour as above. Store in a clean jar in the fridge for up to 5 days.

Makes 1 x 300 ml (10½ fl oz) jar

WASTE TIP

Place egg yolks (or egg whites) in an airtight container and freeze for up to 1 year. Make sure you use them as soon as they are defrosted.

BAKED EGGS

FOUNDATION RECIPE

Serves 2

Breakfast for dinner is often the answer to having nutritious, home-cooked meals in a flash, and this dish is a great way to use up left-overs that you might have in the fridge or freezer. Here we use a simple base of sautéed greens, but see below for other ways you can transform your leftovers into dinner.

3 tablespoons olive oil
1 onion, thinly sliced
3 garlic cloves, crushed
1 long green chilli, thinly
   sliced (optional)
½ teaspoon spice
   fennel seeds
   cumin seeds
   ground coriander
¾ teaspoon salt
½ teaspoon freshly cracked
   black pepper
3–4 cups leafy greens
   English spinach
   silverbeet/Swiss chard with
    stems removed
   rocket (arugula)
½ cup (50 g) chopped pitted
   green olives
4 eggs
50 g (1¾ oz) ricotta
Chilli flakes, for sprinkling

Preheat the oven to 180°C (350°F/Gas mark 4).

Heat the olive oil in a small flameproof casserole dish or cast-iron frying pan over medium heat. Add the onion, garlic, green chilli (if using), spice, salt and pepper and sauté for 4–5 minutes, until the onion is soft and translucent.

Add the leafy greens of your choice and continue to sauté for about 3 minutes. Add the olives and stir through, then taste and adjust the seasoning.

Make four little indents in the mixture and crack an egg into each. Dollop the ricotta over the top and sprinkle with salt, pepper and a pinch of chilli flakes on each egg. Cover and bake in the oven for 15–20 minutes, checking from the 15 minute mark to ensure that the eggs don't overcook, until the eggs are just set.

COMBINATIONS WE LIKE

- Heat 2 cups baked beans (page 233) in the dish or pan with some chopped rosemary, then add the eggs and ¼ cup (25 g) grated parmesan before baking.

- Heat 2 cups mushroom bolognese (page 152) in the dish or pan, then add the eggs and crumble over ¼ cup (55 g) goat's cheese before baking. Serve with a handful of chopped dill scattered over the top.

- Heat 2 cups ratatouille (page 252) in the dish or pan, then add the eggs and ¼ cup (40 g) feta before baking. Tear over a handful of basil before serving.

THE BEST VEGETABLE SLICE

Serves 4–6

Eggs bind other ingredients as they cook, and what you might think are a few random bits and pieces – half a broccoli, a few sprigs of parsley – can become a complete meal when combined with eggs. This recipe is for those occasions when you have a few ingredients left over in the fridge and you want to make them taste great with little effort. Eat it the next day for breakfast, pop it in your lunchbox or gobble it up on a crusty roll with green leaves and plenty of chutney.

Olive oil
140 g (5 oz) chopped/sliced veg
  onion (1 small)
  sliced leeks and their tops
  finely sliced fennel
  thinly sliced capsicum (pepper)
2–3 garlic cloves, crushed
500 g (1 lb 2 oz) grated vegetables
  (a mix works well)
  cauliflower and stems
  broccoli and stems
  zucchini (courgette)
  potato
  mushrooms
1 cup (30 g) chopped soft herbs
  or leafy greens
  parsley
  dill
  rocket (arugula)
  baby or English spinach
1 cup (100 g) grated parmesan
130 g (4½ oz) self-raising flour
6 eggs
¼ teaspoon salt
¼ teaspoon freshly cracked
  black pepper

Preheat the oven to 180°C (350°F/Gas mark 4).

Brush a 20 x 25 cm (8 x 10 inch) baking dish with a little olive oil and line the base with baking paper.

Heat 1 tablespoon of olive oil in a frying pan over medium heat. Add the chopped or sliced vegetables and garlic and sauté for 5–10 minutes, until soft, translucent and sweet. Transfer the mixture to a large bowl.

Squeeze out any excess liquid from the grated vegetables, then add to the sautéed vegetables, along with the herbs or leafy greens. Stir through the parmesan and flour.

In a separate bowl, whisk the eggs until fluffy, then add to the vegetable mixture. Season with the salt and pepper and gently combine. Pour the mixture into the prepared tin and smooth the top with the back of a spoon.

Bake for 30–40 minutes, until firm to the touch. Serve hot out of the oven or allow to cool and store in an airtight container in the fridge for up to 4 days.

COMBINATIONS WE LIKE

These flavours work really well together:

- Capsicum (pepper), cauliflower, potato and parsley
- Onion, zucchini (courgette), broccoli and English spinach
- Leek, mushroom and dill.

BROCCOLI

Broccoli belongs to the cruciferous family, along with kale, cauliflower, brussels sprouts, bok choy and turnips. It is packed full of nutrients and is particularly high in vitamins C and K. It's so good for you it should be on high rotation in all your meals when in season. If you're struggling to get enough greens into your diet, go hard on the broccoli.

Broccoli is great in cold and warm salads, charred on the barbecue, in a pesto and in fritters and vegetable slices. Broccoli florets are not good for preserving, as they end up smelling too sulphurous in the jar; however, never throw the stems away, as they make the most delicious quick pickles.

It's best to wash broccoli just before eating, rather than washing and then storing it, as it doesn't last as well. To store, wrap the unwashed head loosely in a damp cloth or beeswax wrap, leaving the stem free, and refrigerate. Do not store broccoli in a sealed container or plastic bag, as it needs to breathe.

To wash broccoli well, fill your sink with water and add 1 teaspoon salt or bicarbonate of soda (baking soda), or 3 tablespoons vinegar. Soak for a few minutes, then rinse and prepare.

GOES WITH …

Broccoli goes well with its brassica pals brussels sprouts, cauliflower, kale and bok choy. Being part of the mustard family, it also pairs well with bitey flavours, such as Dijon or grain mustard, horseradish, garlic and ginger. Broccoli has a green, grassy flavour that lifts with a little lemon zest or juice, anchovies, preserved lemon or soy sauce, or mellows with creamy additions, such as butter, cream, nuts and cheeses. Broccoli also loves soft and woody herbs so be liberal with your garnishes.

WASTE TIP

Revive tired broccoli by cutting it into pieces with the stem attached and soaking in a bowl of ice-cold water in the fridge for 30 minutes. Drain, dry and use.

USE IT ALL

Broccoli stems are sweet and flavoursome. Add them to stir-fries, use them in pestos or thinly slice and quick-pickle them (using the method for cauliflower stems on page 102).

CHARRED BROCCOLI

We serve this dish at home at least once a week when broccoli is cheap. It's great as a side, tossed through pasta, on toast with ricotta or on top of a homemade pizza. Leftovers are good for 3 days; just give them a flash in a hot pan before serving.

Blanch 1 head broccoli, cut into florets with stems attached, in salted boiling water for 2 minutes or until bright green. Drain and run under cold water, then set aside to dry. Heat 2 tablespoons olive oil in a frying pan over medium–high heat. Add the dry broccoli and sauté for 5–8 minutes, until the edges become a little charred. Add a few tablespoons of chopped olives or capers, or 1 tablespoon finely chopped preserved lemon rind. Anchovies work well, too. Add 1–2 finely chopped garlic cloves, some lemon zest and juice and a few pinches of salt and black pepper. Sauté until it smells delicious and the broccoli is a little soft. Turn off the heat, add chopped herbs of your choice and serve.

If serving over pasta, cook the broccoli for a little longer, covered over low heat, until starting to collapse.

Serves 4 as a side

TIRED BROCCOLI TOASTIES

These toasties were invented in our work kitchen. We pulled some rather limp broccoli from the cool room and used up the last of the ricotta to make what's become a favourite lunch for all the picklers.

Preheat the oven to 160°C (315°F/Gas mark 2–3). Roughly chop 1 head of broccoli into florets, keeping the stems attached, and place in a bowl with 3 tablespoons olive oil, ¼ teaspoon each of salt and pepper and ½ teaspoon chilli flakes. Mix well, spread onto a baking tray and bake for 15 minutes until soft. Remove from the oven and allow to cool. Slather ricotta on slices of sourdough, pile on the broccoli, add a few tablespoons of sliced pickled onion and top with more sourdough. Brush the outsides of the bread with oil or butter and toast in a sandwich press or frying pan until golden.

Makes 3–4

Whole broccoli pesto

WHOLE BROCCOLI PESTO

An almost genius way to serve broccoli without the broccoli haters even knowing. Serve it as you would any herb pesto. We use it as a pasta sauce or you could spoon it over baked potatoes, dollop onto your minestrone, spread on toast for breakfast with a fried egg, or use as a condiment with fritters, slices or in sandwiches.

Wash 250 g (9 oz) broccoli well and chop the florets and stems into pieces. Blanch for 2 minutes in a saucepan of salted boiling water. Drain and run under cold water, then set aside. Place ¼ cup (40 g) almonds or cashews (roasted if you have them), 2 garlic cloves, ½ cup (10 g) flat-leaf parsley (or basil in summer), ½ cup (50 g) grated parmesan, the zest and juice of ½ lemon, 1 teaspoon salt and ½ teaspoon black pepper in a food processor. Add the broccoli and blitz to a chunky pesto. Drizzle in ½ cup (125 ml) olive oil and blitz again.

Stir the pesto through hot pasta with lots of olive oil and more parmesan. Any left-over pesto will keep in a jar in the fridge for up to 1 week.

Makes about 2 cups

LEAFY GREENS

Leafy greens are one of the first signs of spring. English spinach, rocket (arugula), leaf chicory, dandelion – and even the distinctly not green radicchio – brighten every meal. Make them the foundations of salads and slaws, thinly slice them for fritters and our green pockets on page 28, or purée them to make green sauces and pestos. If you can, grow greens in your garden or in a pot on the balcony and you'll always have a leaf or two to add to your meals, with no wastage or packaging.

When it comes to nourishment, vibrant leafy greens knock everything else out of the ring. With spectacular levels of vitamins and minerals, Popeye was really on to something with his spinach-only diet.

English spinach is a favourite and it makes us feel like super-parents seeing the children eat it all week. For a peppery bite, use rocket (arugula), dandelion or leaf chicory. Rainbow and regular silverbeet are also great options in the cooler months (see pages 181–85 for more on silverbeet).

Leafy greens don't last well if they're not stored correctly, so buy less more frequently, and don't let them turn to mush at the back of the fridge. How long they last will depend on how sturdy the leaves are – English spinach won't last as long as silverbeet (Swiss chard), for example.

When stored properly, leafy greens will stay fresh and crunchy for ages. Roll them tightly in a slightly damp tea towel and tuck the ends in. Store them in a sealed container, calico bag or plastic bag in the fridge and you'll be shocked at how long they last. This method is great for herbs too (just not basil or mint).

GO WITH ...

Most leafy greens have a bitter flavour that can range from mild to scowl-inducing. This bitterness stimulates both appetite and digestion, making even the simplest leaf salad essential at the table. To balance bitterness and grassy tastes, pair leafy greens with fruits such as apple, pear, peach and grapes, and creamy nuts such as walnuts, pine nuts and almonds. Leafy greens always go well with soft cheeses, eggs and meats with a sweeter flavour, such as bacon and ham.

WASTE TIP

Don't forget you can add a handful of tired rocket or baby spinach to pestos and green sauces. Once puréed, no one will notice they were wilted!

THE BEST GREEN SAUCE

This bright green sauce, a recipe from our friend Margi, takes about 15 minutes to make and adds plenty of colour and a hit of iron to your plate. It's great to have in the fridge for quick nutritious meals and is a wonderful way to use up a bunch of forgotten greens.

Steam 1 bunch English spinach (stems and all) or ½ bunch silverbeet leaves (remove the stems and reserve to make sautéed silverbeet stems, page 183) in a large saucepan, covered, over low heat. Once soft, turn off the heat and allow to cool. Transfer to a food processor with a clove of chopped garlic, 3 tablespoons olive oil, 1 teaspoon plain (all-purpose) flour and ¼ teaspoon salt and black pepper. Whiz until blended, then add a slurp of milk or cream and whiz again until smooth. If it doesn't look smooth enough, add some more oil and whiz some more. Taste, adjust the seasoning and store in the fridge for 3–4 days.

Makes about 200 ml (7 fl oz)

GREEN EGGS

Add 2 tablespoons green sauce to 2 eggs and whisk with a pinch of salt and pepper. Cook in a saucepan with a knob of butter over a low heat until scrambled. Serve on toast.

GREEN PASTA

Combine 3 tablespoons green sauce with 2 tablespoons cream, extra salt and pepper, lemon zest and chilli flakes to make a simple pasta sauce.

GREEN TOAST

Mash a few tablespoons of green sauce with avocado, then spread on toast and top with crumbled feta and herbs.

GREEN MARINADE

Mix together equal parts natural or Greek-style yoghurt and green sauce with some extra minced garlic and a squeeze of lemon for a marinade for chicken thighs or fish.

Green eggs

WHAT'S-IN-THE-FRIDGE TABBOULEH-STYLE SALAD

This recipe is inspired by how tabbouleh is made, balancing the flavours and textures of greens and grains with a tangy dressing. Use this recipe as a guide, combining something green and bitter, something from the onion family, something crunchy and fresh, such as cucumber or tomato, and a small amount of grains.

Roughly chop 100 g of any combination of leafy greens and herbs – such as baby spinach, rocket (arugula), English spinach, curly endive (frisee), watercress, parsley, dill, coriander (cilantro), celery leaves or fennel fronds – and place in a large bowl. Add a handful of finely sliced red onion, shallot or spring onion and 1 cup finely chopped tomato or cucumber, pomegranate seeds or red grapes. Add 1 cup cooked bulghur, brown rice, farro or quinoa, then gently mix with 2 tablespoons of your best extra virgin olive oil, the juice of ½ lemon, ½ teaspoon salt and a generous grind of black pepper. Mix again with your hands to make sure everything is lightly coated in the dressing.

Serves 3–4 as a side

GREEN POCKETS

Makes 8

These green pockets are the ultimate fast food! They are our version of gozleme and we've been making them for years. If it's the weekend we'll make the simple yoghurt dough, but on a weeknight we'll pick up a pack of Greek pitas (the thicker, doughy sort) or souvlaki bread on the way home from work. We love this interpretation of gozleme because everything goes into the pocket uncooked. It is truly a 15-minute meal. When things get desperate we've even been known to put bolognese in there, with not a green leaf in sight. Of course, the kids loved it.

2 cups (100 g) very thinly
    sliced green leaves
    English or baby spinach leaves
    silverbeet (Swiss chard) leaves
    kale leaves
    rocket (arugula)
⅓ cup (10 g) finely chopped
    soft herbs
    mint
    dill
    parsley
200 g (7 oz) cheese
    ricotta
    crumbled feta
    grated haloumi
    grated mozzarella
⅔ cup (70 g) grated parmesan
½ teaspoon salt
100 ml (3½ fl oz) olive oil
Lemon wedges, to serve

SPICED ONION (OPTIONAL)

½ small onion, very finely diced
2 garlic cloves, minced
½ teaspoon ground cumin
pinch freshly cracked black pepper
1 teaspoon salt
2 teaspoons dried herbs, such as
    oregano, mint or basil

SIMPLE YOGHURT DOUGH

1 tablespoon vegetable oil
1 teaspoon white wine vinegar
1 cup (250 g) Greek-style yoghurt
2½ cups (375 g) plain (all-purpose)
    flour, plus extra for dusting
1 teaspoon bicarbonate of soda
    (baking soda)

Combine the greens and herbs in a bowl. In a separate bowl, combine the cheeses and salt. You can leave the mixture here and it will be yummy and family friendly, but if you want to take it up a notch, it's worth the extra 5 minutes to make the spiced onion; simply combine the ingredients in a small bowl and set aside.

To make the yoghurt dough, combine the oil, vinegar and yoghurt in a bowl and mix well. Sift in the flour and bicarb soda and mix with a wooden spoon until all the ingredients come together to form a dough. Tip out onto a floured work surface and knead for 10 minutes or until very smooth. Divide the dough into eight balls and place under a damp tea towel. Working with one ball of dough at a time, roll the dough into 15 cm (6 inch) circles.

To assemble, spread 2 tablespoons of the cheese mixture over half of each dough circle (or pita bread) and scatter 2–3 teaspoons of the spiced onion mixture (if using) on top. Add ½ cup of the greens and herb mixture, then fold the dough over to make a semicircle. If using homemade dough, pinch the edges to seal. If using pita, wet your hands and dampen the outside of each pocket and seal as best as you can.

Heat the olive oil in a frying pan over medium heat. Working in batches, pan-fry the pockets for 2–3 minutes each side, until golden brown. You can also brush each pocket with olive oil and grill them on the barbecue.

Serve with a squeeze of lemon and a salad if you can be bothered, but there's so many greens inside you hardly need to.

COMBINATIONS WE LIKE

- Kale, parsley, feta and chilli flakes
- Rocket (arugula), mint, haloumi and lemon zest or chopped preserved lemon rind
- Baby spinach, basil, mozzarella and parmesan.

SOFT HERBS

We define soft herbs as being, well, soft … with soft leaves and edible stems. These herbs have a higher water content than other herbs and are lower in aromatic oils. For this reason, they tend to have less flavour when dried, so use them fresh and in abundance.

For the most part, we add soft herbs at the end of cooking to retain their flavour – think of them as a way to liven and freshen up cooked meals. We also add them by the bunch to salads, and Alex uses every kind of soft herb (even the limp, neglected bunches at the bottom of the crisper) to make a whole spectrum of versatile green sauces and pestos (see pages 32–33). Like all leafy vegetables, soft herbs are high in vitamins A, C and K, and each herb is also prized for its medicinal properties, which we extract in home-brewed healing teas (page 229).

Soft green herbs are very delicate and need to be cared for – unfortunately, neglect means they are one of the most wasted ingredients bought at the supermarket. If you can, buy small amounts regularly and please try not to buy herbs wrapped in plastic. Smaller grocers with a high turnover will often sell herbs in bunches without plastic. Even better, grow your own herbs and pick the leaves as you need them.

You can store herbs in a glass of water on the benchtop or in the fridge for a few days. For longer storage, gently wrap them in a slightly damp tea towel and then place in a bag or airtight container in the fridge for 5–7 days. Check on them daily. Mint and basil are the exception here, as their tender, warmth-loving leaves turn black in the cold. Cut stems should be stored in a glass of water in dappled light on the benchtop. Make sure there are no leaves below the water level.

USE IT ALL

If you're left with a small amount of fresh herbs to use up, don't bin them! Chop finely, pop into an ice-cube tray, top with olive oil and freeze. Defrost and use in a salad dressing or add a cube to a hot pan before sautéing fish or potatoes.

KITCHEN FAVOURITES

BASIL

Basil is special and gets its own entry (page 262).

PARSLEY

We use flat-leaf parsley. You hardly see poor old curly-leaf parsley these days, and the flat-leaf variety has more flavour anyway. Parsley has a grassy freshness that goes with just about everything, and pairs well with all other soft herbs. It is particularly good with seafood, potatoes, garlic and eggs.

Nibble parsley to freshen your breath and eat it to eliminate water retention. Parsley stems freeze well and are indispensable in stocks and green sauces.

CHIVES

Common enough but not shy in flavour, chives have a strong allium taste. They are most punchy when freshly snipped, so grow them if you can. Use only as a garnish as their flavour does not hold up in cooking. They go well with cheese and sour cream, and pair perfectly with eggs, potatoes, leafy greens, green beans and white fish.

CORIANDER

Warm and a little citrusy, coriander has travelled the world and appears in many cuisines. One of the best things about a bunch of coriander is the changes in flavour along the stem. The leaves are bright and fresh-tasting, the stems a little more grassy, while the roots have a deeper, more intense flavour. You can save the stems and roots and add them to the spicy kitchen scrap paste on page 239 or the chimichurri on page 33. Coriander is also said to stimulate the appetite.

DILL

The scent and flavour of dill is reminiscent of aniseed. Jaimee, who grew up with a Russian mother and grandmother, remembers everything in her childhood tasting of dill. It goes without saying that dill and sour cream are meant to be; the same is true for cream and yoghurt. Dill goes well with other acidic foods, such as lemon and vinegar, and is therefore a classic addition when it comes to pickling. It is also very good with potatoes, tomatoes, beetroot, cucumber and white fish. Dill is said to calm an upset tummy and act as a mild sedative. We like to add dill stems to our pickled cucumbers and sauerkraut.

MINT

The very definition of a fresh and cooling ingredient, mint is easy to buy, but it's even easier to grow. Its natural sweetness is perfect with fruits, as well as being a great foil to really spicy foods. Add it to the plainest salad (we're talking iceberg lettuce and cucumber) and suddenly you have something perfectly simple and fragrant. Mint is lovely with peas, potatoes, garlic, strawberries and watermelon. There is also plenty of flavour in mint stems and you can use them to flavour a sugar syrup to use in cocktails (page 263).

TARRAGON

Along with dill, tarragon is another flavour from Jaimee's childhood. Tarragon has an aniseed flavour and is pleasantly sour. It goes well with mustard, mushrooms, asparagus and oily fish. We also like it chopped and mixed through mayonnaise in a chicken sandwich. We put tarragon stems with a pinch of salt and sugar into a jar of white wine vinegar and let it sit for a few weeks to flavour the vinegar.

GREEN SAUCES FOR USING UP TIRED HERBS

SPICY GREEN THAI-STYLE SAUCE

Stir through noodle salads or serve with seafood or rice paper rolls.

In a food processor, place 1 cup (50 g) coriander (cilantro) leaves and stems, 1 tablespoon grated ginger, 1 garlic clove, 1–2 long green chillies, 2 tablespoons fish sauce, 2 teaspoons caster (superfine) sugar, ¼ teaspoon salt and the zest and juice of 1 lime. Blitz until chopped but not as smooth as a pesto. If you want to make this a dipping sauce, loosen the mixture with about 1 tablespoon good-quality vegetable oil or more fish sauce. It will keep in a jar in the fridge for up to 2 weeks.

Makes about 1 cup (170 g)

PESTO

Alex believes a house is not a home without pesto in the fridge. Use this base recipe to make a pesto out of any small amount of left-over greens.

Place 80 g (2¾ oz) herb leaves or greens, 40 g (1½ oz) nuts or seeds, 1 garlic clove, 40 g (1½ oz) grated parmesan (if using) and a pinch or two of salt in a food processor and blitz to a paste. With the motor running, add 100–150 ml (3½–5 fl oz) olive oil until well combined. Transfer to a clean jar and store in the fridge for up to 10 days.

Makes about 1 cup (200 g)

COMBINATIONS WE LIKE

- Parsley, walnut, lemon zest and 1 tablespoon lemon juice
- Celery leaves, cashews and parmesan
- Kale, sunflower seeds and parmesan
- The broccoli pesto on page 25

SALSA VERDE

This is lovely with ricotta or goat's cheese on toast, oily fish, a lentil stew or roasted carrots. Or add green chillies and a pinch of ground cumin, coriander and paprika and serve it with tacos or on tortillas.

In a food processor, place 75 g (2½ oz) herbs such as parsley, dill, mint, basil or fennel fronds with 2 small garlic cloves, ⅓ cup (75 g) chopped pickles such as cucumber, dill pickle (gherkin), fennel or jalapeños, 2 tablespoons pickle juice, 2 tablespoons capers or the zest and juice of 1 lemon or lime, a pinch of chilli flakes (or a Thai green chilli if you like heat) and ¼ teaspoon salt. Pulse until roughly chopped, then taste and balance the flavours by adding more salt, some extra chilli or a pinch of sugar if needed. Once you're happy with the flavour, add ⅓ cup (80 ml) olive oil and briefly blitz again until just combined. You can also make this by hand: finely chop the ingredients, then combine in a bowl with the oil. Store in a jar or container in the fridge for 7–10 days.

Makes about 1 cup (250 ml)

CHIMICHURRI

This Argentinian herb sauce is used in cooking and as a table condiment for grilled meats. At Cornersmith, we make our own version whenever we have a load of coriander (cilantro), dill and parsley stems that we don't want to throw out. This recipe comes from our friend and long-time chef, Sabine. It's an absolute winner and we make it almost every week to top tacos and pitas, drizzle over roasted vegetables, marinate chicken or serve with grilled fish. Add a few tablespoons to a salad dressing for your next slaw.

Place about 80 g (2¾ oz) herb leaves and stems – use one type or a mix of coriander, parsley and dill – in a food processor with ½ teaspoon cumin seeds, 1 chopped garlic clove, 2 tablespoons red wine vinegar, ¼ teaspoon salt and a pinch of chilli flakes if you want a little heat. Blend to a paste, then with the motor running, add 100 ml (3½ fl oz) olive oil until combined. Pour into a jar or container, cover with oil and seal. Store in the fridge for up to 2 weeks.

Makes about 1 cup (250 ml)

PARMESAN

From the rearing of animals and milking, to the making and storing, intensive dairy production comes at a hefty environmental cost. To reduce your dairy intake, think of parmesan as you would saffron or truffles – use it wisely to enhance meals, and don't waste a scrap.

We use Australian parmesan, which is a hard, aged cheese made from cow's milk with a thick rind. It's not authentic Parmigiano Reggiano, but we are lucky enough to have some great cheesemakers in Australia who are producing a strong and sharp cheese to savour. We have learned how to use parmesan from Italian home cooks, who save the rinds to use in soups and stews to add flavour, then remove them, dry them off and use them again and again. Treat parmesan as the precious thing it is, and make a little go a long way.

Parmesan's granular and crumbly texture makes it hard to cut finely. It's much easier to grate parmesan or use a vegetable peeler to add shavings to salads. Use very finely grated parmesan to thicken soups and stews, and add it to fritters and meatballs to both bind ingredients and season. Don't buy pre-grated parmesan! Buy it by the block and grate it just before serving; this way the flavour is at its most intense and you'll need less.

In the health department, parmesan is high in protein and calcium, so it is good for your bones.

Store hard cheeses, such as parmesan, in a waxed wrap or cloth to prevent them from 'sweating' and being exposed to the air and turning white. If this happens you can bring your cheese back to life by wrapping it in a piece of damp muslin (cheesecloth) and then in a beeswax wrap and store in the fridge overnight. The next day – ta dah! Your cheese will be fresh again.

GOES WITH …

Nutty, salty, sweet and spicy, parmesan's complex flavour brings other flavours together. Combine it with bitter greens, sweet fruits and black pepper, and everything shines. Season roasted cauliflower, grilled asparagus or charred broccoli with parmesan, or stir it through mashed potatoes just before serving. Add grated parmesan to your breadcrumb mix (page 269) for an umami boost.

WASTE TIP

Save your parmesan rinds! Pop them in a jar or airtight container and store in the freezer, then pull them out as you need them to throw into a minestrone or stew, or make the parmesan broth opposite.

PARMESAN RIND BROTH

This rich and flavoursome stock is packed full of umami and is a waste-warrior's dream, using up parmesan rinds and vegetable scraps to make a delicious broth. Use it to cook pasta (page 187), risotto (page 163) or in minestrone soup (page 189).

Chop 1–2 onions into chunky wedges, then sauté in 2–3 tablespoons olive oil in a saucepan for 10 minutes until lightly caramelised. Add 6–8 smashed garlic cloves and cook, stirring, for 1–2 minutes. Add at least 3 parmesan rinds (it's fine if they are frozen) and a generous handful or two of any stock-friendly vegetable scraps (such as leek tops, parsley stems, mushroom stalks, celery leaves and stalks and lemon peels), plus a generous sprig of thyme and a few bay leaves. Pour in 1.5 litres (52 fl oz) water and bring to the boil, then reduce the heat to low and simmer for 1–2 hours until the stock is rich and flavoursome. Taste, add salt and pepper if needed, then strain and store in the fridge for 5 days, or in the freezer for up to 3 months.

Makes 4 cups (1 litre)

PARMESAN AND CRACKER CRUMBS

We often find half a packet of stale crackers rattling around in the pantry. Whiz them up with parmesan and herbs and they'll have another life as a crumb for fish cakes, chicken or cauliflower schnitzel. This recipe is very basic – you can add 2 teaspoons dried chilli or dried herbs if you want.

Use a ratio of ½ cup (50 g) grated parmesan to 1 cup crushed stale crackers. Combine them in a food processor with ½ teaspoon cracked black pepper and add ½ teaspoon salt if the crackers are unsalted. Pulse on low speed until you have a medium crumb consistency. Store in an airtight container in the fridge for 2 weeks or in the freezer for 3 months.

CORAL'S PARMESAN BISCUITS

One of Alex's many grandmothers, Coral, made parmesan biscuits that are savoury perfection. There is no better snack to serve with wine. Or put these in lunchboxes if your children are fancy.

Place 1 cup (150 g) plain (all-purpose) flour, 2 tablespoons cornflour (cornstarch), 1¼ cups (125 g) grated parmesan, 1 teaspoon salt and ⅛ teaspoon cayenne pepper in a food processor. Add 125 g (4½ oz) butter cut into six pieces and process to a crumbly mixture. Add 1 tablespoon lemon juice and process until the mixture forms a ball. Lightly knead the dough on a floured work surface, then divide it in half and roll into two 30 cm (12 inch) long rolls about 2.5 cm (1 inch) in diameter. Wrap in plastic wrap and freeze until ready to use.

Cut the dough into 1 cm (½ inch) thick slices and arrange on buttered baking trays, leaving a 5 cm (2 inch) gap between each slice. Bake in a preheated 180°C (350°F/Gas mark 4) oven for 15–20 minutes, until golden and cooked through. Immediately loosen the biscuits from the tray and allow to cool.

Makes 30

RICOTTA

Ricotta is such a delicious ingredient to have in the fridge. The best ricotta is homemade, but the next best ricotta often comes in the 1–2 kg (2 lb 4 oz–4 lb 8 oz) baskets at the deli. We're always discussing the best ways to use up all that ricotta.

Half a cup or 125 g of ricotta contains about one-quarter of your daily calcium needs. It is also low in sodium and high in protein. When fresh, its mild taste and creamy texture can be used to replace cream for a lighter option in cakes and pasta dishes.

Our tip is to plan the week's meals and baked goods around the ricotta. Make the ricotta and spinach dumplings on page 39, the baked ricotta opposite and the ricotta and rhubarb tea cake on page 42. And if there's any left, have it on toast with jam or rhubarb compote (page 41) every morning for breakfast.

GOES WITH ...

The taste of ricotta defines fresh. Milky and mild, this curd is best combined with complementary textures as well as flavours. Ricotta sits delicately on leafy greens and mingles happily with eggs. The sweet sourness of orange and sharp acidity of lemon bring out the inherent citrus notes in ricotta for both sweet and savoury dishes. In a similar way, olives bring out ricotta's saltiness. There doesn't seem to be a herb that ricotta doesn't pair well with; just use them sparingly so they don't overwhelm ricotta's more delicate nature.

USE IT ALL

For even small amounts of left-over ricotta, make your own ricotta salata (see opposite).

SALTED LEFT-OVER RICOTTA (RICOTTA SALATA)

Our beautiful cheesemaking friend Kristen Allan makes the most incredible ricotta salata – it takes time, care and patience to achieve those results. This is Alex's cheat's recipe using store-bought ricotta. It's the simple 'I'm busy and forgetful' version that works for us and is yummy grated or crumbled on pizzas, pasta, eggs, charred broccoli, asparagus, roasted pumpkin or chickpea salads. It's also an excellent substitute for parmesan or feta. We really recommend giving this a go: it's not hard and you'll never throw away ricotta again!

Take about ½ cup (125 g) of your left-over ricotta and place it in a fine-mesh sieve to drain out any extra moisture. Place ¼ cup (70 g) pure salt on a flat plate. Form the ricotta into a wedge or ball and roll it in the salt. You want the ricotta to be crusted in a thin layer of salt, so add a little extra if needed. Spread a very clean square of muslin (cheesecloth) or a clean Chux on your workbench and place the salted ricotta in the centre. Wrap well, then place in an airtight container.

Ideally, you should rub the surface of the cheese with more salt and rewrap it every day for 3–4 days, but we usually forget about it for 4–5 days and then find it at the back of the fridge and scream. But it's always OK. The wrapping might get a bit smelly, but the cheese should still smell fresh, so you can just rewrap it in a clean square.

You need to re-salt and rewrap the ricotta three or four times until the ricotta starts to harden. Once this consistency is reached, brush off any excess salt, wrap the ricotta in clean muslin or cloth and store in the fridge. You can eat it immediately or let it sit and age for a month or so. It will last in the fridge for a really long time – many, many months – but if you use it instead of buying parmesan it will get used up very quickly.

Makes 1 small ball of cheese

Salted left-over ricotta (ricotta salata)

BAKED RICOTTA

This recipe comes from Jaimee's mum: a brunch classic from the 90s that will never go out of fashion in our homes. We've used 2 x 250 g layers of ricotta here, with the other ingredients sandwiched between them. Try different herbs, citrus zests and chillies when in season.

Preheat the oven to 180°C (350°F/Gas mark 4). Grease a small ovenproof dish with olive oil. Spread 250 g (9 oz) ricotta into the dish and drizzle over 1 tablespoon olive oil. Combine 100 g (3½ oz) chopped pitted green olives, 1 tablespoon finely chopped preserved lemon rind and 1 bunch chopped parsley leaves in a bowl, then press the mixture on top of the ricotta. Cover with another 250 g (9 oz) ricotta, pressing down lightly. Drizzle the top with another tablespoon of oil and bake for 30 minutes or until the top is golden.

Allow to cool to room temperature before eating. Baked ricotta will keep in an airtight container in the fridge for up to 3 days.

Serves 4–6

SPINACH AND RICOTTA DUMPLINGS IN LEMON BUTTER SAUCE

Makes 20 dumplings

These ricotta dumplings are the near impossible combination of light and luxurious. With their delicious coating of butter sauce, you will hardly notice how easily they slide down until you are devastated they are all gone.

250 g (9 oz) English spinach
1 cup (30 g) chopped parsley
Boiling water
1 egg, beaten
¼ teaspoon ground nutmeg
1 teaspoon salt
2 teaspoons freshly cracked
   black pepper
40 g (1½ oz) grated parmesan,
   plus extra to serve
450 g (1 lb) ricotta, strained
⅓ cup (50 g) plain (all-purpose)
   flour

LEMON BUTTER SAUCE

60 g (2 oz) butter
1 tablespoon olive oil
Zest of 1 lemon (or make
   the dehydrated lemon zest
   on page 204)
1 garlic clove, minced

You can remove the spinach stems if you would like very smooth, rounded dumplings, but we tend to leave them in and have embraced a more textured but less pretty dumpling. If you are going to use the stems, chop them finely and place in a large heatproof bowl. Chop the spinach leaves and add to the bowl, along with the parsley. Pour enough boiling water over the top to cover and let the spinach and parsley wilt for a minute or so. Drain, let cool and squeeze all the moisture out with your hands. Transfer the spinach and parsley to a food processor and purée. Alternatively, use a hand-held blender.

Combine the egg, nutmeg, salt, pepper and parmesan in a bowl, then stir in the puréed spinach mixture. Add the strained ricotta and stir with a wooden spoon until everything is combined. Add the flour and lightly bring the mixture together.

Bring 8 cups (2 litres) salted water to the boil in a large saucepan.

Using a teaspoon, form the mixture into 10 walnut-sized balls. Pop this batch into the boiling water and simmer for 2 minutes or until they float to the surface. While this is happening, make another 10 dumplings. Using a slotted spoon, remove the first batch of dumplings from the water and place on a baking tray, then cook the remaining 10 dumplings.

When you are simmering your last batch of dumplings, make the lemon butter sauce. Melt the butter and olive oil in a saucepan over medium heat and add the lemon zest and garlic. Move the pan around to avoid the garlic burning. Simmer for about 1 minute, then working in batches, sauté the dumplings in the butter sauce for another minute, ensuring that they are well coated in the sauce and a little browned.

Divide the dumplings among four shallow bowls and spoon over the lemon butter sauce left in the pan. Grate a little extra parmesan over the top and serve with a very simple leafy green salad.

RHUBARB

Rhubarb is like a rosy-cheeked grandmother in a cottage garden, and this is why it has never fallen victim to fads. Some things should just be old fashioned and comforting.

Rhubarb is at its best in late summer and early autumn when its stems are thicker and darker and have a higher sugar content. This is when we make compotes to stir through our porridge and bake classic crumbles. But we don't only make dessert recipes because rhubarb is, in fact, a vegetable. We smoke rhubarb to make barbecue sauce and ferment it to make kimchi. Experiment with its savoury potential.

Rhubarb's reputation as being very good for you is not overrated. The root of the plant was used medicinally for thousands of years before it occurred to anyone to cook the stems. Rhubarb is very high in vitamin K and is a good source of vitamin C, fibre and antioxidants.

To store rhubarb, cut off the leaves and discard, as they are high in oxalic acid, which is toxic to humans. Rhubarb stems will last for up to 2 weeks in the fridge, wrapped in a tight bundle with the ends exposed. This stops the stems from drying out and going soft, but allows gas to escape.

GOES WITH ...

Whether it's brown sugar, caster (superfine) sugar or honey, the addition of sweetness will prepare rhubarb for many flavour adventures. In sweet dishes, pair rhubarb with rosewater, apples, berries, vanilla and cream. In savoury combinations, rhubarb goes well with soft cheeses, oily fish, pork and onion, and spices and herbs, such as black pepper, ginger, allspice, sage and rosemary.

WASTE TIP

If you have a stem or two of left-over rhubarb, try pickling it – it's tart and tangy and a great addition to green salads and potato salads. Follow the recipe for the quick pickled grapes on page 171 (and if you like your rhubarb a little sweeter, double the amount of brown sugar).

RHUBARB COMPOTE

This compote is old-fashioned comfort food. Serve spooned over muesli, yoghurt or porridge for breakfast, in smoothies or over ice cream and desserts. If you want to jazz it up, add 1 teaspoon rosewater or cardamom powder, or a little more orange zest.

Chop a bunch of trimmed rhubarb into 2.5 cm (1 inch) pieces. Place the rhubarb, 2 tablespoons honey or maple syrup, ⅓ cup (60 g) brown sugar, a squeeze of lemon or orange juice and 3 tablespoons water in a saucepan. Feel free to add the seeds from ½ vanilla pod or a few slices of ginger. Cover and simmer over low heat for 8–10 minutes, until the rhubarb is soft and falling apart. Stir with a fork and mash for a rough compote, or use a hand-held blender and blitz to a smooth purée. Taste and add more sugar (another tablespoon or two) if needed or another squeeze of citrus if it needs a lift. Store in an airtight container in the fridge for up to 4 days.

Makes about 2 cups (600 g)

ROASTED RHUBARB CHEAT'S RELISH

If you haven't eaten rhubarb as a savoury food, then start here with this cheat's relish. Ready in 10 minutes and perfect with grilled meats, roasted vegetables and fancy cheese.

Trim ½ bunch rhubarb, slice into 5 cm (2 inch) diagonal pieces and place in a small baking dish. Drizzle over 3 tablespoons olive oil and 3 tablespoons red wine vinegar, then scatter over ½ cup (100 g) brown sugar, ½ teaspoon salt, plenty of black pepper and 1–2 teaspoons grated ginger (the last little knob in the fridge door). Mix with your hands to coat the rhubarb in all the flavours. Pop into a preheated 180°C (350°F/Gas mark 4) oven for about 10 minutes, until the rhubarb is soft and caramelised. Store in an airtight container in the fridge for up to 5 days.

Makes 1 generous cup (240 g)

RHUBARB KETCHUP

We've been making this ketchup for over 10 years. Inspired by our preserving hero Pam Corbin, this is an excellent substitute for regular ketchup in the cooler months when there are no tomatoes around. It's the perfect condiment to serve with eggs, roasted meats or burgers.

Heat 1 tablespoon olive oil in a saucepan over medium heat and sauté 1 thinly sliced red onion for 4–5 minutes, until soft and sweet. Add 1 bunch trimmed and roughly chopped rhubarb and sauté for another 5 or so minutes. Add 1 tablespoon brown mustard seeds and 1 teaspoon each of ground cumin, fenugreek seeds and fennel seeds, and mix well. Add 2 cups (500 ml) red wine vinegar, 1¼ cups (230 g) brown sugar and 1½ teaspoons salt. Reduce the heat to low and simmer until thickened.

You can keep the ketchup rustic-looking or blitz with a hand-held blender until smooth. Taste and add more sugar or salt to your liking, then store in a clean bottle or jar in the fridge for up to 3 months.

Makes 2–3 cups (600–800 g)

RHUBARB AND RICOTTA TEA CAKE

Serves 6–8

This cake comes from Cornersmith chef Greer Rochford. It's a twist on a simple butter cake, using ricotta instead of only milk and replacing some of the flour with desiccated coconut. She's used rhubarb in this recipe, but it also works well with other fruit, as long as it's cut into small pieces. This cake is best served warm with cream and compote.

1 cup (150 g) plain
  (all-purpose) flour
½ teaspoon baking powder
½ cup (45 g) desiccated coconut
½ cup (125 g) unsalted butter
¾ cup (150 g) caster
  (superfine) sugar
Zest of 1 lemon, plus 2 teaspoons
  lemon juice
2 eggs
185 g (6½ oz) ricotta
½ cup (125 ml) full-cream
  (whole) milk
125–150 g (4½–5½ oz) rhubarb,
  trimmed and sliced into
  small pieces

Preheat the oven to 170°C (325°F/Gas mark 3). Line a 21 cm (8¼ inch) round cake tin with baking paper. Whisk together the flour, baking powder and coconut in a large bowl and set aside.

In a stand mixer, cream the butter, sugar and lemon zest until light and fluffy, then add the eggs one at a time, beating well after each addition. Turn the mixer to low speed and mix in the ricotta, then add the flour mixture in three goes until just combined. With the mixer still running drizzle in the milk and lemon juice. Turn off the mixer and fold in the rhubarb, then pour into the prepared cake tin.

Bake for 50 minutes or until lightly golden on top and a skewer inserted into the centre comes out clean.

The cake will keep in an airtight container in the fridge for up to 1 week.

COMBINATIONS WE LIKE

You can replace the rhubarb with the same quantity of any fresh chopped fruit, and you can use any type of citrus zest and juice. We love the following flavours:

- Peach and lime
- Berry and lemon
- Pear and orange.

A WHOLE FISH

PEANUTS

GARLIC

A WHOLE LETTUCE

MANGOES

CUCUMBERS

GREEN ONIONS

SHOPPING BASKET 2

It's finally time to eat outdoors: picnics, barbecues and neighbourhood dinners at dusk. In spring, new-season garlic, sweetcorn and crisp cucumbers, as well as all the green things, are in abundance. These are the kinds of vegetables that match the delicate flavour of fish. In this basket, we teach you how to buy and cook fish sustainably, manage the short shelf-life of fresh greens and welcome lighter meals to longer, warmer days.

SWEETCORN

A WHOLE PINEAPPLE

FROM THIS BASKET ...

MEALS

Whole baked fish (page 48)

Fish tacos (page 50)

Rustic fish stew (page 51)

Picnic fish sandwiches (page 51)

Fish cakes (page 53)

Left-over creamed corn toasties (page 57)

Lettuce cups (page 63)

Satay salad bowl (page 76)

SIDES

Cheat's tortillas (page 55)

Charred sweetcorn in their husks (page 55)

Creamed sweetcorn (page 57)

Cornbread (page 58)

Charred or barbecued lettuce wedges (page 61)

Cucumber salad with sesame seeds and peanuts (page 65)

Charred cucumber salad with salad onions and mint oil (page 67)

Roast garlic paste for pizza, pasta and dressings (page 69)

Left-over spring onion pancakes (page 71)

Fried spring onions (page 71)

Miso satay sauce (page 75)

Charred pineapple with honey, salt and lime (page 79)

SNACKS, SWEETS & DRINKS

Toum (Lebanese garlic dip) (page 69)

Poached fruit (page 72)

Peanut butter (page 75)

Candied peanut treats (page 75)

Pineapple soda (page 79)

Whole pineapple cake (gluten free) (page 82)

Mango compote (page 85)

Mango yoghurt cake (page 87)

QUICK PRESERVING IDEAS

Quick pickled sweetcorn salsa (page 55)

Gin-pickled cucumbers (page 65)

Pickled garlic (page 69)

Dijon mustard (page 72)

Vincotto (page 73)

Pineapple hot sauce (page 81)

Quick mango relish (page 85)

NOTHING GOES TO WASTE

Fish stock (page 51)

Corn cob stock (page 55)

Stir-fried left-over lettuce (page 61)

Soy-pickled lettuce (page 61)

Wine vinegar (page 73)

Pineapple skin syrup (page 79)

Mango skin syrup (page 85)

A WHOLE FISH

Our approach to eating fish is the same as with all ingredients: make sustainable choices, eat local, buy whole and use it all. We know our oceans are in crisis. The problem is big, but small changes in our own habits can have a real impact.

It can be overwhelming navigating all the questions that need to be asked when standing at your local fish counter. Where does the fish come from? How was it produced? Is the species overfished? Is farmed or wild better? How do I prepare it and what do I do with the leftovers? We find it's best to arm yourself with knowledge before you hit the shops, to help ensure you make the best choices possible. Read up where you can and follow these tips before buying your next piece of fish.

- Ask your supplier where their seafood comes from. If they don't know, go somewhere else. Sellers will become more informed if they start losing customers.

- Choose sustainable options. There are excellent apps available that indicate which seafood is sustainable and which you should avoid.

- Try something new. As the population grows, our demand for popular choices, such as salmon, tuna and prawns (shrimp), also increases. Swap prawns for mussels, avoid farmed salmon unless you know sustainable practices are used, and eat fish lower down the food chain whose populations regenerate quickly. Often smaller is better, so opt for smaller, oily fish over tuna or swordfish.

- Eat less. Does your paella really need prawns or would roasted capsicums (peppers) and a good homemade fish stock give it the flavour it needs?

- When cooking fish, it's important to respect the whole ingredient. Make it shine and stretch it out to other meals. Buy whole fish that have a healthy ocean population and turn it into two meals. Bake or roast a whole fish and serve half for dinner one night, then save half for another meal.

WASTE TIP

Make sure you keep your fish frames and heads to make a flavoursome stock! See our recipe on page 51.

WHOLE BAKED FISH

FOUNDATION RECIPE

There are many ways to cook a whole fish, including steaming, barbecuing, poaching, pan-frying and baking. This baked fish recipe is an easy place to start. Choose a fish size that suits your household. When feeding four people for two or three nights in a row, we buy a 2 kg+ (4 lb 8 oz+) fish or two 1.5 kg (3 lb 5 oz) fish. The method is the same no matter the size – you just need to adjust the cooking time.

You can serve this with just about anything: we like it with rice, cucumber salad (page 65) and carrot kimchi (page 227), or flatbreads (page 199), chimichurri (page 33) and tabbouleh-style salad (page 27).

1 whole fish
  barramundi
  wild-caught snapper
  flathead
  trevally
Salt and freshly cracked black pepper
Olive oil
4 garlic cloves, crushed
½ lemon, sliced
Handful of mixed herbs
  fennel or dill fronds
  coriander (cilantro) stems
  thyme
  fresh bay leaves
  spring onion (scallion) tops

Preheat the oven to 200°C (400°F/Gas mark 6).

Take your whole fish and pat it dry with paper towel. Season inside the cavity with salt and pepper, drizzle in a little olive oil and stuff with the garlic, lemon and herbs. Score the skin of the fish, being careful not to pierce the flesh. Rub the outside of the fish with a few teaspoons of olive oil and a little salt.

Place the fish on a lightly greased baking tray and bake for 20–45 minutes depending on the size of your fish. As a general guide, a fish weighing less than 1 kg (2 lb 4 oz) needs 18–20 minutes, a 1.5 kg (3 lb 5 oz) fish needs around 30 minutes and a fish closer to 2 kg (4 lb 8 oz) needs 45 minutes. You really don't want to overcook your fish, so check it early and if it's not cooked, return it to the oven for another 5–10 minutes. It's ready when the flesh flakes easily and is white rather than opaque.

Remove the fish from the oven and serve with sides of your choice and plenty of condiments. If you have leftovers, strip the rest of the fish and store it in an airtight container in the fridge. It will last for 2 days, giving you the foundation for dinner over the following 2 nights. Make sure you save the frame, fins and head to make stock (page 51); it's easy to make and so much better than store-bought varieties.

TIP

If you're wrapping your fish in foil and baking paper, add 1 cup (250 ml) wine in with the fish before closing the parcel. Follow the above cooking times.

WHAT TO DO WITH LEFT-OVER COOKED FISH

We are huge fans of leftovers. They often spark some of our best ideas for the next meal. Left-over cooked fish will keep just fine in an airtight container in the fridge for up to 2 days. In addition to the below ideas, you'll find a recipe for fish cakes on page 53 and our lettuce cups with fish on page 63. These are family favourites in both our houses – the kids love them because they're simple, and we love them because they include all our favourite condiments.

CHEAT'S MARINARA

Heat 500 ml (17 fl oz) all-purpose roasted tomato sauce (page 247) or store-bought passata with a splash of fish stock or wine. Once simmering, add 300 g (10½ oz) left-over flaked fish, then cover and heat through. Stir through cooked spaghetti and top with capers, chopped herbs and grated parmesan.

CHEAT'S PAELLA

Turn tomato rice (page 249) into a cheat's paella by substituting the chicken stock with fish stock and adding 300 g (10½ oz) left-over flaked fish in the last 5 minutes of cooking. If you want to show off, add some saffron or paprika.

FISH AND ASPARAGUS RISOTTO

Add left-over flaked fish, asparagus and plenty of dill to the oven-baked risotto on page 163.

FISH PIE

If you've got 200–300 g (10½ oz) left-over flaked fish, you can turn the leek and not-much-chicken pie on page 105 into a leek and not-much-fish pie! As the fish is already cooked, you can just stir it through the sautéed vegetable mix before adding the stock and cream. Then assemble the pie as per the instructions.

NOODLE SALAD

Make the Vietnamese-style noodle salad recipe on page 96 and substitute the poached chicken for the same amount of left-over flaked fish.

FISH TACOS

Served with a simple slaw (page 124), pineapple hot sauce (page 81) and sour cream or guacamole, these fish tacos make a very simple and delicious midweek meal. You can buy corn tortillas or make our cheat's version on page 55.

Heat 2½ tablespoons olive oil in a frying pan over low heat and sauté 1 thinly sliced onion for 5 minutes. Add 1 thinly sliced capsicum (pepper) or fennel and a good pinch of salt. Cook for 20 minutes, until the vegetables are soft. Add 1–2 minced garlic cloves and ½ teaspoon each of chilli flakes, ground cumin, paprika and ground coriander. Sauté for another minute, then add the kernels from 2 sweetcorn cobs. Increase the heat to medium and cook, stirring often, for 5 minutes, until the corn is tender. Check the seasoning and add more chilli flakes or salt if needed. Add 200 g (7 oz) left-over flaked fish and mix well. Add ⅓ cup (80 ml) water or fish stock, cover with a lid and cook for 3–4 minutes, until the fish is hot. Sprinkle with coriander (cilantro) leaves and serve with corn tortillas and your favourite toppings.

Serves 4

PICNIC FISH SANDWICHES

If you like canned tuna sandwiches, you are going to love these. Made with cooked fish, they are more delicious and far more sustainable.

In a bowl, combine 150 g (5½ oz) left-over flaked fish with 2 tablespoons chopped pickled vegetables (cucumber, fennel, zucchini and kimchi all work well). Add 2 tablespoons of the pickle brine and a tablespoon of something creamy, such as sour cream, mayonnaise, cream, yoghurt or toum (page 69), plus 1 tablespoon olive oil, ¼ teaspoon salt and pepper and a pinch of cayenne pepper. If you have a spring onion (scallion), some chives or a few dill fronds, thinly slice these and add them to the mix. Use a fork to whisk the mixture into a rough paste. Spread on slices of white bread, top with crunchy lettuce and serve.

Makes 4

RUSTIC FISH STEW

This recipe is inspired by rustic Italian-style fish stews. Here, we turn a small amount of left-over fish into another hearty meal.

Heat 2½ tablespoons olive oil in a frying pan over medium heat and sauté 1 thinly sliced onion for 15 minutes until soft and sweet. Add 2 minced garlic cloves, ½ teaspoon salt and ½ teaspoon pepper and cook for 5 minutes. Add 3 chopped tomatoes, ½ cup (125 ml) white wine, 2 bay leaves and a sprig of thyme and gently simmer for 10 minutes. Next, add 2 x 400 g (14 oz) tins of drained and rinsed white beans or 2 cups (400 g) cooked white beans and 4 cups (1 litre) fish stock (see opposite).

Simmer low and slow for 30 minutes or until the broth becomes rich and full of flavour. When you're happy with the flavour, add 300 g (10½ oz) left-over flaked fish, the zest of a lemon and a tablespoon of its juice. Simmer for a few minutes until the fish is hot, but not too long as you don't want it to be tough. Taste, season if needed and serve with bread and butter and crunchy green leaves.

Serves 4–6

FISH STOCK

Here is our fish stock recipe. If you have left-over sweetcorn cobs you can add them in, too!

Heat 2½ tablespoons olive oil in a heavy-based stockpot over medium heat and gently sauté 1 roughly chopped onion plus 2 cups (150 g) of any other chopped vegetables that need to be used up: celery leaves and tops, fennel and carrots all work well, as do parsley stems, spring onions (scallions) and leeks. Continue to sauté for 10 minutes, then add 2–3 cloves chopped garlic and gently sauté for another 4–5 minutes. Add your left-over fish frame, fins and head, along with 1 teaspoon black peppercorns and a sprig of thyme or a few bay leaves. Put the lid on, reduce the heat to low and let the fish steam for 5 minutes, shaking the pan every now and then. Take the lid off and add 1 cup (250 ml) white wine if you have it. Bring to a simmer and add up to 4 cups (1 litre) water (just enough to cover the fish). Continue to simmer very gently for 20 minutes. Taste and add ¼ teaspoon salt, then taste again and add more if needed. Strain the stock, set aside to cool and refrigerate. Use the stock as a base for noodle soup (page 190), steamed mussels, a simple paella, risotto (page 163) or the fish stew opposite.

Makes about 4 cups (1 litre)

FISH CAKES

Makes 8

Whole-food cook Jude Blereau's cookbooks taught us how to make fritters and fish cakes when our kids were little, and they've been a family favourite ever since. This is our version using left-over fish and whatever vegetables and herbs are hanging around in the fridge. If you've got left-over mash, it all comes together in a matter of minutes.

400 g (14 oz) cooked potatoes
 or sweet potatoes
Splash of full-cream (whole) milk
salt
¾ cup (75 g) thinly sliced
 crunchy vegetables
 spring onions (scallions)
 sweetcorn kernels
 celery
 fennel
Small handful of finely
 chopped herbs
 dill
 parsley
 fennel fronds
 celery leaves
2 garlic cloves, minced
Zest of 1 lemon or lime
Freshly cracked black pepper
300 g (10½ oz) left-over flaked
 baked fish (page 48)
1 egg
1 cup (100 g) stale breadcrumbs
100 ml (3½ fl oz) good-quality
 vegetable oil such as sunflower
 or rice-bran oil

In a large bowl, mash the potatoes with the milk and a pinch of salt. Add the thinly sliced vegetables, along with the herbs, garlic and lemon or lime zest. Season with salt and pepper and combine well with a fork, then stir through the flaked fish, being careful not to break it up too much, which can make the mixture gluey.

Divide the mixture into eight fish cakes. Whisk the egg in a shallow bowl and tip the breadcrumbs into another shallow bowl. Dip each fish cake in the egg and then coat in the breadcrumbs.

Heat the oil in a frying pan over medium–low heat. Fry the fish cakes in batches for 3–4 minutes each side until crisp and golden.

Drain on paper towel and serve with a crunchy slaw (page 124) and condiments, such as toum (page 69), aioli or hot sauce.

SWEETCORN

In the warmer months, we barbecue or quickly boil sweetcorn and slather it in butter, and every time it tastes of sunshine. Sweetcorn is high in starch and, compared to other vegetables, low in vitamins, but it is rich in antioxidants and fibre. It is often treated as a vegetable, but is, in fact, a cereal grain. It can be turned into a fine or coarse flour or cornmeal, ingredients that Italian and Mexican cooks have been using for centuries. The yellow corn most of us are familiar with is known as sweetcorn, but there are many other varieties.

When sweetcorn is available in spring and summer, buy it in its husk to avoid unnecessary packaging. There are three parts to shucked corn: the husk, the cob and the silks, and each has its uses. (Did you know that there is one corn silk for every corn kernel?) In Mexico, husks are used to wrap and cook tamales, which we encourage you to have a go at making. You can also try wrapping sardines in soaked husks and cooking them on the barbecue.

Polenta, cornmeal and cornflour are all made from ground dried corn kernels in varying degrees of coarseness. Cornmeal can be hard to get hold of outside the United States, so we use fine polenta for our cornbread (page 58) and cheat's tortillas (opposite).

To store, keep sweetcorn cobs in their husks in the fridge for 5 days. For longer storage, remove the kernels and freeze for up to 8 months.

GOES WITH ...

A bursting kernel of corn is sweet with a pleasant hay-like flavour. While there are few better pairings than corn and butter, sweetcorn is also partial to spending time with chicken; bacon, chilli and coriander (cilantro); seafood; garlic; and beans in a classic cowboy combination.

WASTE TIP

Use corn silks to make a tea that is helpful for bladder infections. Simmer the silks from 1–2 sweetcorn cobs in 1 cup (250 ml) water for 10 minutes, then add a little honey and strain before drinking.

You can also fry the silks to add an impressive crunch to corn salads, stews and stir-fries. Deep-fry corn silks in vegetable oil for 5 seconds (they will puff up), then drain, sprinkle over some ground cumin, cayenne pepper and salt, and serve. Try it on top of creamed corn (page 57).

USE IT ALL

Sweetcorn cobs make delicious stock; see opposite. You can add the husks as well; just give them a light char first to create a greater depth of flavour.

CORN COB STOCK

Before the corn cobs hit the compost, make this quick and tasty stock. We use it to cook beans, rice or chicken in, or as the base for a vegetable soup.

Once you've removed the kernels from 2–3 sweetcorn cobs, char the cobs over a gas flame, in a hot chargrill pan or on the barbecue. Place the cobs in a saucepan with 4 garlic cloves (smashed with the skins on), 1 teaspoon black peppercorns and a generous pinch of salt. Add 4 cups (1 litre) water and simmer over low heat for 15 minutes. Taste, add more salt if needed, then strain and use.

Makes 4 cups (1 litre)

CHEAT'S TORTILLAS

Have you ever looked at the ingredients list on a packet of store-bought tortillas? So many additives! Proper tortillas are made only with masa flour, water and a tortilla press. All well and good, but if you don't have either the flour or a press, don't worry, you can still make them. This is our cheat's recipe – these tortillas can be made in a flash.

Combine 1 cup (150 g) fine polenta and 1 cup (150 g) self-raising flour with 1 teaspoon salt and ¾ cup (185 ml) boiling water. Mix with a spatula until a dough forms. When cool enough to touch, knead in the bowl for 2 minutes, form into a ball, then wrap the dough in a tea towel and leave to rest for 30 minutes.

Roll the dough into a thick log and cut into 12 even pieces. This dough is a little sticky, so flour your work surface really well. Roll the dough pieces into balls, then flatten and roll into 15 cm (6 inch) tortillas. Heat a frying pan over medium–high heat and cook each tortilla for about 30 seconds on both sides or until cooked through. Serve immediately.

Makes 12

CHARRED SWEETCORN IN THEIR HUSKS

Make the most of corn's natural packaging by barbecuing sweetcorn in their husks. This will help to keep the kernels juicy.

Preheat a barbecue grill plate to medium. Trim any silks that are hanging out the top of your corn cobs (you don't want these to catch fire). Soak the corn cobs in water for 10–15 minutes and then shake off any excess liquid. Barbecue the corn for 20 minutes, turning every 5 minutes, until the corn kernels are bright yellow and tender when pierced with a knife.

Serve on a platter as is, and let everyone unwrap the corn themselves. Have butter and salt on standby to slather over the corn, or serve with toum (page 69) or chimichurri (page 33).

Serves 1 corn cob per person

QUICK PICKLED SWEETCORN SALSA

Taco Tuesdays step up a notch with this tangy sweetcorn salsa. It's also great with eggs and cornbread (page 58), baked fish (page 48) and salad, or with guacamole and corn chips.

In a bowl, combine 1 cup (200 g) sweetcorn kernels, ⅓ cup (20 g) thinly sliced spring onions (scallions) or red onion and 1–2 thinly sliced long green chillies or jalapeños. Heat 1 tablespoon vegetable oil in a frying pan over medium–high heat. Add the corn mixture in two batches and cook, stirring, for 1–2 minutes – you want to quickly char the ingredients rather than completely cook them through. Once both batches are charred, return everything to the pan and add 3 tablespoons white wine or rice wine vinegar, 1 tablespoon sugar, ½ teaspoon salt and 1 teaspoon cumin seeds. Cook over medium heat for 2–3 minutes, until the corn has absorbed most of the vinegar. Taste and add more salt or a pinch of cayenne pepper if it needs more heat. Allow to cool and either serve straight away or store in a sealed jar or airtight container in the fridge for up to 1 week.

Makes about 300 g (10½ oz)

CREAMED SWEETCORN

Serves 4

Greer Rochford, one of our chefs at Cornersmith, has brought her passion for Mexican flavours into our lives. This is her recipe for creamed corn, and the addition of jalapeño really sets it apart from the rest. It's perfect with eggs for breakfast, as a side with roast chicken or fish, and in toasties the next day for lunch. For a lighter dairy-free version, use corn cob stock (page 55) in place of the milk, and 3 tablespoons olive oil in place of the butter.

4 sweetcorn cobs
1¼ cups (310 ml) full-cream (whole) milk or corn cob stock (page 55), plus extra if needed
110 g (4 oz) butter
1 garlic clove, thinly sliced
1 jalapeño or long green chilli, thinly sliced
Salt and freshly cracked black pepper
Pinch of cayenne pepper (optional)

Remove the husks and silks from the sweetcorn cobs. Separate the husks from the silks and keep both for another use (page 54). Strip the kernels from the cobs and set aside.

Place the cobs in a saucepan with the milk or stock and warm over medium heat (do not boil). Remove from the heat and set aside to let the flavours infuse.

Melt the butter in a saucepan over low heat, add the garlic, chilli and corn kernels and cook, stirring frequently, for 20 minutes or until the kernels are completely soft. You may need to add a little more milk or stock if the corn has absorbed all the liquid.

Strain the milk or stock and discard the cobs. Transfer one-quarter of the cooked corn mixture to the strained liquid and blitz into a slurry using a hand-held blender. Stir the slurry through the remaining cooked corn and cook for a further 5 minutes over low heat. Season with salt and pepper and the cayenne pepper, if you like.

Serve straight away on toast or the cornbread on page 58, with a poached egg and some pickles for breakfast or dinner. It's also a great side dish served with fish or chicken.

The creamed corn will keep in the fridge for up to 5 days; just reheat it in a saucepan with a little extra milk or water.

LEFT-OVER CREAMED CORN TOASTIES

Sometimes we make creamed corn just for the toasties the next day! Simply make them using creamed corn, melty cheese, chilli jam and your favourite bread.

CORNBREAD

Serves 8

When Jaimee was a kid she spent many years in the United States where cornbread is serious business. She remembers it being rich and crumbly and eaten with bowls of chilli. Traditionally, cornbread is made from cornmeal and bacon drippings. In Australia, cornmeal is hard to come by so she has come up with this recipe using fine polenta, butter and plenty of fresh corn kernels. While this is not a purist's version, it is as rich and crumbly as the cornbread she loved.

We eat this cornbread with barbecued fish and slaw or alongside tacos (page 97). You can also serve it with baked beans (page 233) or with eggs for breakfast.

1¼ cups (310 ml) full-cream (whole) milk
2 tablespoons freshly squeezed lemon juice
1 cup (150 g) fine polenta
1 cup (150 g) self-raising flour
1 teaspoon salt
1 tablespoon caster (superfine) sugar
½ teaspoon dried chilli flakes (optional)
100 g butter
1 egg
2 sweetcorn cobs, kernels removed (you will need 350 g/12½ oz)

Preheat the oven to 180°C (350°F/Gas mark 4).

Combine the milk and lemon juice in a jug and allow to stand for 4–5 minutes to curdle.

In a large bowl, combine the polenta, flour, salt, sugar and chilli, if using.

Melt the butter in a 26 cm (10½ inch) ovenproof frying pan over low heat. Turn off the heat.

Whisk the egg in a small bowl, then whisk in the curdled milk. Pour this into the flour mixture, stirring to combine, then add the melted butter and keep stirring until the butter is completely incorporated. Add the sweetcorn kernels and stir gently to combine, then pour the thick batter into the frying pan. Transfer to the oven and bake for 30 minutes or until the cornbread is golden and springy to the touch.

Serve warm. Any leftovers can be toasted and slathered with yet more butter.

A WHOLE LETTUCE

Bagged lettuce leaves have simply got to go. They are reportedly one of the most wasted ingredients in our kitchens – not to mention the amount of packaging that's also thrown away. Instead, we recommend you buy a whole nude lettuce and use it all.

Iceberg, cos (romaine), buttercrunch, oakleaf – whichever lettuce you fancy, only buy enough to get you through the next few days. Even when carefully stored, lettuce leaves do not last long, so use them as soon as you can. Crisp lettuces, such as cos and iceberg, are sturdier than softer, loose-leafed varieties, such as buttercrunch or oakleaf. These soft lettuces should be bought and eaten in the first day or two, while cos or iceberg lettuces can be wrapped in a damp cloth and stored in a sealed bag in the fridge where they'll last 4–5 days. Mixed leaves are best stored out of the bag, in an airtight container lined with paper towel, with another paper towel placed on top of the leaves before closing the lid. Keep any leafy greens away from the coldest part of the fridge, which can quickly turn them soggy.

GOES WITH ...

Crunchy lettuces, such as cos and iceberg, are quite sturdy, making them perfect natural bowls for hot foods such as fried rice, san choy bao or grilled fish and noodles. Their shape and texture holds up well for barbecuing, stir-frying and pickling. More tender-leaved lettuces, such as butter and oak, are best for tossed salads and work well with light, creamy ingredients, such as thin slices of avocado or pear or a crumble of soft cheese and a drizzle of oil.

WASTE TIP

See opposite for tips on how to use up those scraps of lettuce that hang around in the crisper drawer. You can also juice tired lettuce leaves with pineapple, cucumber and ginger for a refreshing drink.

WHAT TO DO WITH LEFT-OVER LETTUCE

STIR-FRIED LEFT-OVER LETTUCE

Cooking lettuce seems counterintuitive, but high heat and quick sautéing or stir-frying makes it shine. It's also a good way to enjoy tired leaves that have seen better days. Add lots of garlic and spring onions (scallions), salt and a little soy sauce and you'll have a green side in a matter of minutes.

Heat 1 tablespoon sunflower oil in a wok over high heat. Add 2–4 thinly sliced spring onions (scallions) and sauté for 30 seconds or so, then add 1–2 minced garlic cloves and a generous pinch of salt. Sauté for another 20 seconds, then add 4 cups (300 g) sliced iceberg or cos (romaine) lettuce and sauté until the lettuce is just limp. Add 1 tablespoon soy sauce, ½ teaspoon sugar and a pinch of chilli flakes and stir well. Top with toasted peanuts or sesame seeds and serve immediately.

Serves 2–3 as a side

SOY-PICKLED LETTUCE

This is a riff on a Korean condiment and is a great way to use up excess or tired-looking lettuce. It takes only 15 minutes to make and goes well with stir-fries, grilled fish, fried rice or noodles.

Place 4 cups (300 g) chopped cos (romaine) or iceberg lettuce in a bowl and sprinkle over 1 tablespoon sugar and ½ teaspoon salt. Let it sit for 10 minutes or so. In a jug, combine ⅓ cup (80 ml) soy sauce, 1 tablespoon rice wine vinegar or apple cider vinegar, 2 teaspoons grated ginger and a pinch of chilli flakes. Use your hands to squeeze out the moisture from the lettuce over the sink – you can be quite rough with it! Place the lettuce in a jar or non-reactive container and cover with the soy and vinegar mixture, pressing down the lettuce to ensure it is completely covered by the liquid. It will be ready in 15 minutes, but will be even better in a few days' time. Store in the fridge for at least 1 month.

Makes 1 x 300 ml (10½ fl oz) jar

CHARRED OR BARBECUED LETTUCE WEDGES

This is insanely delicious. Serve as a side dish, accounting for one wedge per person.

Start by making a garlicky yoghurt sauce. In a small bowl, combine 3 tablespoons olive oil, 1 minced garlic clove, ½ teaspoon salt, ¼ teaspoon chilli flakes and 1 tablespoon yoghurt. Whisk with a fork to emulsify and set aside.

Preheat a barbecue grill plate to high or a chargrill pan over high heat. Cut a cos (romaine) or iceberg lettuce in half lengthways and then into fat wedges. Brush the wedges with sunflower oil, then grill on the hot barbecue or in the pan until charred but not wilted (make sure you turn the lettuce to char each side). Transfer to a plate and drizzle with the garlicky yoghurt sauce, ensuring to brush extra sauce between the leaves. Sprinkle with chopped herbs of your choice and serve.

Serves 6–8 as a side

LETTUCE CUPS

Serves 4

Lettuce cups are on high rotation in our houses in the warmer months. They're quick and easy, fresh and crisp, and can be made with whatever crunchy vegetables you have in the fridge. Add a protein of your choice and you'll have a healthy meal on the table with little effort. Here we've served it with left-over baked fish (page 48), rice, soy-pickled lettuce (page 61) and thinly sliced chilli on the side.

1 tablespoon vegetable oil
2 garlic cloves, chopped
2 spring onions (scallions), chopped
2–3 cups (150–225 g) thinly sliced
   vegetables
   green beans
   carrot
   asparagus
   zucchini (courgette)
   broccoli
   capsicum (pepper)
   wombok
   bok choy
Pinch of salt
300 g (10½ oz) protein
   tofu
   left-over cooked fish
   free-range minced (ground) pork
   poached shredded chicken (page 95)
   beef strips
1 tablespoon mirin or dry sherry
1 tablespoon soy sauce
2 tablespoons hoisin
Iceberg or cos (romaine) lettuce
   cups, to serve
Steamed rice, to serve
Toasted sesame seeds, to serve
Lemon wedges, to serve
Hot sauce or thinly sliced red
   chilli, to serve

Heat the vegetable oil in a wok over high heat, add the garlic and spring onion and stir-fry for less than 1 minute.

Add the thinly sliced vegetables and salt and stir-fry for 2–3 minutes until the vegetables are tender but still bright. Remove the vegetables from the wok, then add the protein and stir-fry until browned and cooked through (if using left-over fish or poached chicken, you'll just need to heat it through). Splash in the mirin or sherry, soy sauce and hoisin. Return the vegetables to the wok and mix through.

Transfer to a serving bowl. Serve with lettuce cups, steamed rice, sesame seeds for sprinkling over, lemon wedges and your choice of hot sauce or chilli and condiments.

CUCUMBERS

Pickles, gin and healthy snacks for kids: the cucumber is the key to our three favourite things. When Alex's backyard exploded with cucumbers one summer, we set to work teaching ourselves how to pickle and ferment on a big scale. Really it was the beginning of Cornersmith, so we will always look at the humble cucumber with a lot of affection.

Actually a fruit, but treated as a vegetable, cucumbers belong to the same family as melons and gourds. They are refreshing, a little grassy, a little sweet and sometimes a little bitter. Made up of 90 per cent water, cucumbers get a reputation for being nutritionally void, but they provide us with antioxidants and anti-inflammatory benefits, plus they keep us hydrated on hot summer days.

There are hundreds of varieties of cucumbers, the most common being the green cucumber that is eaten raw. In Australia, we have plenty of the smooth Lebanese (short) cucumbers with their mild flavour, thin skin and few seeds making them excellent for all our culinary needs. We also have the delicious telegraph (continental) cucumber; however we refuse to buy them because of the wasteful plastic wrap needed to protect them from damage. Both varieties are a good option for sliced pickles.

There are also pickling cucumbers and gherkins, which are short and thick with bumpy skins. These are best fermented or submerged whole in a vinegar brine. They make the best pickles because they have a much lower water content, meaning they stay crunchier for longer.

Cucumbers will last for over a week if stored well. Make sure they are completely dry, then swaddle them in a clean tea towel or cloth bag and place in an old plastic bag before popping in the fridge. They need a little air, but not too much, so don't completely seal them in. Store in the crisper, as the colder parts of the fridge will make them go soggy.

GO WITH ...

Cucumbers match well with mint, yoghurt and melon. Their gentle flavour also pairs nicely with a little acidity from ingredients such as vinegar, goat's cheese, lemon juice, capers, tomatoes, feta and olives. Add a sprinkle of salt, a handful of dill, a little chilli or fennel seeds and the subtle cucumber will sing.

USE IT ALL

If you've bought too many cucumbers, don't let them turn into slimy sea slugs in the fridge! Placing thinly sliced cucumbers in a quick vinegar brine (opposite) will extend their life by weeks and you'll be rewarded with delicious pickles for your cheese sandwiches.

WASTE TIP

If you do end up with tired-looking cucumbers, they're still delicious stir-fried in a hot frying pan; follow the method for the stir-fried lettuce on page 61. Or make the charred cucumber salad on page 67.

CUCUMBER SALAD WITH SESAME SEEDS AND PEANUTS

Jaimee discovered this salad in a dumpling bar in Sydney's Chinatown. It considerably aided the digestion of the many, many dumplings she ate. There's not much to it, but it's so tasty and easy to make, you can serve it even when you're too lazy to think about anything green.

Thickly slice 4 Lebanese (short) cucumbers and place in a serving bowl. Add 1 tablespoon sesame oil and 1 tablespoon soy sauce and top with 2 teaspoons sesame seeds and 1 tablespoon whole toasted peanuts. Add a pinch of salt if you feel it needs it. Allow the salad to sit for 10 minutes before serving.

Serves 4 as a side

GIN-PICKLED CUCUMBERS

This is Alex's fancy grown-up version of our staple bread and butter pickles. When the family is away, she eats these pickles with a boiled egg and rye bread and butter for breakfast, lunch and dinner, and couldn't be happier.

Place 500 g (1 lb 2 oz) thinly sliced cucumbers in a non-reactive bowl and sprinkle over 2 teaspoons pure salt. Mix with your hands to evenly disperse the salt, then let the cucumber sit at room temperature for at least 2 hours (or overnight if you can) to draw out excess moisture. Strain and discard the excess liquid.

To make a brine, combine ½ cup (125 ml) white wine vinegar, 2 tablespoons caster (superfine) sugar, ½ teaspoon salt and 3 tablespoons water in a saucepan and place over low heat. Stir to dissolve the sugar and salt and bring to simmering point. Turn off the heat, add a few strips of lemon peel and ½ teaspoon lightly crushed juniper berries and let it sit for 15–20 minutes, until the brine has cooled down and the flavours have infused. Once cool, add ½ cup (125 ml) gin and stir well.

Gently pack the cucumber into two 300 ml (10½ fl oz) clean jars. Pour over the brine, making sure the lemon peel and juniper berries are evenly dispersed among the jars and the cucumbers are completely submerged in the liquid. Poke any air bubbles with a knife or a chopstick and seal. Allow the cucumber to pickle in the fridge for 3 days before eating. Eat within 3 months.

Makes 2 x 300 ml (10½ fl oz) jars

CHARRED CUCUMBER SALAD WITH SALAD ONIONS AND MINT OIL

Serves 3–4 as a side

For a salad with only three parts, there is plenty of flavour here. Charring is a smart way to rescue those cucumbers that have seen better days, and this dish has a surprisingly moreish flavour. The raw onion and the mint make for a bitey and cooling contrast. We serve this alongside whole baked fish (page 48) or koftas (page 251) and flatbreads (page 199).

4 Lebanese (short) cucumbers
1 teaspoon salt
1 bunch mint
100 ml (3½ fl oz) good-quality vegetable oil, such as sunflower oil, plus a little extra for cooking
1–2 tablespoons freshly squeezed lemon juice
1 salad onion, green stalk included and thinly sliced

Start by cutting up your cucumbers into 3 cm (1¼ inch) chunks on the diagonal. Sprinkle with the salt and leave to stand for 10–15 minutes.

Meanwhile, make a mint oil by picking a small handful of the mint leaves and placing them in a mortar with a pinch of salt. Using the pestle, grind the leaves until the mint is completely smooth. Slowly add the vegetable oil while mixing with the pestle. Add 1 tablespoon of the lemon juice and taste, adding more if needed.

Heat a touch of oil in a frying pan over high heat. Drain the salted cucumbers, pat dry, then add to the pan in small batches and briefly char for 3 minutes on all sides. Remove from the pan and allow to cool completely, then combine in a serving bowl with the onion.

Tear the remaining mint leaves over the top, drizzle with the mint oil and serve.

GARLIC

A member of the lily family and related to onions and leeks, garlic has been cultivated for thousands of years. Said to have fortified the Olympians of Ancient Greece and once thought to be very good for warding off evil, garlic has been used for every imaginable purpose. In the kitchen it has become a necessity.

When we let ourselves run out of garlic, we know our lives have fallen apart. Garlic was one of the first ingredients we tried to eat seasonally and locally, as we realised the market was flooded with imported garlic, which is often bleached and unnecessarily packaged. Peeled, plastic-wrapped garlic is not a sustainable choice and is to be avoided. Because garlic is a seasonal crop, it was one of the first ingredients we learned to preserve. It's worth buying a decent amount and preserving it for later. Look for garlic that is firm to touch and don't buy garlic that has sprouted, as this is a sign it's been on the shelf for too long.

Garlic contains magnesium and copper, along with vitamins B6 and C and trace amounts of nearly everything that is good. Garlic's health-giving benefits can be attributed to its sulphur compounds. So potent is garlic's effectiveness that consuming even a little is beneficial. It's anti-inflammatory, antibacterial and antimicrobial, so can be used topically to treat infections and internally to treat inflammation. In addition, garlic supports cardiovascular health, reduces arthritic symptoms and may support bone density.

Moisture and light will cause mould to grow on garlic, so store it in a cool, dry, dark place in a wire basket or an open paper bag. Whole heads of garlic will keep for many months if unbroken. Once you do break open your garlic, use the cloves within 10 days.

GOES WITH ...

Raw garlic is sharp with plenty of heat. A tiny amount will make dips and sauces zing, and it is particularly well suited to cooling and raw ingredients, such as cucumber, zucchini (courgette), leafy greens, tomatoes and fresh herbs. The longer you cook garlic the sweeter it becomes, giving complexity to slow-cooked meats, legumes and vegetables.

WASTE TIP

Put 3–4 peeled garlic cloves in a jar and cover with 1 cup (250 ml) apple cider vinegar. Let it sit for a few weeks, then use the garlicky vinegar in stir-fries, salad dressings and marinades. Sip a teaspoon of it when you feel a sore throat coming on!

PICKLED GARLIC

The jars of minced garlic in supermarkets are full of additives and taste nothing like garlic should. This is our version, although we leave the cloves whole and mince them as needed.

Break up 3 heads of garlic and blanch the unpeeled cloves in a saucepan of boiling water for 1 minute (this is to prevent the garlic turning blue in the vinegar). Drain and run under cold water, then peel the cloves. In a jug, combine 300 ml (10½ fl oz) apple cider vinegar, ¼ cup (55 g) caster (superfine) sugar and a pinch each of salt and ground turmeric. Whisk until dissolved.

Fill a sterilised jar (page 278) with the peeled garlic cloves, adding 2 bay leaves and a few peppercorns if you like. Cover with the pickling liquid, making sure the cloves are submerged. Remove any air bubbles, seal and store in the fridge for up to 3 months.

Makes 1 x 500 ml (17 fl oz) jar

ROAST GARLIC PASTE FOR PIZZA, PASTA AND DRESSINGS

Having roast garlic paste on hand will take the flavour of any savoury dish up a notch. Use it wisely as a little goes a long way. We spread it on pizza bases with sliced potato or on toast topped with tomato. You can add a teaspoon to a salad dressing or a tablespoon to the base of soups and stews.

Preheat the oven to 170°C (325°F/Gas mark 3). Remove 1 cm (½ inch) from the tops of 4 heads of garlic, so the tips of the cloves are exposed. Remove any excess papery skin, then place in a small baking dish. Pour 1 tablespoon olive oil over each head of garlic, then cover the dish tightly with foil. Roast for 1 hour, until the garlic is soft and golden. Once cool enough to handle, squeeze the roasted garlic cloves into a bowl and mash with a fork. You can add a little more oil if you like and a pinch or two of salt. Transfer to a clean jar, cover with oil (as you would pesto) and store in the fridge for up to 1 week.

Makes about ½ cup (125 g)

TOUM (LEBANESE GARLIC DIP)

Toum is so quick to make, it's easier than popping down the shops and buying it! Serve alongside carrot, cucumber and celery sticks, on flatbreads, in sandwiches or with falafels, or use a few tablespoons to marinate lamb or chicken.

In a food processor, blitz 6 peeled garlic cloves with ½ teaspoon salt to form a paste. Add 1 tablespoon lemon juice and blend until combined, then add 1 tablespoon ice-cold water and blend until smooth. With the food processor running very slowly, pour in 300 ml (10½ fl oz) vegetable oil in a steady stream until you have an emulsified and thick dip. Add up to 100 ml (3½ fl oz) ice-cold water to loosen the dip into a creamy consistency. Keep in an airtight container in the fridge for up to 3 days.

Makes 2 cups (500 g)

Roast garlic paste, pickled garlic and toum

GREEN ONIONS

Spring is the time for young green onions, meaning onions that are harvested before maturity. Depending on when they are pulled from the earth they either have no bulb, or one that is small and tender. Green onions go by a confusing number of names which make for endless conversations where nothing is decided. Below is our guide to identification, naming and using green onions.

SHALLOTS OR SPRING ONIONS?

No one agrees what to call these things, so here we are going to call them spring onions (also known as scallions). Spring onions are either harvested as very young onions or they are grown as a distinct variety that never forms a bulb. They have tubular stems that are about 40 cm (16 inches) in length, ending in a white part with a little skirt of roots. Their flavour is milder than more mature onions, but spicier than chives.

SALAD ONIONS

Salad onions are more mature than spring onions, with a sturdier green stem and a small white bulb, both of which are edible. The bulbs are far sweeter and milder than mature onions, but we cook them the same way as any other onion. Because of their mild flavour, they are also lovely raw in salads and sandwiches.

All onions are rich in prebiotic fibres that are great for your gut health, but can be an irritant to those who are sensitive. Spring onions are high in vitamins A, C and K, while salad onions also contain antioxidants, making them most nutritious when consumed raw.

GO WITH ...

Salad onions go well with ricotta, cream and eggs – basically a quiche. They also pair wonderfully with other spring greens and herbs. Spring onions often appear alongside garlic, ginger and chilli. Thinly slice them and add as a garnish over stir-fries and omelettes.

WASTE TIP

Don't toss those tired spring onions left in the bottom of the crisper; instead use them to make the left-over spring onion pancakes opposite.

USE IT ALL

The green tops of salad onions have a very strong flavour and are woody in texture. Thinly slice them and sauté until soft and collapsed, then serve with soups, rice and salads.

LEFT-OVER SPRING ONION PANCAKES

It always seems like there are a few too many spring onions in a bunch, so make these pancakes with the excess. They are a classic breakfast food in China, and we also serve them alongside stir-fries or the baked fish on page 48.

Mix 1 cup (150 g) plain (all-purpose) flour and ½ teaspoon salt in a bowl and make a well in the centre. Bring ¾ cup (185 ml) water to the boil, leave it to cool for 1 minute, then add to the flour, stirring to combine with chopsticks or a spoon. When cool enough to handle, knead the dough on a lightly floured workbench for about 5 minutes until very smooth. Wrap the dough in a tea towel and rest for 30 minutes.

In a bowl, combine 1–2 teaspoons crushed Sichuan peppercorns or freshly cracked black pepper, 3–4 very thinly sliced spring onions (scallions), 1 minced garlic clove, 2 tablespoons plain (all-purpose) flour and 2 tablespoons vegetable oil.

Roll the dough out to a thin 30 cm x 15 cm (12 inch x 6 inch) rectangle. Brush generously with oil and evenly spoon over the spring onion mixture. Starting at a short end, roll the dough into a sausage, then cut it into 12 even-sized pieces. Take each piece and with the spiral facing up, use the palm of your hand to flatten each piece into a disc. Roll the flattened discs into 10 cm (4 inch) circles and set aside on a sheet of baking paper.

Heat 3 tablespoons vegetable oil in a frying pan over medium heat and when the oil is hot but not sizzling, fry the pancakes on each side for about 3 minutes until golden. Serve immediately.

Makes 12

Left-over spring onion pancakes

FRIED SPRING ONIONS AND FLAVOURED OIL

Crispy and toasty fried spring onions are great sprinkled over noodles. The spring onion oil makes a wonderful dipping sauce when mixed with soy.

Heat 400 ml (14 fl oz) vegetable oil in a saucepan over medium heat until very hot. Meanwhile, thinly slice a bunch of spring onions (scallions). Place in a bowl and sprinkle over ½ teaspoon salt. Working with a handful at a time, press the spring onion onto a tea towel to remove some moisture, then add to the hot pan and stir-fry for about 1 minute (don't let them brown). Using a spoon, scoop out the spring onion and drain on paper towel. Repeat until all the spring onion is cooked. Set the oil aside to cool.

Preheat the oven to 60°C (140°F/Gas mark ¼). Lay the spring onion on a baking tray and dry in the oven for 15–20 minutes. Allow to cool, then store in an airtight container in the pantry for up to 1 week. Strain the cooled oil through a fine sieve into a jar and store in the pantry for up to 3 months.

Makes 400 ml (14 fl oz) flavoured oil and 1–2 cups fried spring onion

WHAT TO DO WITH LEFT-OVER WINE

DIJON MUSTARD

Making mustard sounds much harder than it is. Here's a simple way to make Dijon mustard at home.

Roughly chop a small onion and 2 garlic cloves and place in a saucepan with ¾ cup (185 ml) white wine and ⅓ cup (80 ml) apple cider vinegar. Add 1 teaspoon peppercorns and a bay leaf, then gently bring to the boil and simmer for 5 minutes. Remove from the heat and set aside for 15 minutes for the flavours to infuse, then strain the liquid into a bowl and discard the solids. Pour the liquid back into the pan and set over low heat. Once the mixture starts to slowly bubble, gradually sift in ½ cup (45 g) mustard powder, stirring constantly with a spoon or whisk to avoid any lumps forming. When the mixture is completely smooth, add 1½ teaspoons salt, 3 teaspoons honey, 1 teaspoon vegetable oil and a pinch of ground turmeric, then stir until smooth and starting to thicken. Keep stirring until the mustard becomes thick and shiny (remember it will thicken more once it cools, so be careful not to overcook it). Taste for seasoning – it should be sharp-tasting at this stage because of the mustard powder, but this will mellow over time. If you'd like to flavour your mustard, remove from the heat and stir through 1 tablespoon chopped rosemary, thyme, sage or finely grated horseradish.

Pour the mustard into a clean jar and seal. Store in the fridge for 2–3 weeks before eating to let the flavours develop, then keep for up to 3 months.

Makes 1 cup (250 g)

POACHED FRUIT

A little left-over wine with some sugar and spice thrown in makes for an excellent poaching syrup for fruits. Wine intensifies the flavours and preserves the fruit so it lasts longer in the fridge. Serve over ice cream or cakes, or with a spoonful of thick cream.

Heat 1 cup (220 g) sugar, 2 cups (500 ml) wine and 1 cup (250 ml) water in a large saucepan over low heat until the sugar has dissolved. Add in your choice of aromats and fruit (see below), then cover the surface of the liquid with baking paper or a small plate to keep the fruit submerged.

Gently simmer until the fruit is tender and cooked through, but not falling apart. Cooking times will vary depending on the fruit and its ripeness, so keep a close eye on it. Once the fruit is poached to perfection, remove it from the pan and reduce the poaching liquid until it is thick and syrupy. Serve over the fruit with something creamy.

Pair red wine with:
brown sugar and spices such as ginger, cinnamon, allspice and star anise; and fruit such as pears, plums and cherries, as well as dried fruits.

Pair white wine with:
raw sugar, citrus peels and thyme or bay leaves; and fruit such as peaches, nectarines, rhubarb and berries.

VINCOTTO

This sweet or savoury wine syrup translates to 'cooked wine'. It is equally good drizzled over ice cream, cakes and roasted beetroot, or used as the base of a dressing.

Pour 3 cups (750 ml) fruity red wine into a saucepan and add ½ cup (110 g) caster (superfine) sugar, a pinch of salt, 30 g (1 oz) sliced ginger, 1 teaspoon crushed cardamom pods, 1 cinnamon stick and a few allspice berries or cloves. Simmer over low heat, stirring to dissolve the sugar, then bring to the boil over high heat. Boil for 5 minutes, then reduce the heat to medium and simmer for 20–30 minutes, until the wine has reduced by one-quarter and looks glossy and syrupy. Strain through a fine-mesh sieve into a clean jar or bottle and seal. The vincotto will keep in the fridge for up to 6 months.

Makes 1 cup (250 ml)

WINE VINEGAR

To make your own vinegar, you'll need a live vinegar with the active culture, or 'mother', in it. You can buy this at health-food stores. Use 1 cup (250 ml) live vinegar for every 3 cups (750 ml) wine.

Place your wine and vinegar in a large sterilised jar (page 278). Cover with muslin (cheesecloth) or a clean Chux and secure with an elastic band. Let it sit unrefrigerated for at least a month and up to 2 or 3 months, until it tastes tart and acidic. Don't be alarmed if a slimy jellyfish begins to appear on the surface. This is the mother growing and it's a very good sign.

As you begin to use your vinegar, you can top it up with more wine; just make sure you stick to the ratio of three parts wine to one part vinegar. Feel free to mix your wines, but keep whites and reds separate.

Makes 4 cups (1 litre)

PEANUTS

Peanuts are an excellent crop that we should be eating more of. While we think of peanuts as part of the nut family, they are technically a legume, making them a naturally sustainable crop that takes nitrogen from the air and releases it back into the soil as it grows. Peanuts (unlike almonds, which need enormous amounts of water), adapt to the water levels available to them. This makes them a better choice for Australia's increasingly hot, dry climate. These little heroes are also considered a zero-waste crop, as every part of the plant, from the roots to the hulls, are turned into other useable products.

If that isn't enough to convince you, peanuts are incredibly high in protein, making them an excellent addition to our increasingly plant-based diets. They are loaded with monounsaturated fats for healthy heart function and are high in vitamin E and folate.

Peanuts need to get out of the salty snack aisle and become a main player in our kitchens. They need to rebrand and we are here to help!

Always buy locally grown peanuts, and when buying spreads and butters choose brands that contain peanuts, salt and nothing else.

Most bulk stores sell peanuts with and without their shells. Unshelled peanuts will last for several months stored in a cool, dark place, but shelled peanuts should be stored in the fridge or freezer, because their high oil content causes them to go rancid when exposed to heat and light.

GO WITH ...

Raw peanuts taste more like a bean, but toast them and they fully realise their nutty, sweet potential. Peanuts also have a meaty taste, which can make even the lightest salad feel substantial. Peanuts love cool cucumber and most seafood. Pair toasted peanuts with spicy ginger and you have more than enough flavour to start a stir-fry. Their flavour also works well with lime, cinnamon and chillies, and cool herbs such as mint and coriander (cilantro). And the toasted flavours of peanuts and the rich floral flavours of honey are meant to be together.

PEANUT BUTTER

Whenever we buy a big container of peanuts, we make a jar of this butter. It's basically like bought peanut butter, but without any additives and a quarter of the price.

Place 2 cups (240 g) roasted peanuts in a food processor and blitz to a butter. This will take a little longer than you think, but it's fun to watch the peanuts turn to crushed peanuts, then to crumbs, then to a big dry ball and then finally to a peanut butter consistency. Blitz in 2–4 tablespoons honey if you want to use it with sweet things, or a pinch or two of salt. Store in a jar in the pantry or fridge until it gets eaten!

Makes 300 g (10½ oz)

MISO SATAY SAUCE

As long-time lovers of a good satay sauce, we wanted to perfect a homemade version that we could whip up midweek. This is a simplified recipe with minimal ingredients – instead we've used miso to bring complexity. We like to brush it over grilled tofu, vegetables or chicken skewers, or serve it with the satay salad bowl on page 76.

Place ½ onion in a food processor along with a roughly chopped garlic clove, 1 tablespoon grated ginger, 1–2 chopped red chillies, ¼ teaspoon ground turmeric and 2 teaspoons ground coriander. Blitz until very finely chopped.

Heat 2 tablespoons vegetable oil in a frying pan over medium heat and sauté the spice paste for 5 minutes – you want it to be softened and cooked but not browned. Remove from the heat and add 1 tablespoon miso paste, 1 tablespoon soy sauce, 1 tablespoon brown sugar, 2 tablespoons freshly squeezed lime juice and 3 tablespoons crunchy peanut butter. Set the pan over low heat, stirring well to make a paste. Add ½ cup (125 ml) water and simmer and stir until the paste thickens. You may need to gradually add up to another ½ cup (125 ml) water to achieve a sauce-like consistency. Use warm or leave to cool and store in the fridge in an airtight container for up to 1 week.

Makes 1 cup (250 ml)

CANDIED PEANUT TREATS

These candied peanuts are so good you'll have to hide them from yourself or you'll eat the whole lot.

Place 2 cups (280 g) unsalted peanuts (or use 1½ cups/80 g peanuts and ½ cup/75 g sesame seeds), 1 teaspoon each of salt and ground cinnamon, 1 cup (220 g) raw sugar, 1 tablespoon cocoa powder and ⅓ cup (80 ml) water in a good-sized frying pan over medium heat. Stir well and cook for about 15 minutes, until the mixture becomes dry and dusty-looking. It'll take time but you'll know when it happens! Stop stirring and allow a sugar syrup to form on the bottom of the pan, then stir the nuts again to make sure they are well coated in the gloss. Cook for a further 5–10 minutes, stirring often, until the nuts are roasted and glossy but not burnt. Mix through ¼ teaspoon cayenne pepper if you like it hot, then pour the mixture onto a baking tray lined with baking paper and allow to cool. Break into pieces and store in an airtight container or jar in the pantry for up to 1 week.

Makes snacks for 8 or a good stash for 1

SATAY SALAD BOWL

Serves 4

This is a substantial salad and a filling meal on its own. While you do need to cook the ingredients separately to avoid things going limp, it is well worth the extra effort. The pleasure of this dish is not just in the flavour but also the textures. Use what's on hand and change ingredients according to the seasons. You could swap the tofu out for a little poached chicken, baked fish or stir-fried pork mince.

1 potato
200 g (7 oz) crunchy vegetables,
  cut into thin matchsticks
  asparagus
  snow peas (mangetout)
  carrots
  green beans
  broccolini
300 g (10½ oz) protein
  firm tofu, cut into 2 cm
    (¾ inch) cubes
  poached and shredded chicken
    (page 95)
  left-over baked fish, flaked
    (page 48)
  cooked spiced pork mince
    (page 265)
2 tablespoons vegetable oil
  (optional)
2 Lebanese (short) cucumbers,
  cut into batons
2–3 hard-boiled eggs, sliced
  into quarters
Salt and freshly cracked
  black pepper
1 quantity Miso satay sauce
  (page 75)
¼ cup (35 g) toasted unsalted
  peanuts, to serve
Coriander (cilantro) leaves,
  to serve

Cook the potato in a saucepan of boiling salted water until tender. Remove using a slotted spoon and set aside to cool.

Add the crunchy vegetables to the boiling water and blanch for 1 minute. Drain and refresh under cold running water and shake dry. Set aside to cool completely.

If using tofu, heat the vegetable oil in a frying pan over medium–high heat and sauté the tofu in batches for 2–3 minutes, until crispy on all sides. Drain on a plate lined with paper towel and allow to cool to room temperature.

Slice the potato and place it in a serving bowl with the cucumber, egg and tofu, chicken, fish or pork. Season with salt and pepper. Pour over the satay sauce, garnish with toasted peanuts and coriander and serve.

A WHOLE PINEAPPLE

Native to South America, the pineapple got its strange name because colonial Europeans had a habit of comparing something unfamiliar with something they knew from back home, and thought that the pineapple resembled the pine cone.

The fruit of the pineapple is actually made up of 100–200 individual flowers fused together around a central stem. The diamond pattern on a mature pineapple is the remains of these flowers.

Pineapple is low in starch so it does not continue to develop its sugars after harvesting. For this reason, pineapple should be cut when fully ripe. A ripe pineapple will give a thud sound if you tap it and it shouldn't look too green.

Pineapples are very high in vitamin C and there is more than 100 per cent of your recommended daily intake in 1 cup. They are also extremely high in a mineral called manganese, which is essential for bone health. Plus, even conventionally grown pineapples use few pesticides or chemicals in their production. Do you really need any more reasons to cut up a pineapple after dinner and serve it for dessert?

Keep pineapple at room temperature with the skin and top on for about 3 days. Cut pineapple will keep in an airtight container in the fridge for a week.

GOES WITH ...

Pineapple goes well with bananas and kiwi fruit, mangoes and coconut. It is also perfect with spicier pairings of chilli, cinnamon, pepper and coriander. We love pineapple with all seafood. Whether pineapple should ever be seen on a pizza is a matter for your own household to discuss. In both our homes the kids have worn us down – we have surrendered.

WASTE TIP

Don't toss the pineapple skins – they're full of flavour and can be easily made into a delicious drink or syrup (see opposite).

PINEAPPLE SODA

This is based on the Mexican beverage 'tepache', a sweet and sour drink with an unexpected hit of heat. This is a simple ferment so don't be afraid to give it a go. The results are sweet, spicy and naturally fizzy. Enjoy ice cold.

Place the skins from ½ a pineapple, ¼ cup (55 g) brown sugar, 1 cinnamon stick and 1 fresh jalapeño or hot red chilli in a clean 500 ml (17 fl oz) jar and fill with water. Cover with muslin (cheesecloth) and secure with a rubber band. Stir 2–3 times a day over 2 days, during which time the sugars will convert to lactic acid.

Strain the soda into a jug and discard the solid ingredients. Wash out the jar and pour the strained soda back in, but this time secure with the lid to capture the carbon dioxide that will build in the jar and make your soda fizzy. Leave at room temperature for 2 days before drinking and refrigerate for up to 1 week.

Makes about 400 ml (13½ fl oz)

PINEAPPLE SKIN SYRUP

There is so much flavour in pineapple skin that it would be a crime to throw it away. Make this syrup and add pineapple flavour wherever you drizzle it. At Cornersmith we drizzle it over our whole pineapple cake (page 82), fruit salads and ice cream, and use it in marinades, salad dressings and cocktails.

Place washed and roughly chopped pineapple skin (along with the core if you haven't eaten it) in a saucepan with 2 cups (500 ml) water, 1 cup (220 g) caster (superfine) sugar, 1 star anise, 4 allspice berries, 2 cloves and ¼ teaspoon black peppercorns. Set over low heat and simmer for 15–20 minutes, then strain. If you want a thicker syrup, place it back on the heat and reduce further. Pour the syrup into a clean jar or bottle and store in the fridge for up to 1 month.

Makes about 350 ml (12 fl oz)

CHARRED PINEAPPLE WITH HONEY, SALT AND LIME

Serve these charred pineapple wedges with a Mexican-style feast, grilled seafood or your Christmas ham, or thinly slice and toss through a red cabbage, cucumber and snow pea slaw. For a delicious sweet version, leave out the chilli and salt and serve on top of rice porridge, muesli, yoghurt or ice cream.

Trim the peel from a whole pineapple (reserve the skins to make syrup; see opposite) and cut the flesh into long, thick wedges. Heat a frying pan over medium–high heat, then, working in batches, char the wedges in their own juices for 3–4 minutes, until golden and caramelised. Make sure you keep checking so they don't burn. Squeeze in the juice of 1 lime to help make a zesty caramel sauce form in the pan. Once the wedges are charred and oozy, transfer them to a platter, drizzle with 1–2 tablespoons honey, then sprinkle over ½ teaspoon flaked salt and a little black pepper, ½ teaspoon chilli flakes and the zest of 1 lime. Scatter a few mint leaves over the top and serve.

Serves 6–8

PINEAPPLE HOT SAUCE

Makes 4 cups (1 litre)

We teach this hot sauce recipe in our chilli preserving workshops at Cornersmith. It's a great base recipe for making spicy sauces from excess fruit. We make this mostly with pineapples and green chillies, but peaches, plums or green tomatoes work really well, too. If you are using pineapple, make sure you save the skins for the pineapple soda or pineapple skin syrup on page 79.

50–150 g (1¾–5½ oz) long
    green or red chillies (depending
    on how hot your chillies are),
    roughly chopped
35 g ginger, grated
2 garlic cloves, grated
Zest and juice of 2 limes or
    1 lemon
800 g–1 kg (1 lb 12 oz–2 lb 4 oz)
    skinned pineapple, chopped into
    3 cm (1¼ inch) chunks, or use
    peaches
    mangoes
    green tomatoes
    cherries
    plums
1 cup (250 ml) apple cider vinegar
3 tablespoons caster (superfine)
    sugar
1 tablespoon salt

Place the chilli, ginger, garlic and lime or lemon zest in the bowl of a food processor and blitz to a paste. With the motor running slowly, pour in the lime or lemon juice.

Add half the chopped pineapple and blitz until smooth, then add the remaining pineapple and blend again to form a smooth paste.

Pour the paste into a saucepan and stir through the vinegar, sugar and salt. Bring to a gentle simmer and cook for 15–20 minutes, until you have a thick sauce.

Pour the sauce into sterilised bottles (page 278) and keep in the fridge for up to 8 weeks. Alternatively, heat-process the bottled sauce for 15 minutes (page 278) and store in a cool, dark place for up to 1 year. Once opened, store in the fridge and use within 4 months.

TIP

You can also add coriander roots, shallots or spring onions (scallions) when blending.

WHOLE PINEAPPLE CAKE (GLUTEN FREE)

Serves 8

This is a delicious morning or afternoon tea cake and a staple at the Cornersmith cafe. We love it because it uses the whole fruit and extracts as much flavour as possible from the pineapple's flesh, core and skin. You can also just use pineapple cores if you have an excess left over from another recipe – char them on a grill to intensify their flavour and sweetness before you purée them. Feel free to experiment with this recipe using oranges, lemons or other fruit purées.

1 pineapple
1½ cups (150 g) almond meal
2¾ cups (250 g) desiccated
    coconut
1 teaspoon baking powder
6 eggs
250 g (9 oz) caster (superfine)
    sugar
Toasted coconut flakes, to serve
Natural or Greek yoghurt,
    to serve

Preheat the oven to 160°C (315°F/Gas mark 2–3) and line a 30 cm (12 inch) loaf (bar) tin with baking paper.

Cut the skin off the pineapple and set aside, then cut the flesh and core into small cubes and blitz them in a food processor until smooth. You'll need 400 g (14 oz) of pineapple purée for the batter.

Whisk together the almond meal, desiccated coconut and baking powder in a large bowl and set aside. In a stand mixer with the whisk attachment, whisk the eggs and sugar on medium speed until pale and fluffy (or you can do this in a large bowl with a hand whisk). Add the pineapple purée to the egg mixture and whisk for another minute. Slowly add the dry ingredients in batches, whisking well after each addition. Pour the mixture into the prepared tin and bake for 50–60 minutes, until golden brown and a skewer inserted into the centre of the cake comes out clean.

Meanwhile use the pineapple skin to make the pineapple skin syrup on page 79.

Leave the cake to cool in the tin on a wire rack for 10 minutes before turning out. Serve straight away or keep in an airtight container in the fridge for up to 1 week. Serve warm or toasted with the pineapple skin syrup, toasted coconut and yoghurt.

MANGOES

Native to India and a relative of the cashew, the mango is the unofficial fruit of summer. Messy mango eating is something of a ritual on a hot day and it is possibly the only fruit that any of us buy by the case.

There is variation in the sweetness and texture of mangoes depending on the variety and season. The best mangoes are picked ripe off the tree, but they only have a 24–48 hour shelf life, so most commercially grown mangoes are picked unripe and ripen after harvest. The colour of the skin is not a good indication of ripeness; instead choose mangoes that have a sweet fragrance and a little give when touched. If you need to ripen mangoes at home, place them in a brown paper bag for a day. Keep mangoes that you intend to eat within a day or two in the fruit bowl. Mangoes for later use should be refrigerated, where they'll last for up to 2 weeks.

Mangoes are high in vitamins A, B6, C and E. They also contain a significant amount of copper, which helps the body absorb iron and maintain healthy immune function and bones.

GO WITH ...

The mango's heady sweetness is well matched to bold flavours: add a squeeze of lime, a handful of coriander (cilantro) and you have a simple salad, or balance it with spicy flavours, such as chilli, cumin, cinnamon and ginger. Avocado and coconut share mango's creaminess. Mango and white fish are meant to be together, so serve the relish opposite with the whole baked fish on page 48.

WASTE TIP

Use leftover mango skins and stones to make a syrup to use on cakes or in cocktails (see opposite).

USE IT ALL

If you find yourself with too many mangoes, you can dehydrate them to enjoy as snacks (page 172–3).

MANGO SKIN SYRUP

If you eat mangoes like we eat mangoes, you'll end up with skins and pips aplenty. Both have lots of flavour that you can't chew through, but you can extract. Making this syrup is bottling the essence of mango. Drizzle over cakes, fruit salad and ice cream, or invent a cocktail and use this as the base.

Wash and roughly chop the mango skin from 1–2 mangoes and place in a saucepan with the mango pips, 2 cups (500 ml) water and 1 cup (220 g) caster (superfine) sugar. Add a few slices of ginger or the last knob in the fridge and some lemon or lime peel. A little lemongrass is nice, too. Set over low heat and simmer for 15–20 minutes, then strain. If you want a thicker syrup, place it back on the heat and reduce further. Pour the syrup into a clean jar or bottle and store in the fridge for up to 1 month.

Makes about 350 ml (12 fl oz)

MANGO COMPOTE

If you have a few browning mangoes in the house, their over-ripe sweetness is perfect for this simple compote. Ripe or even slightly under-ripe mangoes also work.

Place the flesh of 2 mangoes, 1 tablespoon honey or maple syrup, 1 tablespoon freshly squeezed lemon juice and 3 tablespoons water in a saucepan. You could also add either ¼ teaspoon vanilla essence, the zest of 1 lime, 1 tablespoon crushed lemongrass or a few mint stems. Simmer over low heat for 5–8 minutes, until the mango is soft and falling apart. Remove from the heat and mash with a fork for a rough compote or blend to a smooth purée. Taste, and add more sweetness if needed or another squeeze of lemon if it needs a lift. Serve spooned over yoghurt for breakfast, in smoothies or over ice cream and desserts. Keep in a jar in the fridge for up to 4 days.

Makes 1 x 400 ml (14 fl oz) jar

Mango skin syrup

QUICK MANGO RELISH

Fresh, sweet and spicy – if summer was a condiment, well, this relish would be it. Whip up a small batch, keep it in the fridge and serve with baked fish or tacos, alongside curries or in a white bread and butter ham sandwich.

Chop 2 mangoes into 3 cm (1¼ inch) cubes (set aside the stones and peel to make the mango skin syrup opposite). Thinly slice a small onion, 2 spring onions (scallions) or a few shallots. Heat 2½ tablespoons olive oil in a frying pan over medium heat, add the onion and sauté for 5 minutes or until soft and sweet. Add 1 tablespoon freshly grated ginger, 1 teaspoon mustard seeds, ½ teaspoon salt and ½ teaspoon chilli flakes. Sauté until fragrant, then add the chopped mango and mix well. Add 3 tablespoons apple cider vinegar and 2 tablespoons caster (superfine) sugar and stir to dissolve. Simmer over low heat for 15–20 minutes, until the relish is thick and glossy. Allow to cool a little, then transfer to a container or jar. It will keep in the fridge for at least 2 weeks.

Makes 1 x 500 ml (17 fl oz) jar

MANGO YOGHURT CAKE

Serves 8

This light and fluffy cake is super easy to make. Its beauty is in its simple flavour, which can be tricked up with the addition of a teaspoon or two of spices and herbs, such as ground cinnamon, wattleseeds, thyme or rosemary. Thinly slice whatever fruit you have to hand to make this seasonal. Instead of almond meal, you could use the same amount of a mix of rolled oats and desiccated coconut for the topping.

3 eggs
¾ cup (165 g) caster (superfine)
   sugar
½ cup (125 ml) vegetable oil, plus
   extra for greasing
1 cup (250 g) natural yoghurt
Zest of 2 lemons, 2 limes or
   2 oranges
1–2 teaspoons spices or herbs
   (optional)
1½ cups (225 g) self-raising flour
½ teaspoon baking powder

TOPPING

1 mango, sliced into thin wedges
⅓ cup (60 g) brown sugar
40 g (1½ oz) almond meal

Preheat the oven to 170°C (325°F/Gas mark 3) and line or grease a 23 cm (9 inch) springform cake tin with baking paper or oil.

Using a hand whisk, briefly mix the eggs and sugar in a large bowl until pale and a little fluffy, then slowly whisk in the vegetable oil, followed by the yoghurt, citrus zest and spices or herbs, if using.

In a separate bowl, whisk together the flour and baking powder, then add this mixture to the wet ingredients and whisk to combine. Pour into the prepared cake tin.

To make the topping, toss together the mango slices, brown sugar and almond meal in a small bowl, then arrange on top of the cake.

Bake for 50 minutes, until a skewer inserted into the centre of the cake comes out clean. Rest in the tin for 5 minutes, then use a knife to slide around the edge of the cake and remove it from the tin.

Any left-over cake will keep in an airtight container for up to 3 days.

A WHOLE CHICKEN

A WHOLE CAULIFLOWER

FENNEL

LEEKS

SHOPPING BASKET 3

Buying whole ingredients, such as a whole chicken, a whole cauliflower or fennel with its long fronds attached, is really the most practical way to shop and cook. Buying whole is economical, it reduces packaging and helps organise your meal planning. This basket features a free-range chicken, which we know isn't cheap, but here we teach you how to stretch it out to many meals, so the expense is manageable and your footprint is minimised. Oats, tahini and sesame seeds are our pantry staples in this chapter, which make everyday breakfasts and snacks come together without additives or fuss.

ROLLED OATS

TAHINI

BERRIES

SESAME SEEDS

FROM THIS BASKET ...

MEALS

Ava's sticky kimchi chicken pieces (page 92)

Chicken and vegetable dumplings (page 92)

Jude's mum's Hungarian chicken (page 93)

Chicken meatballs (page 93)

The magic poached chicken (page 95)

Vietnamese-style chicken salad (page 96)

Taco Tuesday spiced shredded chicken (page 97)

Chicken sandwiches (page 97)

Whole cauliflower bake (page 100)

Cauli schnitzels (page 102)

Leek and not-much-chicken pie (page 105)

Muesli four ways (page 113)

SIDES

Roasted cauliflower florets (page 103)

Raw cauliflower salad (page 103)

Braised whole leeks (page 105)

Shaved fennel, orange and black olive salad (page 107)

Roasted fennel with citrus zest and chilli (page 107)

SNACKS, SWEETS & DRINKS

Cauliflower fritters (page 102)

Strawberry shrub cocktail (page 109)

Berry jam drops (page 109)

Easy homemade muesli bars (page 113)

QUICK PRESERVING IDEAS

Turmeric-pickled cauliflower stems (page 102)

Berry jam (page 109)

Strawberry and fennel shrub (page 109)

NOTHING GOES TO WASTE

Roast chicken scrap stock (page 97)

Sautéed cauliflower stems and leaves (page 103)

Sautéed leek tops (page 105)

Spicy fennel top green sauce (page 107)

Tired berry sauce (page 110)

A WHOLE CHICKEN

Once upon a time, a whole chicken on the family table was considered a luxury and there would be no wastage. These days chicken is commonplace, and to meet consumer appetites chickens are bred hard and fast. Standard conditions are not pretty and the result is a young flavourless bird. We think it is time to change our habits. The trouble is that most of us don't know how to make multiple meals out of one whole chicken. So, we choose convenient cuts such as thighs and breasts, overlook issues of animal welfare and packaging, and totally forgo flavour.

Our approach to buying chicken is to only purchase birds that we know have been raised well. Don't rely on packaging promises as they can be misleading. We don't buy meat at major supermarkets, but if that is your only option, buy the best-quality organic bird they have. These birds are more expensive; however, making one chicken last for many meals will keep your shopping expenses down.

When we buy a whole chicken we usually use it in one of three ways:

- Poach it whole and shred it, using small amounts of meat for multiple dinners and lunches.

- Joint it and use the various cuts for two full meals (page 92–93). This is the kind of skill any home cook can acquire – it's economical, sustainable and essential for reducing food waste.

- Cook it for a special dinner, where we make a one-meal-only roast chicken with all the trimmings.

Whatever way you choose to deal with a chicken, be sure to keep the carcass for making stock. Doing so will give you a whole other meal.

JOINT A WHOLE CHICKEN FOR TWO MEALS

Consider the cost of buying an ethically raised chicken as an investment from which you can make a few meals, and its affordability becomes more apparent. The key to getting multiple meals from one bird is to joint it. Before you stop reading, hold on! We are not butchers: we taught ourselves how to do this by watching YouTube. It isn't hard – we promise. Watching a video online will teach you how to break the chicken into eight pieces: two legs, two thighs, two wings and two breasts. And don't worry if your cuts don't look like the butcher's; ours don't either.

The breast meat is low in fat and great for mincing and lightly poaching. By adding other ingredients, the meat from even one breast can easily be stretched to feed two or more people. The thighs, legs and wings are higher in fat and, therefore, bigger on flavour. Slow-cook them with other vegetables for one-pot meals that will feed many mouths.

Here are our recipes for transforming one chicken into two complete meals, simply by using the cuts wisely.

AVA'S STICKY KIMCHI CHICKEN PIECES

Ava is a teacher at Cornersmith and a genius at creating the tastiest meals from what is at hand, using the last scraping of something or making the most of left-over ingredients. This recipe is great for using the legs, thighs and wings of your chicken.

Preheat the oven to 200°C (400°F/Gas mark 6). In a large mixing bowl, combine 3 tablespoons vegetable oil, 8 crushed garlic cloves, ½ teaspoon each of salt and cracked black pepper, 90 ml (3 fl oz) kimchi juice from the bottom of your kimchi jar (or lemon juice if there is no kimchi in the house) and 100 g (3½ oz) marmalade. Add 2 chicken thighs, 2 chicken wings and 2 chicken drumsticks to the sauce and toss well so the pieces are evenly coated. Roast for 40 minutes, basting the chicken every 15 minutes with the sauce, until golden and sticky. Serve with sautéed greens, fried rice (page 159) and lots of kimchi.

Serves 2–4

CHICKEN AND VEGETABLE DUMPLINGS

These simple dumplings use only 200 g (7 oz) breast meat to serve four people. Served in a homemade broth, they make a wholesome and comforting meal. You can also use this mixture in the fried dumplings on page 157.

In a food processor, place 200 g (7 oz) raw breast meat (you could also use thigh or leg meat), 150 g (5½ oz) shredded cabbage, 1 egg, 1½ teaspoons fresh or dried chilli, 1 teaspoon minced ginger, 1 minced garlic clove and ¼ teaspoon salt and pepper and blend until smooth. Transfer to a bowl and, with wet hands, form into 10–12 walnut-sized dumplings.

Bring 4 cups (1 litre) stock to a simmer. Add the dumplings one at a time to the simmering stock and poach for 5 minutes. Remove with a slotted spoon and divide among four bowls. Bring the broth back to a simmer and add 1–2 cups cooked rice or pasta and 1 cup (100 g) thinly sliced seasonal vegetables. Cook for 3–4 minutes, until the vegetables are tender, then ladle over the dumplings and serve.

Serves 4

JUDE'S MUM'S HUNGARIAN CHICKEN

Thank you, Jude, for this perfect one-pot meal. It's now entering its third generation of nourishing our families. Serve with a cauli bake (page 100) alongside for an even more substantial meal.

Use six pieces of chicken for this recipe: thighs, legs and wings. Heat 1 tablespoon olive oil in a flameproof casserole dish over medium heat. Add the chicken in batches and cook for 5–7 minutes, until browned all over. Remove the chicken and set aside. In the same dish, sauté 1 sliced onion for 4–5 minutes, until soft. Add 1 teaspoon sweet paprika and ½ teaspoon smoked paprika and cook, stirring, for 30 seconds. Return the chicken to the dish, add a few handfuls of sliced mushroom and/or 1–2 thinly sliced potatoes, 1 cup (250 ml) stock of your choice and season with salt and pepper. Reduce the heat to low, cover and gently simmer for 1 hour. Throw in a handful of English spinach or green beans in the last 5 minutes of cooking.

Serves 4

CHICKEN MEATBALLS

This recipe uses a small amount of chicken breast and plenty of seasonal vegetables and herbs to make meatballs that are light and tasty but still full of chicken flavour. Serve with flatbreads, salad and the tomato rice on page 249 or the pilaf on page 161. Alternatively, add them to a crusty roll to make your own meatball sub.

Use the ratio 100 g (3½ oz) raw chicken meat to 100 g (3½ oz) roughly chopped seasonal vegetables and herbs, which makes about eight meatballs. Scale up depending on how many mouths you're feeding. For four, we usually double the amount to make 16 meatballs.

Place 200 g (7 oz) chicken meat (breast or thigh from your jointed chicken) in a food processor with 200 g (7 oz) roughly chopped vegetables and herbs – a combination of leek (including the green tops) and cauliflower works well, but you can also use carrot, celery, fennel, onion, green onion, cabbage, chives, parsley or coriander (cilantro) leaves and stems. Add 2 sliced garlic cloves, 2 tablespoons thyme leaves, 1 teaspoon salt, 1 teaspoon cracked black pepper, the zest of 1 lemon and ¼ cup (25 g) breadcrumbs (see page 269 for our mix) and blitz until well combined. You can leave the mixture a little chunky for texture, or blitz until smooth if someone in your household hates vegetables.

Use a tablespoon measurement to roll the mixture into walnut-sized meatballs. Heat 3 tablespoons olive or vegetable oil in a frying pan over medium heat and cook the meatballs for 3 minutes on each side or until golden and cooked through.

Makes 16

THE MAGIC POACHED CHICKEN

FOUNDATION RECIPE

Makes 4–5 cups (400–500 g) shredded chicken, plus 4 cups (1 litre) or more chicken stock

We spend so much time discussing how to make multiple meals out of one beautiful free-range chicken that it's almost a competition between us to see how far we can stretch one bird. Poaching a chicken on a Sunday evening when you know you have a busy week ahead creates all kinds of magic, plus it means there's less dinner panic and no takeaway!

There are so many different methods for poaching a whole bird, and they all give slightly different results. After years of practice, we find this method the most straightforward – it gives a slightly firmer meat, which is great for chicken sandwiches or added to salads, tacos or fried rice. The recipes overleaf make the most of your shredded chicken and are really easy to pull together after work on a weekday. Plus, you end up with a good amount of tasty stock, which can be turned into a whole other meal (see page 190–91 for tips on making soup).

1 whole free-range organic chicken
1 unpeeled onion
½ head garlic
Stock-friendly vegetables that
    need to be used up
    half a broken carrot
    fennel tops
    leek tops
    celery stalks and leaves
    ½ tomato
1 bundle herbs tied with kitchen
    string
    parsley stems
    thyme
    bay leaves
    coriander stems and roots
    oregano
    rosemary
1 tablespoon black peppercorns

Rinse your chicken and place it in a medium saucepan with the onion, garlic, vegetables, herbs and peppercorns. Cover with just enough water to submerge the chicken. Slowly bring to the boil, then reduce the heat to very low so the liquid is just bubbling, and simmer for 1 hour. Turn off the heat and allow to cool for 15 minutes in the stock. Using tongs, remove the chicken from the pan and place in a large bowl.

Place the stock back over low heat and when the chicken is cool enough to handle, start stripping the meat (Alex is like a scavenger with chicken meat and doesn't let a single strand out of her sight!). As you're stripping the chicken, chuck the bones, skin and any bits you're not going to eat into the stock. Adding the skin back in means you'll get a rich, darker and slightly cloudier stock – not a clear, light broth – but it adds so much flavour and it seems a shame to throw it in the bin.

Simmer your stock over low heat for another 1–2 hours, occasionally skimming the scum that rises to the surface. The longer you cook it, the less stock you will have, but the richer and more flavoursome it will be. Strain the stock into a bowl, taste and add a little salt if needed. Allow to cool slightly, then store in the fridge for up to 5 days or in the freezer for 3 months.

Once your shredded chicken meat is cool, store it in an airtight container in the fridge for 3–4 days. Use the meat first and then use the stock for a meal later in the week.

WHAT TO DO WITH POACHED SHREDDED CHICKEN

Having poached shredded chicken in the fridge is a good place to start when thinking about what's for dinner. Here are a few ways to turn a small amount of cooked chicken into a meal.

SATAY SALAD

Follow the recipe on page 76, and swap out the tofu for the same amount of poached shredded chicken, smother with satay sauce and you're set!

OVEN-BAKED RISOTTO

Follow the recipe on page 163, and in the last 5 minutes of cooking add 1 cup (150 g) poached shredded chicken to warm through.

FRIED RICE

Follow the recipe on page 159, and add 1 cup (150 g) poached shredded chicken in the last few minutes of cooking for a quick and more substantial meal.

LETTUCE CUPS

Follow the recipe on page 63, and swap out the fish for the same amount of poached shredded chicken.

NOODLE SOUP

Add 1 cup (150 g) poached shredded chicken to brothy soups to make them heartier, such as the ramen on page 191 and the pasta in broth on page 187.

VIETNAMESE-STYLE CHICKEN SALAD

If you have poached chicken ready to go, this is a dinner that can be pulled together with very little effort. The dressing is also a good one to have up your sleeve, because it also doubles as a dipping sauce.

In a large bowl, combine 3 cups (225 g) very thinly sliced cabbage, 1 cup (75 g) thinly sliced fennel, 1 cup (150 g) grated carrot (you can also use radish or daikon), ¼ cup (25 g) quick pickled ginger (page 239; optional) and 1 cup (30 g) picked herb leaves (mint, basil, coriander/cilantro). Add 1–2 cups (100–200 g) cooked shredded chicken (this could be from your poached chicken, left-over from a roast or you could grill and shred two chicken breasts or thighs) and 2 cups (150 g) cooked vermicelli noodles, if you like.

In a jar, mix 3 tablespoons freshly squeezed lime juice, ⅓ cup (80 ml) fish sauce, 1 tablespoon rice vinegar, 2 tablespoons caster (superfine) sugar, 1 tablespoon sesame oil, 1 minced garlic clove and ½ finely chopped red chilli. Shake well to combine. Gently dress the salad and top with toasted peanuts or sesame seeds.

Serves 4

TACO TUESDAY SPICED SHREDDED CHICKEN

Taco Tuesday is a regular in our houses, using up bits and pieces from the fridge and pantry. And as long as there is sour cream and taco shells, the kids are happy. Condiments are really what make this meal. Pull out the sambal from page 261, the spicy pickled cabbage from page 120 and even the carrot kimchi on page 227, or use anything hot and flavoursome that you have in the fridge. The chicken isn't the hero, it's just a nice addition – and in a sustainable kitchen, it's important to start thinking about meat as a condiment rather than the main event.

Heat 1 tablespoon vegetable oil in a frying pan over medium heat and sauté 1 small chopped onion and 1 crushed garlic clove. Add ½ teaspoon each of ground cumin, dried oregano, paprika, salt, black pepper and chilli flakes, and give everything a stir. Add 1–2 cups (100–200 g) shredded chicken and flash in the hot pan until well seasoned and hot.

Serve the tacos with the chicken, a light fresh slaw (page 124), something creamy, such as sour cream, guacamole or grated cheese, and your condiments of choice. A quick rice or bean dish completes this meal – try the refried beans on page 233 or the tomato rice on page 249.

Serves 4

CHICKEN SANDWICHES

A chicken sandwich is a pretty simple pleasure. Just like the fish sandwiches on page 51, we use left-over chicken to make these. Pack them into school lunchboxes or for days at the beach or the park.

Place 1½ cups (150 g) shredded chicken in a bowl with ⅓ cup (80 g) mayonnaise, ¼ cup (40 g) finely diced red onion, ¼ cup (30 g) finely sliced celery, 2 tablespoons chopped celery leaves or parsley and ¼ teaspoon each of salt and pepper. Use a fork to whisk the mixture into a rough paste. Spread on a baguette or your favourite bread.

Makes 3–4

ROAST CHICKEN SCRAP STOCK

Save the bones from a roast chicken, or roast the chicken carcass after jointing a whole bird (this takes 15 minutes at 200°C/400°F/Gas mark 6). If you've got an hour or two before bed, then let the stock simmer straight after dinner. Otherwise, store the roasted chicken bones/carcass in an airtight container in the fridge for up to 3 days. Alternatively, stockpile bones/carcasses for up to 3 months in the freezer to make a larger batch of stock at a later date.

Place your roasted chicken bones/carcass in a medium saucepan, so that they fit snugly, and just cover with water. The less water, the richer your stock will be. If you have ½ onion, an old carrot or a few parsley stems in the fridge add them too, although it will still be delicious if you don't. Bring to the boil, then reduce the heat to the lowest setting and simmer for 1–2 hours. Strain the stock into a bowl, taste, and add a little salt if needed. Allow to cool slightly, then store in the fridge for up to 5 days.

You now have a rich stock with which to make dinner later in the week, such as broth with noodles or rice and finely chopped vegetables.

Makes about 4 cups (1 litre)

A WHOLE CAULIFLOWER

The cauliflower is the bouquet you didn't realise you had at the bottom of the crisper. Its creamy head, or 'curd', is made up of underdeveloped flower buds that store within them a gentle earthy flavour. Being one of the mildest tasting members of the brassica family, the cauliflower is an obliging ingredient, taking up many different cooking techniques and flavours. Blanching, steaming or cooking in stock will result in a creamy-tasting cauliflower, while roasting and frying will bring out a stronger, sweeter flavour.

Cauliflower comes in green and purple and even orange – if you see them in the market, buy them just because they are pretty. Most often, we use the everyday white variety with the leaves still attached. Don't be afraid to buy the whole cauliflower and refuse the plastic wrapped smaller portions. Look for smaller heads if you can't face a heavy weight. Cauliflower is a great source of vitamin C and has a decent amount of vitamin K, folate and fibre.

Store whole cauliflower in a bag in the fridge or wrap the head in a big beeswax wrap and leave the stem sticking out the bottom – it will last for 7–10 days.

GOES WITH...

The sweet and mellow flavours of cauliflower scream out for salty ingredients, such as preserved lemons, capers, parmesan, olives, anchovies and bacon. Add a creamy element, such as nuts, butter, tahini, cream, milk or cheese, and everything is in harmony. Cauliflower absorbs spices well – think of Indian or Middle Eastern flavours like coriander, cumin, mustard seeds, ginger, turmeric and fenugreek.

WASTE TIP

Keep your cauliflower stems to make the turmeric-pickled cauliflower on page 102.

USE IT ALL

Make the sautéed cauliflower stems and leaves on page 103. You can also thinly slice the leaves and stems to use in stir-fries or add them to your kitchen scrap sauerkraut (page 120).

WHOLE CAULIFLOWER BAKE

Serves 4–6

Baking vegetables in a cheesy béchamel is very decadent. This cooking technique suits all sorts of vegetables (see some of our suggestions below), and it is also a wonderful way to turn the fibrous parts of vegetables into velvety, creamy bites.

We use this recipe to make a simple potato bake, but also to turn silverbeet (Swiss chard) stems and surplus celery stalks into a meal. In this version, we use the whole cauliflower – leaves, stems, the lot. The leaves and stems are fibrous, but sauté them into submission and they will give you great texture and flavour. Serve with a light green salad for a yummy easy dinner.

1.5 kg (3 lb 5 oz) whole cauliflower with leaves attached
1 tablespoon butter
1 tablespoon olive oil

CHEESE SAUCE

2 cups (500 ml) full-cream (whole) milk
60 g (2 oz) butter
40 g (1½ oz) plain (all-purpose) flour
1½ cups (150 g) grated mature cheese, such as tasty, cheddar or gruyere
Salt and freshly cracked black pepper, to taste

Strip the leaves and remove the stems from the cauliflower and chop both into 2 cm (¾ inch) pieces. Chop the florets into bite-sized pieces and set aside.

Bring a large saucepan of salted water to the boil. Meanwhile, melt the butter and oil in a frying pan over medium heat. Add the leaves and stems, along with a pinch of salt, then increase the heat slightly and sauté for 15 minutes or until tender.

When the water comes to the boil, add the cauliflower florets to the saucepan and simmer for 2 minutes. Drain and set aside. The leaves and stalk should be finished sautéing now, but taste and cook for a little longer if they are still tough. Set aside.

Preheat the oven to 180°C (350°F/Gas mark 4).

To make the cheese sauce, heat the milk to just below boiling point. In another saucepan, melt the butter and flour over low heat and stir to make a roux, but do not let it brown! Add the warm milk, ½ cup (125 ml) at a time, and stir constantly with a wooden spoon or whisk until you have a thick white sauce. Add the grated cheese and salt and pepper to taste, and stir until melted.

Spread the cauliflower leaves and stems in the base of a small baking dish and top with the florets. Pour the cheese sauce all over the cauliflower and bake in the oven for 30 minutes. Serve hot.

COMBINATIONS WE LIKE

- Silverbeet (Swiss chard) stems: If you have stripped the leaves off a bunch of silverbeet, then save the stems to make a gratin. Slice into 3 cm (1¼ inch) pieces, sauté over medium heat with 1 tablespoon olive oil for 5–7 minutes until soft, then bake in the sauce as above
- Celery: Yes, celery is absolutely delicious cooked in this way. Use 1 whole bunch and sauté in the same way as the silverbeet stems (though you may need to increase the cooking time until the celery is tender and sweet), then bake in the sauce as above.

CAULIFLOWER FRITTERS

This is how Alex got her kids to eat cauliflower! Fried and a little cheesy, these fritters are a fantastic quick vegetarian meal served with the tabbouleh-style salad on page 27. They're also great in lunchboxes the next day.

Grate ½ cauliflower head, including the stem, into a bowl (approximately 350 g/12 oz grated cauli). Add ¼ cup (35 g) flour (chickpea flour/besan if you have it), ⅓ cup (30 g) grated parmesan, 1 teaspoon ground cumin, ½ teaspoon dried thyme, a few pinches of salt and pepper and 1 beaten egg. Mix well. Squash the mixture into walnut-sized balls, and shallow-fry in 1 cm (½ inch) hot vegetable oil until crispy and golden.

Makes 16

CAULI SCHNITZELS

Schnitzels don't always have to be chicken. These are a hit with everyone. Serve them with a green salad, garlicky mayo and a wedge of lemon to make a healthy pub meal at home.

Preheat the oven to 170°C (340°F/Gas mark 3). Trim the leaves from a whole cauli and set aside for another meal. Cut the head into 3 cm (1¼ inch) 'steaks', keeping the stem attached (don't worry if they fall apart a bit, you can crumb any stray florets as well). You can also cut the cauliflower in half and then into smaller steaks if it's easier. Rub the steaks and florets all over in a little vegetable oil.

In a shallow bowl mix 50 g (1¾ oz) plain (all-purpose) flour with 1 teaspoon sweet paprika and ½ teaspoon salt. Crack 2 eggs into another shallow bowl and whisk together with 2 teaspoons Dijon mustard. In a third shallow bowl, place 150 g (5½ oz) breadcrumbs (store-bought, or ours from page 269). Dip each steak into the flour, egg, then breadcrumbs.

Heat some vegetable oil in a frying pan over medium heat, add the steaks and cook for 3–4 minutes each side until the crumbs are golden brown. Transfer to a baking tray and bake for 20–30 minutes until the cauliflower is tender. Serve hot.

Serves 4

TURMERIC-PICKLED CAULIFLOWER STEMS

Instead of throwing cauliflower stems in the bin, pickle them!

Chop any cauliflower you're not going to use into bite-sized pieces (including the stems) and put into a 300 ml (10½ fl oz) clean jar or container.

Heat ½ cup (125 ml) white wine vinegar, ½ cup (125 ml) water, 2 tablespoons raw sugar, ¼ teaspoon salt, ½ teaspoon caraway seeds and ½ teaspoon black peppercorns, plus a small pinch of ground turmeric and chilli flakes, in a small saucepan over medium heat. Stir to dissolve the sugar and bring to the boil, then pour over the cauliflower. Allow to sit in the fridge for a few days before eating; it should last for 2–3 weeks in the fridge. Serve with falafels, garlic dip and flat breads, stirred through a grain salad or in a sandwich.

Makes 1 x 300 ml (10½ fl oz) jar

ROASTED CAULIFLOWER FLORETS

Serve these with everything. They are excellent in tacos or on top of a pilaf, and they are a good pal to both falafel and fried eggs. Toss them through salads or squish into a cheese toastie with chilli jam.

Preheat the oven to 200°C (400°F/Gas mark 6). Cut 300 g (10½ oz) cauliflower into florets with the stems attached. In a bowl, place 1 teaspoon curry powder, 1 teaspoon ground cumin, 1 teaspoon ground coriander, ½ teaspoon salt and 50 ml (1¾ fl oz) olive oil and mix well. Add the cauliflower florets to the bowl and mix with your hands to make sure the cauliflower is well coated. Spread the cauliflower in a single layer on a baking tray and roast for 15–20 minutes, until golden.

Serve as is, or sprinkle with chopped herbs, toasted nuts and a squeeze of lemon.

Serves 2–3

SAUTÉED CAULIFLOWER STEMS AND LEAVES

Think of this side as a wilted green to accompany a family pie, the occasional roast chicken, or cauli schnitzels (see opposite). Any leftovers can be thrown into an omelette the next day. Using caraway and mustard seeds brings out the earthy flavours of cauliflower, but swap them for fennel seeds and grated ginger and this dish will go just as well with dal and rice.

Chop the leaves and stems from 1 small–medium cauliflower into 2–3 cm (¾–1¼ inch) pieces.

Heat 3–4 tablespoons olive oil in a large frying pan over medium heat. Add the leaves and stems and sauté for 5 minutes, then add 2 finely chopped garlic cloves, ½ teaspoon salt and 1 teaspoon caraway seeds.

Sauté for 10 minutes or until the stems are starting to soften. Add 2 teaspoons mustard seeds and sauté for a further 5 minutes. Serve.

Serves 4

RAW CAULIFLOWER SALAD

Here grated cauliflower is masquerading as a grain and it's doing a terrific job. This salad is satisfying on its own or as part of a meal of shared plates.

Coarsely grate ½ cauliflower head with a box grater and place in a large mixing bowl. Add the zest of 1 lemon, 2 tablespoons very finely chopped preserved lemon, 2 tablespoons chopped dill, ½ teaspoon each of ground cumin, sumac, chilli flakes and salt and gently mix to combine. Drizzle with olive oil and lemon juice and scatter with a decent amount of chopped herbs, and pickled or roasted grapes (page 171).

Serves 3 as a side

LEEKS

The Romans thought leeks would improve their voices, the Ancient Egyptians depicted leeks on wall carvings, and in modern-day Wales they are the national vegetable.

It is only recently that leeks started to be used as a seasoning ingredient like its cousin, the onion. It is such a missed opportunity not to savour leeks as a hero ingredient, and the common practice of using only the white part and throwing the green tops away seems mad to us. It's so wasteful to throw out half a vegetable! The green part is definitely more fibrous and requires longer cooking, but slice it thinly and you can use it just as you would the white part. If you learn nothing else in these pages, may it be that you never discard the green part of the leek again!

There are many ways to prepare whole leeks: cut them into largeish pieces and roast them, use them when making kimchi or stock, put them in fritters and soups or sauté them.

Leeks contain a good amount of fibre, vitamin K and magnesium. Like other vegetables in the onion family, they are high in flavonoids that protect our blood cells from damage.

Leeks usually need a good clean. Cut them in half and then slice them lengthways and wash under running water to clean off the dirt. Store uncut and dry leeks in the fridge for 2 weeks. They may go a little wrinkly, but once cooked they come good. You can also slice leeks and freeze them in an airtight container for 3 months.

GO WITH ...

The mild allium taste of leeks pairs with so many other flavours. Of course, onions and garlic are natural companions and make for a sweet base to many dishes. Leeks also match with other sweet-tasting ingredients, such as bacon, chicken, pumpkin and cream, to bring out the best in each other. Earthier flavours, such as potato, thyme, bay, mustard, cauliflower and potatoes, make for a rich yet balanced combination.

USE IT ALL

Leek tops are a delicious addition to the kitchen scrap sauerkraut (page 120).

BRAISED WHOLE LEEKS

When in season, leeks should be used as a feature vegetable. This lovely side dish has a silky texture and mildly sweet flavour.

Preheat the oven to 180°C (350°F/Gas mark 4) and line a baking tray with a piece of baking paper large enough to fold over the leeks. Remove the roots from 2 leeks and cut each leek into thirds. Split each third lengthways and give them a good rinse. Shake dry and place on the baking paper in the tray to snugly fit. Dot 25 g (¾ oz) butter over the top and sprinkle with ½ teaspoon each of salt and pepper. Combine 2½ tablespoons olive oil and 1 teaspoon Dijon mustard in a jar and pour over the leek. Spoon over 2½ tablespoons water, then fold the baking paper over to make a parcel and bake for 30–35 minutes, until the leek is tender and sweet. Serve as a side with roast chicken or as one of a few vegetarian dishes made to share.

Serves 4–6 as a side

LEEK AND NOT-MUCH-CHICKEN PIE

Here we revisit the classic chicken and leek pie, using every last bit of the leek and not much chicken – we promise you'll hardly notice.

Preheat the oven to 180°C (350°F/Gas mark 4). Wash and finely slice 2 whole leeks, then sauté the green parts in 3 tablespoons olive oil in a large frying pan over medium–low heat for 5 minutes. Add the white parts plus 3 chopped garlic cloves and sauté for a further 5 minutes until very soft. Remove the leek from the pan and set aside. Heat 1 tablespoon olive oil in the pan and add 200 g (7 oz) diced chicken meat (breast or thigh) and cook for 5 minutes until just browning. Add 200 g (7 oz) diced vegetables (such as cauliflower, potato and corn) and cook for 5 minutes. Return the leeks to the pan and stir.

Meanwhile, in a small bowl or jug, mix ½ cup (125 ml) cream, ½ cup (125 ml) chicken stock, 1 teaspoon salt, 1 teaspoon pepper and the leaves of 4 thyme sprigs. Pour this over the leek mixture in the pan, sprinkle over 1 tablespoon plain (all-purpose) flour and mix together. Cook for 5 minutes until the sauce has slightly thickened. Remove from the heat and allow to cool a little.

Line a 23 cm (9 inch) shallow pie tin with puff pastry (or the sour cream pastry on page 185), line the pastry with baking paper and baking beads and blind bake for 10 minutes. Remove the beads and baking paper, spoon the mixture into the tin and cover with your chosen pastry. Bake for 30–35 minutes, then serve with a salad.

Serves 4–6

SAUTÉED LEEK TOPS

We make this every time we have leeks in the house, and use it in omelettes, stirred through pasta, or just as a simple green side. You can also add it to the vegetable slice on page 23, the green pockets (with fresh parsley) on page 28 and the galette (with spinach) on page 185.

Make sure your leek tops are well washed and dry, then finely slice. Heat 2 tablespoons olive oil per leek top in a frying pan over medium heat and add the leek. Stir constantly for a few minutes until the leek tops release some water. Reduce the heat to low, cover and allow the leek to sweat for 10 minutes. Uncover and season with a pinch of salt and 1 crushed garlic clove per leek top. Stir and continue to sauté for 10 minutes or until a little browned at the edges.

FENNEL

You'll probably notice that fennel is everywhere in these pages. We love the wild variety that we forage in local parks, as well as the common fennel with its fat bulb and feathery fronds.

The mythology of fennel and the joys of cooking it are entwined. Prometheus, who stole fire from the gods to give to humans, smuggled a smouldering ember off Mount Olympus in the hollow part of a fennel stalk so humans might keep warm and have the pleasure of cooking their food. Fennel has a slightly aniseed flavour that is most distinct when eaten raw (it is subtler when cooked). Fennel contains the minerals calcium, potassium and magnesium and has been eaten since ancient times to aid digestion.

GOES WITH ...

Part of the carrot family, fennel shares some of the grassy notes of its relatives, but it's the aniseed flavour that dominates and this should be highlighted. Fennel pairs with almonds, pistachios, sunflower seeds, olive oil, olives, lemon and oranges. Fennel also works well with crunchy sweet produce, such as cabbage, apples and celery, and creamy dairy including butter, cream and sharp cheese, along with eggs.

USE IT ALL

Use the fronds and stems to make the green sauce opposite. You can also put fennel stems in a fermenting brine (page 168) and use them sliced through salads or on sandwiches.

SHAVED FENNEL, ORANGE AND BLACK OLIVE SALAD

A few simple ingredients, chosen for their strong flavours and compatibility, make for a quick but elegant salad.

Using a mandoline or sharp knife, very thinly slice a medium fennel bulb. Segment an orange by cutting away the skin and pith (save the peel and dry it; page 204) and removing the top and bottom of the orange. With a sharp knife, make a cut on each side of one segment along the membrane. The segment should pop out. Make your way around the whole orange, then add the segments to the fennel and add ½ cup (90 g) wrinkly salted black olives. Season with salt and lots of pepper, a really good drizzle of olive oil and the rest of the juice left in the segment-less orange. Top with chopped parsley and serve.

Serves 3–4

SPICY FENNEL TOP GREEN SAUCE

It's a shame to throw away fennel stems and fronds when they have so much flavour. This sauce is a cross between a chimichurri and a gremolata, and it will boost the flavour of whatever you serve it with. Fish is a natural partner, as are leafy green salads or the lentil salad on page 135. It's also great drizzled over boiled potatoes.

Place 1 cup (100 g) fennel fronds and thinly sliced fennel stems in a food processor with 2 sliced garlic cloves, 2 good pinches of salt, a pinch of black pepper, the zest and juice of 1 lemon and 1 teaspoon chilli flakes or 1 chopped fresh chilli. Blitz to a paste and, with the motor running, add 100–150 ml (3½–5 fl oz) olive oil and blend to a smooth paste. Taste, and add more salt if needed.

Makes about 1½ cups (375 ml)

ROASTED FENNEL WITH CITRUS ZEST AND CHILLI

Make this: it's simple and delicious and gets devoured in our cooking classes. Then, if you manage to have any leftovers, you can make an antipasto-style pickle, just like what you find at Italian delicatessens.

Preheat the oven to 180°C (350°F/Gas mark 4). Slice 2 fennel bulbs into long wedges and 1 onion into sixths. Put the vegetables in a baking dish, drizzle with 100 ml (3½ fl oz) olive oil, and sprinkle with 1 teaspoon each of salt, pepper and fennel seeds, along with the juice and zest of 1 orange. You can add ½ teaspoon chilli flakes if you like. Mix together with your hands until the fennel is well coated. Roast for 30–40 minutes, or until the fennel is soft, sweet and starting to brown at the edges. Serve with finely chopped fennel fronds or parsley.

Store any leftovers in a container or jar and cover with the brine on page 256. Seal and store in the fridge for up to 2 weeks. Serve on toast with goat's cheese, tossed through green leafy salads or pasta, or on an antipasto board or pizza.

Serves 4 as a side

BERRIES

Most of our favourite berries are not even berries at all! Botanically speaking, a berry is a fruit produced from a single ovary of a flower, making pumpkins and grapes berries, but not strawberries; however, if the gardeners and botanists can forgive us, we will side-step this technicality and refer to berries as they do in the shops.

The world's most popular berries are strawberries followed by blueberries (a true berry, if we are going to be accurate) and raspberries. There are many more in the 'berry' family: blackberries, cranberries, boysenberries, mulberries … depending where you live a large variety will be commercially available or growing wild.

The biggest problem with the berries we buy at the shops is the plastic packaging they come in. As consumers, we need to speak up for change. Talk to your grocer or market seller about alternatives. Also, global demand for berries year-round promotes the sale of imported berries and out-of-season growing. Check which berries are grown locally and when they are seasonally available. If you can, have an adventure and go to a berry farm to pick your own and freeze them to eat and cook later.

All berries are high in fibre and vitamin C, and strawberries, blueberries and raspberries are rich in magnesium too. There is a lot of fuss about blueberries and their antioxidants, but really all berries are good for you.

Store berries for up to 5 days on a higher shelf in the fridge as they need good air circulation. You can freeze them by spreading them in a single layer on a tray in the freezer until frozen, then transfer them to a container and keep for up to 3 months.

GO WITH …

It is a universal truth that all berries pair well with dairy. Ice cream, whipped creams, yoghurt, even cheeses will complement. Stone fruits and berries are good combined in tarts or served fresh together. Basil goes well with strawberry and blueberry. Try tearing the leaves over a bowl of fruit and serve with cream.

WASTE TIP

Make the tired berry sauce on page 110 to serve on ice cream or yoghurt or add to smoothies and cakes.

BERRY JAM

There's not enough natural pectin in strawberries to make a well-set jam, but the addition of a granny smith apple and lemon zest and juice will help this jam set. Or use blackberries, which are very high in pectin! For a savoury twist, add a generous sprig of rosemary or thyme or a teaspoon of fennel seeds when you're softening the fruit.

Place 500 g (1 lb 2 oz) hulled and roughly chopped strawberries and 1 grated granny smith apple in a saucepan with the zest and juice of 1 lemon and ½ cup (125 ml) water. Simmer over low heat until the fruit is soft, sweet and falling apart. Add in 300 g (10½ oz) sugar and stir to dissolve. Turn up the heat and cook for 20 minutes, until the jam is glossy and heavy. Allow to cool, then pour into a clean jar and keep in the fridge for up to 1 month.

Makes about 2 cups (640 g)

STRAWBERRY AND FENNEL SHRUB

A shrub is an old-fashioned preserved fruit cordial. Vinegar not only makes the fruit juice last, but also adds a refreshing acidic kick. Use the leftover strawberry pulp in a muffin mix (page 276) or add a little sugar to it for an instant cheat's compote.

Place 500 g (1 lb 2 oz) hulled and chopped strawberries, ¾ cup (165 g) caster (superfine) sugar and 1 teaspoon fennel seeds in a food processor and blend until smooth (or use a hand-held blender). Pour the mixture into a saucepan, place over very low heat and stir to dissolve the sugar. Add 3 tablespoons water and keep stirring. Bring to a gentle simmer, then turn off the heat and allow to cool. Check the consistency – it should look like a sauce – and add up to 3 tablespoons more water if needed.

Strain the mixture into a bowl through a fine-mesh sieve or a sieve lined with muslin. Add 3 tablespoons red wine vinegar to the liquid in the bowl, taste and add up to another 3 tablespoons if you prefer a tarter flavour. Reserve the pulp for another use.

Pour the shrub into a clean glass bottle and keep in the fridge for up to 2 weeks.

Make 2 cups (500 ml)

STRAWBERRY SHRUB COCKTAIL

Make a cocktail using the strawberry and fennel shrub opposite.

Fill a glass with ice. Pour over ⅓ cup (80 ml) of the shrub and top with sparkling water. You could also combine 30 ml (1 fl oz) of shrub with 30 ml (1 fl oz) white rum and the juice of 1 lime for a kind of daiquiri.

Makes 1

BERRY JAM DROPS

This is Greer Rochford's granny's very special signature recipe. While Greer reckons she can't make these as well as her granny, they're still a firm favourite in the Cornersmith cafe, and in our kids' lunchboxes. They're even better with homemade berry jam!

Preheat the oven to 175°C (345°F/Gas mark 3). Line a baking tray with baking paper. In a large bowl, whisk together 3 cups (450 g) plain (all-purpose) flour, 1 cup (125 g) arrowroot or tapioca flour and 2 teaspoons baking powder. Sift three times and set aside.

In a stand mixer with the paddle attachment, cream together 225 g (8 oz) unsalted butter and ¾ cup (165 g) caster (superfine) sugar until light and fluffy. While still mixing, add 2 eggs, one at a time, followed by 2 tablespoons honey. Slowly mix in the flour mixture until the dough comes together. Turn out onto a workbench and divide the dough into 50 g (1¾ oz) balls. Place on the prepared tray. Make a small depression in each ball and fill with 1 tablespoon jam. Bake for 12–15 minutes, until golden brown. Allow to cool a little, then store in a jar or airtight container for at least 1 week.

Makes about 20

TIRED BERRY SAUCE

Makes 2 cups (500 ml)

We spoon this sauce over ice cream, add it to smoothies and milkshakes, and serve it with cakes, crêpes and muesli. Make it when berries are cheap and ripe or when they're starting to go a bit mushy in the fridge.

500 g (1 lb 2 oz) tired strawberries, hulled and chopped
2 tablespoons caster (superfine) sugar
1 tablespoon honey
½ teaspoon vanilla extract

Place the berries in a bowl with the sugar. Squish the berries with your hands and then let them sit for an hour or so.

Transfer to a small saucepan and add the honey and vanilla. Simmer over low heat for 10–15 minutes, until thick and shiny.

Either use as is or blend until smooth. Store in a jar in the fridge for up to 5 days.

COMBINATIONS WE LIKE

- Swap the strawberries for blueberries and replace the vanilla with ½ teaspoon ground cinnamon and the zest of 1 orange
- Swap the strawberries for raspberries and replace the vanilla with the zest of 1 lime and a generous sprig of mint
- Swap the strawberries for blackberries and replace the vanilla with ½ teaspoon ground cinnamon, allspice or nutmeg

ROLLED OATS, SESAME SEEDS AND TAHINI

The years when our kids were young were a blur of porridge, apple crumbles and homemade muesli. We would not have survived if not for rolled oats. They are affordable and extra nutritious and a great way to start the day. Oats have been shown to lower cholesterol when eaten regularly because they are high in beta-glucans and soluble fibre. Raw rolled oats have a creamy taste and when soaked or cooked in liquid they become muculent, which is healing for the gut.

Buy oats from bulk-supply shops, so you can bring your own containers, or when at the supermarket opt for oats in big cardboard boxes. Oats contain oils, so they are best stored in an airtight container in the fridge.

Another pantry staple is sesame seeds. We use them when making bread, sprinkled in salads or over rice dishes and in many, many baked goods. Their flavour is nutty and a little grassy when raw, but they take on an aromatic toasty flavour when heated. Sesame seeds are a good source of protein, fibre and monounsaturated fats.

Because sesame seeds are so rich in oil, they can burn very quickly if left unattended. Go low and slow when toasting any seeds and especially with sesame.

Tahini is a paste made from 100 per cent sesame seeds. It is a staple in Middle Eastern cooking. We both use tahini in salad dressings, marinades, baking and very often on toast with honey. Tahini is made from hulled or unhulled seeds. Hulled tahini is lighter and smoother, while unhulled is coarser and sometimes more bitter.

ONE MUESLI MIX, FOUR RECIPES

RAW MUESLI MIX

This is a versatile recipe that builds on a few simple ingredients. Use this raw muesli as a base and throw in those last few dried apricots and bottom-of-the-packet sesame seeds or whatever needs to be used up! This recipe is your foundation for making the following muesli recipes.

In a bowl, combine 1 cup (100 g) rolled oats, 1 cup (65 g) shredded coconut or puffed rice (or a mix of both), 1 cup (150 g) mixed pepitas (pumpkin seeds), linseeds, sunflower seeds, sesame seeds, walnuts, sliced or chopped almonds or hazelnuts and ¼ teaspoon ground cinnamon. Store in an airtight container or jar in the fridge for up to 1 month.

Makes about 3 cups (400 g)

TIP

Add a handful of this muesli to your crumble mix to give it some extra crunch.

TAHINI-ROASTED MUESLI

Toast the raw muesli mix with tahini and honey to turn it into a healthy crunchy granola.

Preheat the oven to 150°C (300°F/Gas mark 2). Combine 50 g (1¾ oz) brown sugar, ⅓ cup (70 g) coconut oil, 80 g (2¾ oz) honey and 70 g (2½ oz) tahini in a saucepan and place over low heat. Stir constantly until melted, then stir the mixture through one quantity of raw muesli mix.

Spread the mixture on a baking tray and roast for 10 minutes. Take the muesli out and give it a good stir with a fork. Roast for another 10–15 minutes, until golden brown. Remove from the oven, give it another stir and then allow to cool completely on the tray.

Once cool, store in an airtight container or jar for 2–3 weeks in the pantry. If the muesli starts to get a little soft you can re-roast it for 5–10 minutes.

Makes 500–600 g (1 lb 2 oz–1 lb 5 oz)

TIP

If you want to give this a healthy Coco-Pops vibe, add 2 tablespoons cocoa powder to the dry muesli mix.

BIRCHER MUESLI

Soak the raw muesli mix overnight for a fresh and fruity breakfast.

Place one quantity of raw muesli mix in a bowl or container and cover with 400 ml (14 fl oz) apple or orange juice, kefir or milk of your choice. You want your oats to be just covered, not drowning in liquid. Cover and soak overnight.

In the morning, stir through 1 grated apple, skin and all, and ½ cup (125 g) natural yoghurt. If you're not using juice, stir through some honey or maple syrup. Top each bowl with toasted nuts and fresh fruit or fruit compote, such as the strawberry sauce on page 110 or the rhubarb compote on page 41.

Serves 4

EASY HOMEMADE MUESLI BARS

These are hands down the best homemade muesli bars we have ever eaten – and the kids agree too!

Preheat the oven to 160°C (315°F/Gas mark 2–3). Grease a 16 cm x 26 cm (6¼ inch x 10½ inch) baking tray or line it with baking paper. Combine ½ cup (135 g) tahini, ½ cup (175 g) honey and ⅓ cup (70 g) coconut oil in a small saucepan and melt over low heat. Stir the wet mixture through one quantity of raw muesli mix, coating well (omit the nuts if making for school lunchboxes). Add ⅓ cup (50 g) LSA or wheatgerm (you can buy these in the health-food aisle) and 60 g (2 oz) chocolate buttons or dried fruit and stir well to combine.

Press the mixture into the baking tray to flatten, then cover with baking paper and press the mixture firmly with the palm of your hand. Bake for 20–30 minutes, until golden brown. Allow to set in the fridge overnight, then slice into 12 bars (or make them bigger if you like). Keep in an airtight container in the fridge for up to 2 weeks.

Makes 12

RAW MUESLI MIX

BIRCHER MUESLI

TAHINI-ROASTED MUESLI

EASY HOMEMADE MUESLI BARS

SAUSAGES

LENTILS

A WHOLE CABBAGE

APPLES

POTATOES

SHOPPING BASKET 4

In this basket, meals come together using simple everyday ingredients. Potatoes, onions, sausages and apples are bought so frequently that they are often taken for granted, and statistically are wasted more often. But their secret power is their affinity with one another, and their ability to make the task of cooking for yourself and others truly satisfying. Plant-based proteins, such as lentils, are put front and centre in our meals, while meat products like the beloved sausage step back into a supporting role.

ONIONS

FROM THIS BASKET ...

MEALS

Quick cabbage curry (page 120)

As you like it pancake (page 123)

Sweet potato fritters (page 129)

Giant potato rosti (page 131)

The simplest potato gnocchi (page 133)

Red lentil and potato dal (page 135)

Easy lentil salad (page 135)

Lentil stew (page 137)

Potato pizza with garlic, rosemary and sausage (page 139)

SIDES

Sautéed cabbage and apple (page 120)

Slaws (page 124–7)

Potato pikelets (page 129)

Tiny sausage meatballs (page 139)

SNACKS, SWEETS & DRINKS

Potato peel chips (page 129)

Sausage rolls (page 141)

Homemade scrolls (page 146)

QUICK PRESERVING IDEAS

Spicy pickled cabbage (page 120)

Quick pickled red onion (page 143)

NOTHING GOES TO WASTE

Kitchen scrap sauerkraut (page 120)

Caramelised onions (page 143)

Sticky onion relish (page 143)

Super-quick stewed apple (page 145)

Rescued apple chutney (page 145)

Left-over apple skin caramel (page 145)

A WHOLE CABBAGE

All the vegetables of the mighty brassica family originate with the wild cabbage. It has been boiled and baked, fermented and shredded for centuries. The cabbage has saved millions from starvation, its leaves have wrapped the wounds of soldiers and given relief to nursing mothers. Unassuming as it is, the cabbage is a treasure.

Walk past the plastic-wrapped portions in the supermarket and take home a whole cabbage. Here is a vegetable that has over half the recommended daily intake of vitamin C and K in just one cup. There are plenty of ideas in this chapter to encourage you to cook with cabbage. And look further – eastern Europe, the Mediterranean countries, China and Japan are all great lovers of cabbage and have a wealth of dishes to explore.

Store a whole cabbage wrapped in a lightly damp cloth for up to 1 month in the fridge. Don't take the outer leaves off and don't wash the cabbage until you are ready to use it. Cut the cabbage as you use it and rewrap the unused portion. Or if you have only a small amount left, shred it and keep in an airtight container. Once the cabbage is cut it will start to lose its vitamin C, so eat it within a week.

GOES WITH ...

Cabbage's mild peppery and sulphurous notes contrast nicely with the sweet tartness of apple, unripe pear and currants. Cabbage and pork sausages or bacon make a rustic combination for simple but tasty fare. Cabbage also pairs well with other humble ingredients such as rice, onions, garlic and carrots. For herb and spice combinations, you can always rely on cabbage and black pepper, dill, caraway, mustard, horseradish or ginger.

WASTE TIP

Use the tired outer leaves from your cabbage to make kitchen scrap sauerkraut (page 120).

KITCHEN SCRAP SAUERKRAUT

This is a great way to make a small batch of sauerkraut, using 500 g (1 lb 2 oz) of produce all up. Use the outer leaves of the cabbage for this recipe – they are all too often thrown away.

Shred the leaves and a little extra from the cabbage head to yield 300 g (10½ oz). Make up the remaining 200 g (7 oz) with ½ grated apple and a grated carrot or whatever is rattling around. In a large bowl, massage all the produce with 1 teaspoon pure salt until the water in the cabbage is released. You know you have broken down the vegetables enough when you can squeeze a fistful and lots of water runs out.

Pack into a clean 500 ml (17 fl oz) jar, leaving a 2 cm (¾ inch) gap at the top. Seal and leave to ferment for 3–7 days at room temperature (for more fermenting tips, see page 278). Open the jar daily to allow gas to escape, and taste: it's ready when it has a pleasantly tangy flavour that's a little salty and quite sour. Store in the fridge for up to 3 months.

Makes 1 x 500 ml (17 fl oz) jar

Kitchen scrap sauerkraut

SAUTÉED CABBAGE AND APPLE

There isn't much to this recipe but it's everything a winter side should be: rustic and comforting.

Finely slice 300 g (10½ oz) cabbage and 1 apple. Heat 3 tablespoons butter in a frying pan over medium heat until melted. Add the apple and sauté for 5 minutes or until the edges are a little brown. Add the cabbage, ½ teaspoon salt and 1 teaspoon black pepper and sauté until the cabbage has completely softened and looks buttery.

Serves 2–3 as a side

SPICY PICKLED CABBAGE

A simple quick pickle to add to sandwiches or salads.

Finely slice any left-over cabbage you have lying around and put into a 600 ml (21 fl oz) clean jar or container.

Heat 1 cup (250 ml) white wine vinegar, 1 cup (250 ml) water, ⅓ cup (70 g) raw sugar, ½ teaspoon salt, 1 teaspoon caraway seeds, 1 teaspoon peppercorns and a pinch of chilli flakes in a small saucepan over medium heat. Stir to dissolve the sugar and bring to the boil, then pour over the cabbage. Leave in the fridge for a few days before eating; it should last for 2–3 weeks.

QUICK CABBAGE CURRY

This is a riff on a curry that's popular in Sri Lanka. For those who are new to cooking, this is one to have up your sleeve for an affordable, quick and delicious meal.

Shred 500 g (1 lb 2 oz) white cabbage and slice 1 onion. Sauté the onion in 2 tablespoons ghee, butter or vegetable oil until soft and translucent, then add the very thinly sliced roots and stems from a bunch of coriander (cilantro), 2 minced garlic cloves, 1 tablespoon minced ginger, 2 teaspoons curry powder and 1 teaspoon salt. Sauté for a few more minutes until fragrant. Add the cabbage and stir until it has softened and combined well with the onion and spices. Add 1 cup (250 ml) coconut milk, reduce the heat to low and cook for 10 minutes or until slightly reduced. Stir through coriander leaves and the juice of 1 lime. Top with toasted coconut flakes and serve with rice.

Serves 4

AS YOU LIKE IT PANCAKE

Makes about 8

This Japanese savoury pancake recipe comes from Cornersmith chef Tutu. It's a take on okonomiyaki and is a staple on our cafe menu and a favourite for us at home. 'Okonomi' roughly translates to 'as you like it', making this the perfect master recipe to swap in and out what you like or what you need to use up!

400 g (14 oz) cabbage, very thinly
    sliced, preferably on a mandoline
200 g (7 oz) thinly sliced or
    grated veg
    leeks (white and green parts)
    onion
    carrot
    potato
    zucchini (courgette) (squeezed
      dry)
    kimchi (squeezed dry)
1⅓ cups (200 g) plain (all-purpose)
    flour
1 teaspoon baking powder
1 teaspoon salt
½ teaspoon freshly cracked
    black pepper
2 eggs
1 tablespoon good quality
    vegetable oil
Quick pickled ginger (page 239),
    to serve
Slaw of your choice (page 124),
    to serve
Sweet and sour sauce,
    such as teriyaki, to serve
Mayonnaise, to serve

Combine the cabbage and thinly sliced veg in a bowl and set aside. In another bowl, combine the flour, baking powder, salt and pepper. In a third bowl, whisk the eggs and 160 ml (5¼ fl oz) water. Pour the wet mixture into the dry mixture and stir to combine, then gradually fold the sliced vegetables through the batter; the mixture will loosen as you mix.

Heat the oil in a large frying pan over medium–high heat. Working in batches, scoop ½ cup portions of batter into the pan and flatten to 10 cm (4 inch) pancakes. Fry the pancakes for 3 minutes each side or until golden brown and cooked through. Serve with pickled ginger, a fresh slaw, a sweet and sour sauce of your choice and a little mayonnaise.

TIP

At Cornersmith we don't buy imported ingredients or sauces, which forces the chefs to get creative in the kitchen. Tutu reduces left-over pickling brine into a thick sweet and sour syrup, which the chefs use as the sauce to drizzle over the okonomiyaki. To try this at home, pour your strained pickle brine into a small saucepan and simmer until it reduces by half and thickens. Taste, add a little sugar or salt if it needs it, then pour into a clean jar. Store in the fridge for pretty much forever.

A LESSON IN MAKING SLAW

Serves 4

Knowing how to make a top-notch slaw brings salad to the table at every meal. Once you're confident with it, you can pull together interesting salads with very little effort. Think of this recipe as a guide to combining seasonal vegetables that are already in your fridge, nuts or seeds that are in the pantry, herbs from the garden and delicious dressings using ingredients you already have.

The key is to cut your vegetables into similar sizes and shapes. A mandoline or sharp knife will give a mix of lovely, thinly shaved vegetables; a vegetable peeler is great for ribbons; use a box grater for root vegetables; or chop your veggies into thin batons, which takes a little longer to prep, but the results are well worth it.

¼ small green or red cabbage
   (about 200 g/7 oz), thinly sliced
1 cup (100 g) thinly sliced
   seasonal vegetables
   brussels sprouts
   fennel
   kale
   wombok
1 cup (100 g) thinly sliced very
   crunchy vegetables or fruit
   snow peas (mangetout)
   sweetcorn
   green beans
   celery
   radish
   carrot
   apple
   pear
1 bunch soft herb leaves (save the
   stems for the chimichurri on
   page 33)
   dill
   coriander (cilantro)
   parsley
Large handful of toasted nuts
   or seeds
   almonds
   walnuts
   peanuts
   sesame seeds
   pepitas (pumpkin seeds)

Place the cabbage, vegetables and fruit in a salad bowl and gently mix to combine. Drizzle over the dressing (see below) and scatter the herbs and toasted nuts or seeds over the top. Mix again and serve immediately.

TIPS

Add ½–1 cup cooked grains or pulses, such as chickpeas (garbanzo beans), quinoa, white beans or barley, to make your salad more of a meal.

For an extra kick, add ¼ cup quick pickles to the slaw; try quick pickled red onion (page 143), Vietnamese-style pickled carrot (page 227), quick pickled celery (page 193) or spicy pickled cabbage (page 120).

A LESSON IN MAKING DRESSING

A classic slaw dressing couldn't be simpler. All you need is:

- 3 tablespoons oil (a mix of olive and good-quality vegetable oil)
- 1 tablespoon of something acidic, such as lemon juice, red or white wine vinegar, apple cider vinegar or left-over pickling brine
- 1 teaspoon Dijon mustard
- a good pinch of salt and freshly cracked black pepper
- a dash of something sweet to balance everything, such as a pinch of sugar, honey, maple syrup or marmalade.

DRESSING TIPS

For a creamy slaw, add 1–2 tablespoons natural yoghurt, tahini or mayonnaise.

For a spicy slaw, leave out the mustard and add chilli paste or hot sauce, 1 crushed garlic clove or 1 teaspoon finely grated ginger.

A slaw made with red cabbage, fennel, apple, dill, pickled red onion, lentils and a creamy dressing.

SEASONAL SLAWS WE LIKE

AUTUMN

Brassicas all work well together. Make a brussels sprout, cabbage and kale slaw with dill and add an autumnal fruit, such as thinly sliced apple or grapefruit segments, with toasted walnuts or almonds.

WINTER

Root vegetables make a great slaw. Grate raw beetroot (beets), carrots and daikon or kohlrabi with ginger and add toasted sesame seeds or pepitas (pumpkin seeds).

SPRING

Combine cabbage, fennel, zucchini (courgette), snow pea (mangetout) and parsley with a little chopped preserved lemon and some cooked barley.

SUMMER

For a light and refreshing slaw on a hot day, try long, thin strips of wombok, cucumber and capsicum (pepper), plus sweetcorn, chilli and coriander (cilantro) with sliced spring onion (scallions) and toasted peanuts.

CABBAGE

HERBS

DRESSING

PICKLES

NUTS OR SEEDS

GREENS

POTATOES

Gnocchi, hash browns, soups, mash, chips, fritters, pizza ... with simple cooking methods, the versatile potato can be turned into a multitude of nutritious meals from breakfast to dinner. It is an excellent vegetable to have in the kitchen.

Potatoes get a bad rap when it comes to nutrition, but they are a great all-rounder, giving you a little of a lot of things. They are high in fibre and a source of vitamin B6, making them good for your nervous system and brain function. Potatoes are surprisingly high in vitamin C too, and were eaten in the past to prevent scurvy on long sea voyages.

If you can afford organic potatoes, you will notice a flavour difference. You will find a much wider variety at farmers' markets and small grocers – look out for Dutch cream, King Edward, moonlight and purple Congo. If you're restricted to supermarkets, the bigger brands tend to carry all-rounders such as sebago and desiree, and cocktail potatoes which are excellent for fast cooking.

Different potatoes give different results, so here is a quick guide to potato types and their uses:

- Waxy: Dutch cream and kipfler – good for potato salads and roasting
- Floury: Desiree, King Edward and coliban – good for gnocchi, mash and chips
- All-rounders: Sebago and pontiac – good for fritters and mash.

Although sweet potatoes aren't actually potatoes (they're from the root vegetable family as opposed to the tuber family), they can be used interchangeably with regular potatoes. They are sweet and carroty in flavour and provide a more sustained energy hit than regular potatoes. They, too, are high in fibre and also boast incredibly high levels of vitamin A.

All potatoes and sweet potatoes should be stored in a cool, dark place. Warm temperatures encourage sprouting, while light prompts greening. Don't seal your potatoes in plastic bags or containers, as they need oxygen. It's best to store them in a cloth or paper bag. Buying your potatoes unwashed means they will keep longer as the dirt protects them from light. Remember, new potatoes with very thin skins won't last very long, so cook them soon after buying.

If your potatoes do start sprouting, don't panic and throw them away. As long as the potato is still firm, it'll be fine; just remove the sprouts and carry on.

WASTE TIP

We are often asked what to do with potato and sweet potato peels. Our first piece of advice is to stop peeling your potatoes! There are nutrients and flavour in those peels, plus vegetable peels contribute to a huge amount of unnecessary waste in landfill. Wash your potatoes really well and then cook as normal, but with the skins on. If you can't break the habit of peeling your potatoes, see opposite for what to do with peels.

WHAT TO DO WITH LEFT-OVER MASH

If you've got a little mash left over, don't throw it out. Here are our three favourite ways to turn it into something even more tasty. You can freeze mash in containers for up to 2 months and then reheat it on the stovetop or in a microwave.

POTATO PIKELETS

You can enjoy these pikelets as is, make them more savoury by adding salt and 1–2 tablespoons chopped chives or other soft herbs, or make them sweet by adding 1 teaspoon sugar and serving them topped with stewed apples and maple syrup.

In a bowl, combine 1 cup (230 g) left-over mash, 1 beaten egg and ¼ cup (35 g) self-raising flour to make a thick batter. Stir through your savoury or sweet additions, if using. Heat 2–3 tablespoons butter or vegetable oil in a frying pan and spoon in 2 tablespoons batter per pikelet. Cook over low heat for 3–4 minutes each side, until golden brown.

Makes 6

SWEET POTATO FRITTERS

Inspired by Ottolenghi's sweet potato fritters, ours make use of left-over sweet potato mash. Perfect for a light dinner with a salad on the side.

In a bowl, combine 1 cup (250 g) left-over sweet potato mash with 1 cup (110 g) sliced spring onion (scallion). Add ⅓ cup (50 g) plain (all-purpose) flour, 1 teaspoon chilli flakes and ½ teaspoon salt and mix together by hand. Don't overwork the mix. Scoop out ¼ cup (60 g) portions of the mash mixture and form into 5 cm (2 inch) flattened fritters. Heat 2 tablespoons olive oil in a frying pan over medium heat. Fry the fritters for 3 minutes each side, then drain on paper towel and serve warm.

Makes 6

FISH CAKES

Follow the recipe on page 53 for our favourite way to use up left-over mash.

WHAT TO DO WITH LEFT-OVER PEELS

ADD PEELS TO BREAD DOUGH

We add left-over cooked peels to the soda bread on page 219, in place of the grated pumpkin.

Boil 1 cup (50 g) well-washed potato peels in 3 cups (750 ml) water for 20 minutes, until tender but not mushy. Strain and pat dry with paper towel, then add to your bread dough.

POTATO PEEL CHIPS!

Pop your potato peels in the oven while you're preparing dinner – they only take 10 minutes and are very nice with a glass of wine.

Place the peels from 1 kg (2 lb 4 oz) potatoes in a small bowl, add 1 tablespoon olive or vegetable oil, ¼ teaspoon salt and ¼ teaspoon smoked paprika. Add a pinch of cayenne pepper if you want a little heat. Mix with your hands, then spread out on a baking tray and bake in a 200°C (400°F/Gas mark 6) oven for 10–12 minutes, until crispy and browned.

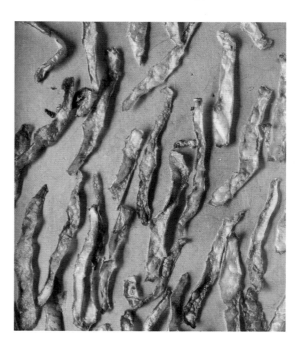

GIANT POTATO ROSTI

Serves 4–6

Made with 1 kg (2 lb 4 oz) potatoes, this pan-sized rosti or potato pancake is a breakfast-for-dinner staple. Serve with eggs and avocado in the morning or as a welcome addition to any spread or barbecue. After a long day, simply pile a green salad on top and dinner is ready, or serve on a crusty bread roll for a fancy chip butty!

1 kg (2 lb 4 oz) potatoes
Scant teaspoon salt
⅓ cup (80 ml) vegetable oil

Grate the potatoes on the big side of a box grater into a large bowl. Working in two batches, tip the grated potato into a clean tea towel, form into a sausage and squeeze out all the moisture. You may need to do this a few times to get the potato as dry as possible. Once all the liquid has gone, tip the potato back into the bowl and add the salt. Mix gently with your hands to combine.

Heat 3 tablespoons of the vegetable oil in a 25 cm (10 inch) frying pan over medium–low heat. Tip the potato in and use a spatula to spread it evenly across the base of the pan. Cook for 10–12 minutes, until an even golden-brown crust forms on the bottom.

You'll need to flip the rosti, which is hard with one this size. The easiest way to do this is to cover the pan with a plate and tip it upside down. Add the remaining oil to the pan and slide the rosti back in, pressing down again to flatten, and cook the other side for another 10–12 minutes. Don't have the heat too high or it will burn before the inside cooks properly. Slide out onto a plate and let the rosti rest for a few minutes, before cutting into wedges and serving.

COMBINATIONS WE LIKE

- Mix it up and use half grated regular potato with half grated sweet potato
- Or to add some spicy sweetness, try half grated regular potato with half grated parsnip.

Gnocchi with sausage meatballs and passata

THE SIMPLEST POTATO GNOCCHI

Serves 4 hungry people

This is a weekend meal and a nice way for everyone to be involved in the kitchen. It's magic that such basic ingredients – potato, flour and water – can make such a wonderful meal. Generally, we serve our gnocchi with passata (page 247) and shavings of salted ricotta (page 37), but it's also very good with a sprinkling of sausage meatballs (page 139) and a green salad.

1.2 kg unpeeled floury potatoes, such as pontiac, King Edward, desiree or sebago
salt
Up to 1⅓ cups (200 g) plain (all-purpose) flour, plus extra for dusting
Olive oil, for drizzling
Sauce of your choice

Place the whole potatoes in a large saucepan, cover with cold water, add a pinch of salt and bring to the boil. Gently boil until they are tender in the middle, but not falling apart. Drain and allow to cool a little.

When the potatoes are just cool enough to handle, peel them, cut them in half and pass them through a potato ricer into a large bowl. If you don't have a potato ricer, you can grate them on the medium side of a box grater or scrape them apart with a fork.

Add 1½ teaspoons salt and 150 g (5½ oz) of the flour to the warm potato and gently mix with your hands to just bring everything together. Add a little more flour if the dough seems sticky; you're looking to make a soft and just-combined dough (too much flour will result in tough gnocchi so only use as much as you need).

Lightly flour your workbench and tip out the dough, then very gently knead a few times until the dough is soft and smooth. Form it into a ball, wrap in plastic wrap and leave in the fridge to rest for 30 minutes.

Line a baking tray with baking paper and set aside. Lightly flour your workbench again, cut the dough into six pieces and then roll each piece into a long, thin sausage. Using a knife, cut 2–3 cm (¾–1¼ inch) pieces of gnocchi (they should look like pretty little pillowy rectangles). Place each piece of gnocchi onto the baking tray, making sure they don't touch each other.

Bring a large saucepan of salted water to the boil and cook the gnocchi in small batches until each piece floats to the surface. Remove with a slotted spoon, then drain and place in a baking dish with a little drizzle of olive oil. Shake the dish as you add each spoonful of cooked gnocchi, so that the pieces are coated in oil and don't clump together.

Once your gnocchi are cooked, add the sauce of your choice and serve straight away with a light fresh salad.

OTHER SAUCES WE LIKE

- Lemon butter sauce (page 39)
- Basil Pesto (page 263).

LENTILS

Lentils were one of the first crops grown during the transition to agriculture, and they also might be one of the crops that can save it. Like all legumes, lentils take the abundant nitrogen from the atmosphere and fix it where it is needed in the soil. By doing this, lentils make the soil fertile, reducing or eliminating the need for chemical fertilisers and herbicides.

As a smaller plant, lentils have lower water needs and are suited to the hotter, drier climate we are all facing. Good for farmers and good for us, lentils are an excellent source of protein (we use brown lentils to make less-meat burgers; see page 267). They also contain micronutrients (the ones we need smaller amounts of), such as folate and magnesium. Compared to other proteins, lentils are economical and quick to cook.

There are hundreds of varieties of lentils, but in Australia we predominantly grow red lentils (and most of those are exported) and green lentils. Red lentils are hulled, split and polished, and very quick to cook. One cup (200 g) will yield about 3 cups (600 g) cooked lentils. Unlike red lentils, brown lentils keep their shape during cooking. One cup (215 g) brown

lentils will give you about 3 cups (645 g) cooked lentils. Proper Puy lentils are grown strictly in the region of Le Puy, but you can get varieties grown elsewhere. They have a distinct mottled appearance and peppery flavour. One cup (200 g) puy lentils will give you about 2 cups (400 g) cooked.

After harvesting, lentils are dried and can be stored for long periods of time, although it is recommended that you use up your lentils within a year. Store them in the pantry in an airtight container, and make sure they are kept dry.

GO WITH ...

Lentils are the least fussy of ingredients: they will sit at the table with anyone. Their earthy, nutty flavour welcomes fatty, sweet, salty and spicy companions alike. A little onion and garlic make a meal of lentils; bacon and lentils also often hang out. Lentils take on warm spices, such as ginger and turmeric, cardamom and cumin, and woody herbs, such as rosemary and thyme.

RED LENTIL AND POTATO DAL

Dal is a vital dish for young cooks to learn how to make, as you can create a delicious meal when money is tight and you are just starting out in the kitchen. Across India, dal is made in myriad ways with different pulses and vegetables – you could eat a different dal every day of the year. This recipe is a great place to start. In this version we use red lentils and potato, but you could use cauliflower, sweet potato or pumpkin instead.

Rinse 1 cup (200 g) red lentils in a bowl of water, swishing them around before draining. Place the lentils in a saucepan with 4 cups (1 litre) water and ½ teaspoon grated or ground turmeric. Place over medium heat, bring to a simmer and cook for 15–20 minutes.

Meanwhile, in another saucepan, heat 2 tablespoons ghee, butter or vegetable oil over medium heat. Sauté 1 diced onion in the oil for 2 minutes, then add 2 tablespoons grated ginger and 2 thinly sliced garlic cloves and continue to sauté until the onion is translucent. Add 8 fresh or 12 dried curry leaves, 1½ teaspoons cumin seeds and 1 tablespoon black mustard seeds and stir until the seeds begin to pop. Cut 2 potatoes into 3–4 cm (1¼–1½ inch) cubes and add to the pan, stirring to coat in the spices. Add 400 g (14 oz) passata (page 247) or canned tomatoes, ¾ teaspoon salt and 1–2 cinnamon sticks. Cover and cook over low heat for 20 minutes.

By this time, your lentils are probably ready. Turn off the heat and let the lentils sit there waiting. Don't drain them! When the potatoes are tender, add the lentils and the remaining cooking liquid and cook, uncovered, for 5 minutes.

Remove the cinnamon sticks, then taste, season with salt and pepper as needed and squeeze in the juice of ½ lemon or lime. Serve with steamed rice and plenty of coriander (cilantro), Indian pickles and sambal.

Serves 4

EASY LENTIL SALAD

This salad can be served as a side dish or on its own. Keep an eye on the lentils while cooking to ensure that they don't turn mushy, and be generous with the flavours. Double the quantity to feed a crowd.

Pour 1.2 litres (35 fl oz) water into a saucepan, add 1 smashed garlic clove, 2 bay leaves and 1 teaspoon black peppercorns and bring to the boil. Add 375 g (13 oz) brown lentils and cook for 15 minutes or until just tender. Drain in a colander and rinse under cold water, shaking dry. Once drained, transfer to a bowl and season with 1 teaspoon salt, 1 teaspoon pepper and 1 tablespoon olive oil. Add ½ cup of either the quick pickled red onion (page 143), green olives, capers or diced preserved lemon, and 75 g (2½ oz) currants. In a small jar or jug, place 100 ml (3½ fl oz) olive oil, 30 ml (1 fl oz) lemon juice, 1 tablespoon lemon zest, 1 teaspoon caster (superfine) sugar, 2 minced garlic cloves and ¼ teaspoon ground nutmeg, and shake or stir until well combined. Pour this dressing over the lentils, add a large handful of chopped parsley, toss all together and serve. The salad will keep in an airtight container in the fridge for 4 days.

Serves 4 as a side

LENTIL STEW

Serves 4–6

A lentil stew is not fussy; it is not sophisticated. A lentil stew has only one intention and that is to comfort and satisfy. This is a dish that can and should be cooked by those who are just learning, as well as those who have cooked for years. The ingredients are simple, and only a little care is needed with the onion; the rest looks after itself. This stew is meant to feed many; double it to feed even more. Serve over mashed potatoes or polenta, or season the stew with the tiny sausage meatballs on page 139.

1½ cups (300 g) brown lentils
4 garlic cloves, 1 smashed,
   3 minced
3 tablespoons olive oil
2 onions, thinly sliced (or
   ½ cup/100 g Caramelised
   onions, page 143)
2 bay leaves
1 tablespoon freshly cracked black
   pepper (or less if you like)
1 tablespoon brown sugar
½ cup (125 ml) marsala wine (or
   red wine plus ½ teaspoon sugar)
800 g (1 lb 12 oz) passata (page
   247) or canned crushed tomatoes
½ teaspoon salt, to taste

To cook the lentils, rinse them first and place them in a large saucepan with 6 cups (1.5 litres) water and the smashed garlic clove. Bring to the boil, then reduce the heat to a simmer and cook for 15 minutes or until just tender.

Heat the olive oil in a cast-iron pan or heavy-based saucepan over medium–low heat. Add the onion, bay leaves and pepper and cook, stirring frequently, for 15 minutes or until starting to caramelise. This is your base flavour, so take the full 15 minutes. Add the minced garlic and stir for another minute, until fragrant. Add the brown sugar and pour in the marsala (or wine and sugar), and allow to reduce for 2 minutes. Everything should smell sweet and rich. Keep stirring!

Add the drained lentils and stir for a few seconds more. Finally, pour the passata or tomatoes and 2 cups (500 ml) water into the pan, season with the salt and cover. Cook over low heat for 45 minutes. Uncover and cook for a further 5–10 minutes to reduce the sauce and thicken the stew. Taste and season as needed and serve hot.

SAUSAGES

With over 4,000 recorded years of sausage eating in human history, there is no dismissing their place at the table. Originally, sausages made use of left-over cuts of meat and offal. With added salt and smoking techniques, sausages could be put aside for leaner times. Waste free and preserved – we could hardly approve more! But sausages have come a long way from their frugal origins and are now something of a problematic food in our diets.

Australians cook and eat more than 1 billion sausages a year. That's about 44 per person, per year. It's the meal that we can all cook without even knowing how to cook. It's what gets served up at school fetes, on election day, for kids' birthday parties and when the neighbours come around.

Unfortunately, our increased appetite for sausages comes with multiple issues. Firstly, we can only keep up with the demand for this many sausages using factory-farmed animals. Today's sausages also have so much salt added that a single one contains half our recommended intake for the day. Plus, the fat content isn't doing anyone's heart any favours.

This worldwide obsession with sausages isn't going away, so we need to rethink. We want to take on the sausage and figure out how best to enjoy them when the sausage sizzle is probably not the healthiest nor the most sustainable choice. For this, we look to other food cultures to learn how to use sausage meat more like a condiment than the main event.

Cantonese lap cheong is a perfect example of how to make a little bit of sausage go a long way. Rather than anyone sitting down to a plate of these sweet and smoked sausages, they are used to boost flavour and fragrance in meals. This is the approach we should take when eating all meats. It's about reducing our meat consumption, but still enjoying the flavours.

CHOOSING SAUSAGES

Yikes! Have you read the ingredients list on a packet of supermarket sausages? There are a lot of numbers, and a lot of other things that are basically salt in disguise.

Your best bet is to make your own sausages or buy them from small, trusted butchers who are doing the right thing. If you are buying sausages at the supermarket, choose the ones that have the least amount of ingredients. That cheap tray of sausages has hidden costs to our health, the environment and animal welfare that don't get accounted for. Spend a little more and learn how two sausages can make a meal.

POTATO PIZZA WITH GARLIC, ROSEMARY AND SAUSAGE

Homemade pizzas for dinner always go down well. This one features the winning flavour combination of garlic, sausage and rosemary.

Preheat the oven to 200°C (400°F/Gas mark 6). Boil 2 whole potatoes in their skins until just tender. Use 1 quantity of the scroll dough on page 146 and roll out two 30 cm (12 inch) pizza bases (or use ready-made bought pizza bases) and set aside.

In a small bowl, mix ¼ cup (60 ml) olive oil with 2–3 minced garlic cloves (or the roast garlic paste on page 69) and ½ teaspoon salt. Brush the garlicky oil generously over each pizza base. Add thin slices of cooked potato and divide lightly browned tiny sausage meatballs (opposite) between the pizzas (they are best not cooked all the way through as they will cook more in the oven). Sprinkle the pizzas with a little chopped rosemary and shavings of ricotta salata (page 37) or your favourite cheese. Bake for 15 minutes and serve with a few rocket (arugula) leaves scattered over the top.

Makes 2 pizzas

TINY SAUSAGE MEATBALLS

These tiny sausage meatballs are a surprise burst of salt, fat and flavour to add to your meals. When feeding four, you can use just two or three sausages to make 30 tiny meatballs instead of the usual serving of two sausages per person. These meatballs are no harder to make than frying a sausage, and they can be used to top pizzas (opposite) or added to gnocchi (page 133), a pasta bake, fried rice (page 159), lentil stew (page 137) or baked beans (page 233).

Squeeze the meat out of 2–3 sausage casings directly into a bowl. If your sausages are fancy and full of other flavours, there's no need to add anything more. To plain sausages you can add ½ teaspoon dried herbs or some minced garlic. With damp hands, bring the mince together into a ball. Roll the meat into small grape-sized meatballs and set aside.

Heat a splash of vegetable oil in a frying pan over high heat and fry the meatballs in batches of 10, shaking the pan to ensure even cooking, for 2 minutes or until crisp, browned and cooked through. Remove from the pan, drain on paper towel and add to your meal.

Makes 30 tiny meatballs

SAUSAGE ROLLS

Makes 15 party-sized sausage rolls

Good old sausage rolls are still favourites in school canteens and at sporting events, but the ingredients lists for some supermarket sausage rolls are alarming. This recipe is easy to make and contains 50 per cent vegetables. It maintains that sausage-roll flavour, but with far less meat, salt and fat.

For this recipe, we use a basic homemade pastry; it honestly takes five minutes to make and while it does need to rest for 30 minutes, you can use this time to make the mix and preheat the oven. We still buy premade pastry when we're pushed for time (the same goes for wonton wrappers and pizza bases). When you do buy store-bought pastry, look for brands that contain the least amount of ingredients, choose butter over margarine and avoid palm oil.

200 g (7 oz) sausages
200 g (7 oz) grated vegetables
   cabbage
   cauliflower
   zucchini (courgette) (squeezed
    dry)
   carrot
   celery
½ cup (30 g) breadcrumbs
   (page 269, or use regular fresh
   breadcrumbs)
2–4 tablespoons chopped herbs
   parsley
   thyme
   coriander (cilantro)
   oregano
1 garlic clove, minced
   (use 2–3 cloves if using
   plain sausages)
1 tablespoon tomato sauce or
   Worcestershire sauce
1 egg, plus a little beaten egg or
   milk for brushing
Sesame seeds, for sprinkling

BASIC PASTRY

345 g (12 oz) plain (all-purpose)
   flour, plus extra for dusting
½ teaspoon sea salt
250 g (9 oz) cold unsalted butter,
   diced
½ cup (125 ml) iced water

To make the pastry, place the flour and salt in a food processor and pulse until combined. Add the butter and pulse until the mixture resembles breadcrumbs. With the motor running, slowly pour in the iced water and pulse until the mixture forms a ball.

Turn the dough ball out onto a floured workbench and lightly knead. Flatten the dough into a disc, then wrap and rest in the fridge for 30 minutes.

Preheat the oven to 180°C (350°F/Gas mark 4).

Squeeze the mince from the sausage casings into a bowl, add the grated vegetables, breadcrumbs, herbs, garlic, tomato or Worcestershire sauce and egg and combine well. If you want to check the seasoning, make a little meatball and fry it in a frying pan, then taste and adjust the flavours where needed.

Roll out your pastry on a floured workbench to 30 cm x 40 cm (12 inch x 16 inch).

Cut the pastry into two 15 cm x 40 cm (6 inch x 16 inch) rectangles. Form the sausage mixture into two long logs and place them down the centre of each strip of pastry. Fold the pastry over to seal and create long sausage rolls.

Brush each sausage roll log with egg wash or a little milk and sprinkle with sesame seeds. Cut the logs into 7–10 cm (2¾–4 inch) sausage rolls and bake for a good 30 minutes or until golden brown.

TIP

The sausage roll mixture can also be used to make meatballs. After you've combined the ingredients, roll the mixture into balls and either fry or bake until golden brown. We serve these with flatbreads and a tangy cabbage, carrot and apple slaw.

ONIONS

Onions are indispensable in the kitchen. So much so that they are almost overlooked as an ingredient. Onions grow wild in many regions of the world and are one of the earliest cultivated crops. For this reason, there are few cuisines with recipes that do not start with an onion. As the base of a meal, onions are the foundation of flavour. In cooking, the volatile oils of an onion turn to sugar and give sweetness. When raw, the flavour remains sharp.

Onions have been used medicinally for centuries, treating everything from the plague to preventing stroke. Onions are nutrient-dense with sulphur compounds and high levels of vitamin B6 known to be good for heart health. They are also rich in vitamins B and C and the mineral potassium.

While there are many varieties of onion, the main difference to understand is between dry and green. Dry onions have matured in the ground until their tops dry out, while green onions (page 70) are pulled while they are still young with their fresh green stalks attached.

Dry onion varieties include:

- Brown onions: The most common and often the most affordable, these onions have a flaking golden skin and are sweetly sulphurous in flavour.

- Red onions: Also called Spanish onions, these onions have a bright purple–red skin and are sweeter than brown onions. They are often eaten raw in salads and sandwiches, or as a garnish.

- White onions: Creamy white in colour and pungent in scent and flavour, white onions are stronger and have less sugar than brown onions.

GO WITH ...

Pairing flavours with onions will depend on whether you are using them raw or cooked. Raw onion goes well with tomato, avocado, fish, olive oil, vinegar, garlic, basil, parsley, rocket (arugula) and cabbage. Cooked onions are the perfect match for sausages, butter, eggs, mushrooms, capsicum (pepper), potatoes, lentils, beans, bacon, rosemary, sage, thyme and cheese.

WASTE TIP

There's no need to ever throw half an onion away again! Use it to make the quick pickled onion opposite.

CARAMELISED ONIONS

Maybe this is the very best way to eat onions. All their sweetness and subtlety are realised through caramelising. It isn't hard, but it is patient work. This is a clever thing to do on a Sunday so you are prepared for the week ahead. Caramelised onions make a great flavour base for soups and stews, or stir them through pasta with parmesan, pop in cheese toasties or use them to make the sticky onion relish below.

Start by peeling and chopping 5 large onions. You can do this any way you like really – diced is good – but if you are going low and slow with your cooking, then we prefer to cut an onion in half and then slice along the grain. Heat ½ cup (125 ml) olive oil in a frying pan over medium heat. When the oil is hot but not sizzling, add the onion, 2 bay leaves, ½ teaspoon salt and 1 teaspoon cracked black pepper.

Reduce the heat to low and cook, stirring frequently, for 45–60 minutes. The onion will go from transparent to soft and dark golden, even a little blackened at the edges, and sticky. Transfer to an airtight container and allow to cool, before sealing and storing in the fridge for up to 5 days.

Makes about 2 cups (400 g)

STICKY ONION RELISH

Made with the caramelised onions above, this relish is rich, smoky, sticky and flavoursome. It's intense in flavour, meaning you only need a small amount. Because all the work is done caramelising the onions, all you need to do is add a few extra ingredients and cook for 10–15 minutes. Eat in a toastie, wrap or burger, with a tart or pie, or make it the star attraction at a barbecue.

Place 1 cup (200 g) caramelised onions, 3 tablespoons red wine vinegar, 1½ tablespoons brown sugar, ¼ teaspoon salt, ¼ teaspoon smoked paprika and a pinch of cayenne pepper in a small frying pan or saucepan and simmer over medium–low heat for 10–15 minutes, until the mixture is glossy, thick and delicious. Keep in a sealed jar or airtight container in the fridge for at least 1 month.

Makes about ¾ cup (160 g)

QUICK PICKLED RED ONION

Make this for the colour alone! It will bring a sweet and tart vibrancy to all that it touches. This also works with brown and white onions; just add ¼ teaspoon ground turmeric for colour.

Very thinly slice ½ red onion and set aside. In a small bowl or container place 3 tablespoons vinegar (either white wine, apple cider or rice wine vinegar), 3 tablespoons boiling water, 1 tablespoon caster (superfine) sugar, a big pinch of salt, a few chilli flakes and a few peppercorns. Whisk with a fork to dissolve the sugar and salt. Add the onion to the brine and in 20 minutes you'll have pickled onions to pop in toasties, on top of tacos or toss through salads. These will last for a few weeks in the fridge.

APPLES

If you can find unwaxed apples at the market, please buy them; it's like finding a pot of gold. Generally only available during their true seasons – autumn and winter – unwaxed apples taste amazing and are full of nutrients and probiotics, living up to the 'apple a day keeps the doctor away' adage. The shiny apples we see in the supermarkets all year round have been waxed and kept in cold storage to make them last for the year. Their shiny appearance makes them look fresh and firm, but it's often masking a floury, tasteless piece of fruit.

Our advice when buying shiny waxed supermarket apples is to only buy new season – good shops will label them as such – which means you're buying apples as close to their natural season as possible and limiting the amount of time they've been in storage. In our houses, apples are off the menu from late spring to early autumn. Luckily, there's an abundance of other fruits to eat over these warm months.

Buy enough apples for snacks, lunches and salads for the week ahead and then buy an extra kilo (2 or so pounds) for stewing for desserts and breakfast options. Apples like a cool and dry place. They'll last for a week on the bench; just keep them away from bananas and potatoes. Alternatively, keep them in the crisper drawer in the fridge.

To de-wax an apple, fill your sink with water and add 1 tablespoon bicarbonate of soda (baking soda) and 3 tablespoons vinegar. Give the apples a good scrub and then rinse again.

GO WITH …

Sweet, sour and crunchy apples are the perfect match for creamy textures. Cheddar, cottage cheese, ricotta, nut butters, custard and butter all work well. In sweet dishes, pair apples with warming spices, such as cinnamon, allspice, wattleseed, ginger and vanilla. Apples also like dark spirits.

For savoury dishes, apples go well with crunchy vegetables, such as fennel, celery, radish, carrot, beetroot (beets) and cabbage. They pair well with savoury flavours including mustard, ginger, coriander, dill and lemon. Apples add a sweet, tart crunch to salads – try them in a Waldorf salad (page 193) or a slaw (page 124). Grate an apple into your sauerkraut (page 120) or sauté them with cabbage and butter for a warming vegetable side dish. You could adjust the grape pickle recipe on page 171 to make tart apple slices to mix into salads or serve with cheese, or make your own dried apple slices for lunchboxes, trail-mixes and baking (page 172–3).

WASTE TIP

Apples are a rich source of probiotics. Most of this goodness is contained in the core and seeds, so get into the habit of eating your apple cores! The following pages are tips on how to make the most of the whole fruit.

If your apples don't get eaten or do end up a bit wrinkly, chutneys or apple sauce are great ways to use up what's leftover.

SUPER-QUICK STEWED APPLE

This is a quick and easy way to use up whole apples. We add stewed apple to muesli and yoghurt or use it to make a simple midweek crumble.

Grate 500 g (1 lb 2 oz) unpeeled apples. Melt 1 tablespoon butter in a saucepan over low heat. Add the apple, 2 tablespoons maple syrup, honey or sugar, the zest and juice of ½ lemon or orange and ¼ teaspoon ground ginger or cinnamon if you like. Pour in 200 ml (7 fl oz) water and cook, stirring often, for 15–20 minutes, until soft and sweet. Cool and store in the fridge for up to 5 days.

Makes about 2 cups (500 ml)

RESCUED APPLE CHUTNEY

We used to make this chutney a lot when the kids were little, using up all the apples from the fruit bowl with only one little bite taken out. This recipe is a good way to rescue fruit that is floury, bruised or wrinkled. Try it with pears, plums or even pumpkin. Change the spices to whatever you have in the pantry.

Heat 3 tablespoons olive, sunflower or vegetable oil in a saucepan over medium heat and sauté 1 thinly sliced small onion (or that ½ onion leftover in the fridge) with 1 teaspoon salt until soft and sweet. Add 1 teaspoon brown or yellow mustard seeds, ½ teaspoon ground cinnamon, a pinch of ground cloves (or use 2 whole cloves), a pinch of cayenne pepper if you like a little heat and 1–2 tablespoons grated ginger. Mix well, then throw in 3 roughly chopped apples with the skin on, ½ cup (125 ml) red, white or apple cider vinegar and ¼ cup (55 g) sugar of your choice and stir again. Reduce the heat and gently simmer until you have a thick and glossy chutney (add a little water if the chutney starts to look dry). Taste, and add extra spices or sugar if needed. Allow to cool a little, then spoon into an airtight container or jar and store in the fridge for up to 1 month.

Makes about 2 cups (500 ml)

Rescued apple chutney

LEFT-OVER APPLE SKIN CARAMEL

Another excellent waste reduction idea that's come out of our Cornersmith kitchen is to make this apple skin caramel after making a big batch of plum and apple jam. Spoon it over ice cream, crumble or apple tart, or add to cakes and muffins.

Place the apple skins from 4 apples, 1 cup (220 g) sugar, 1 cup (250 ml) water and some aromatics (such as a few star anise, cloves or slices of ginger) in a saucepan over low heat, stirring until the sugar has dissolved. Bring to a simmer, then remove from the heat and let the skins infuse for an hour or so.

Strain the syrup through a fine-mesh sieve into a small, clean saucepan. Bring the syrup back to a simmer over low heat, swirling the pan occasionally to distribute the heat. Once it reaches a nice caramel colour, remove from the heat. Gently stir in about 3 tablespoons water (depending on your desired consistency, you can add more). If left it will become toffee. At this point, you can add a little cream to make butterscotch or sprinkle in a little salt.

Makes 1 cup (250 ml)

HOMEMADE SCROLLS

Makes 6–8

We are so thankful that our chef Greer shared this recipe with us. Filled with apple and cinnamon, these scrolls, hot out of the oven, are great with a cuppa; alternatively, pack them full of caramelised onion and cheese and serve them with soup. You can also use this versatile dough to make simple bread rolls and pizza bases. You will need to start this recipe the day before, but it's well worth it.

275 ml (9½ fl oz) milk, plus extra for brushing

7 g (¼ oz) instant dried yeast (you can also use 15 g/½ oz fresh yeast)

2 eggs

1 teaspoon salt

45 g (1½ oz) caster (superfine) sugar

60 g (2 oz) unsalted butter, at room temperature

500 g (1 lb 2 oz) bread flour, plus extra for dusting

Canola or vegetable oil, for greasing

1 teaspoon ground cinnamon

1½ cups (400 g) stewed apple (page 145)

½ cup (85 g) sultanas

⅓ cup (80 ml) left-over apple skin caramel (page 145) or ⅓ cup (115 g) jam or marmalade of your choice, warmed, for glazing

Using a stand mixer fitted with the dough hook attachment, mix the milk, yeast, eggs, salt, sugar, butter and flour on low until the ingredients are combined. Turn the mixer to a medium speed and mix until you see a dough beginning to form. Use a pastry scraper to scrape any mixture left on the side of the bowl during the mixing process. Depending on your mixer, you may need to finish the dough by hand as it becomes thicker or hold onto the mixer in the final stages.

Turn the dough out onto a lightly floured workbench and knead with your hands until it comes together into a smooth ball. Grease a stainless steel or ceramic bowl with oil and add the dough. Cover with a lid or beeswax wrap and leave in the fridge overnight to rise.

The next day, roll out the dough on a lightly floured workbench to a 30 cm (12 inch) square. Mix the cinnamon through the stewed apple and then spread this evenly over the dough. Sprinkle the sultanas on top. (For alternative filling options, see below.)

Carefully roll the dough into a log, then cut into rough 2.5 cm (1 inch) thick rounds – you should get 6–8. Place the rounds on a tray lined with baking paper, cover with a tea towel and leave for 1 hour to rise.

Preheat the oven to 180°C (350°F/Gas mark 4). Brush the scrolls with milk before baking to give them a lovely glossy finish. Bake for 15–20 minutes or until golden, then remove from the oven and glaze immediately with the warmed caramel or jam. The scrolls are best eaten on the day they are made, but they will keep for 1–2 days in an airtight container – just reheat them in a low oven.

COMBINATIONS WE LIKE

- Spread the dough with a thin layer of tomato paste, then sprinkle over 1 cup (100 g) grated cheese and ½ cup (80 g) chopped ham
- Spread the dough with 1½ cups (300 g) caramelised onions (page 143) and sprinkle with grated cheese
- Spread the dough with a thin layer of pesto and top with a small handful of chopped pitted olives and 1 cup (100 g) grated cheese
- Mix 1 cup (250 g) ricotta and ½ cup (165 g) jam in a bowl and spread over the dough.

GRAPES

GREEN BEANS

DRIED FRUITS

RICE

KALE

SHOPPING BASKET 5

Things are getting very wholesome with this basket. Rice, kale, dried fruits …
this is a homage to our whole-foodie 20s and the parenting goals of our dreams.
The thing is, though, we are not believers in eating something just because it's good
for you. These recipes might be healthy, but they are first and foremost delicious
and bring warmth and nourishment to cooler days.

MUSHROOMS

FROM THIS BASKET ...

MEALS

Mushroom bolognese (page 152)

Mushroom, rice and greens pie (page 154)

Fried mushroom dumplings (page 157)

Rice fritters (page 159)

Breakfast rice porridge (page 159)

Pilaf (page 161)

Oven-baked risotto (page 163)

SIDES

Mushroom duxelles (page 153)

Fried rice (page 159)

Bright green garlicky kale (page 165)

Black pepper green beans (page 167)

The most delicious way to cook tired
green beans (page 167)

SNACKS, SWEETS & DRINKS

Kale chips (page 165)

Dried fruits (page 172)

Wholemeal dried fruit slice (page 175)

Clear-out-the-pantry cookies (page 176)

QUICK PRESERVING IDEAS

Dried mushrooms (page 153)

Use it all green bean relish (page 167)

Fermented garlicky green beans (page 168)

Quick pickled grapes (page 171)

NOTHING GOES TO WASTE

Mushroom salt (page 153)

Kale pesto (page 165)

Kale, seaweed and sesame seasoning mix
(page 165)

Roasted wrinkly grapes (page 171)

Tired grape and date paste (page 171)

MUSHROOMS

The mushrooms we see popping up on the forest floor are only the fruiting parts of the incredible network of mycelium that spreads underground, living off decay and in return conditioning the soil. This ability to recycle is even being used to clean up toxic waste and recycle plastics. Mushrooms have been eaten for centuries for their distinctly savoury and 'meaty' flavour, and their health-promoting properties.

In autumn, mushroom foraging is a beautiful thing to do. We go with an experienced forager who can safely identify mushroom varieties for us. Never pick mushrooms unless you are 100 per cent certain they are safe to eat. For the most part we buy cultivated mushrooms from specialty growers. Mushrooms are a very good source of potassium and selenium, which is a powerful antioxidant, as well as vitamin B.

Store button, field and Swiss brown mushrooms in a paper bag in the fridge for up to 1 week. Store more delicate varieties, such as oyster and shiitake, in a single layer covered with a barely damp tea towel in the fridge for 1 week.

GO WITH ...

Mushrooms' earthy flavour and spongy texture soak up other flavours so well. Garlic, lemon and ginger, as well as butter and cream, love mushrooms. Herbs such as tarragon and dill are particularly complementary to their slight anise flavour. Mushrooms and bacon are a good match, but otherwise we don't really pair mushrooms with meat as they are 'meaty' enough.

WASTE TIP

If you are using shiitake mushrooms or making stuffed mushrooms, save the stems to make a very quick dashi broth. Add stalks to 2 cups (500 ml) water, a few kale stems if you have them and a small piece of dried seaweed. Simmer for 15 minutes. Use this dashi to make quick noodle dishes at home.

A BATCH OF MUSHROOM BOLOGNESE

For a more sustainable kitchen, meat eaters need to reduce their consumption by half, particularly when it comes to beef. Spaghetti bolognese is a staple in so many homes, and our own children were raised on it. And while we're not condemning spag bol, we have both cut back on the amount of times it appears on the table. This recipe looks like a meaty stew, but definitely tastes like mushrooms. Make up a batch and then use it to make any of the following dishes.

The secret to this recipe is to add the ingredients one stage at a time. This builds up a more complex flavour and creates a ragu texture, rather than stewed mushrooms.

Heat 100 ml (3½ fl oz) olive oil in a large frying pan over medium–low heat and sauté 2 finely chopped onions and 2 finely chopped celery stalks or leeks with a good pinch of salt for 10 or more minutes until very soft and sweet. Add 2 crushed garlic cloves, 2 teaspoons smoked paprika, 1 teaspoon black pepper and 1 tablespoon dried thyme or oregano (if using fresh, add a little more) and sauté for a few minutes until fragrant. Add 1 cup (250 ml) red wine and 1 tablespoon miso and stir well, then simmer for a few more minutes. Gradually add 3 teaspoons plain (all-purpose) flour, a teaspoon at a time, stirring constantly to make a thickened gravy-like sauce.

Add 1 kg (2 lb 4 oz) grated button or field mushrooms, a large handful at a time, allowing each handful to cook down into the sauce before adding more. Once all the mushrooms are in, add 2 tablespoons tomato paste (concentrated purée), 1 cup (250 ml) beef bone, chicken or vegetable stock and 1 tablespoon Worcestershire sauce and simmer over low heat for at least 15 minutes. Taste, adjust the seasoning where needed, and add more stock if you feel like the mixture is too thick.

Makes 4 cups (900 g)

MUSHROOM PASTA

Serve this exactly as you would a meat bolognese: pile 2 cups (450 g) on spaghetti with lots of grated cheese.

MUSHROOM PIE

Take 2 cups (450 g) of this bolognese to make the mushroom, rice and greens pie on page 154.

MUSHROOM LASAGNE

Follow the summer harvest lasagne recipe on page 254 and swap out the ratatouille for 2 cups (450 g) mushroom bolognese. This will make a rich and meaty-tasting family favourite.

MUSHROOM POCKETS

Replace the roasted root vegetables in the curried vegetable pockets on page 216 with 1½–2 cups (350–450 g) mushroom bolognese. Leave out the curry powder and add a tablespoon of grated cheese to each pocket.

Mushroom pasta

MUSHROOM DUXELLE

We teach this recipe during our annual mushroom foraging and preserving workshop, and it's a smash hit. Duxelle is a concentrated mushroom paste, which can be used to flavour soups, stews and sauces. Use ½ cup (110 g) in a risotto or a white wine sauce for pasta, or add a dollop as a topping for a jacket potato. It can also be spread on bread (like a pâté), and served with sliced pickles or fried eggs.

Very finely chop, grate or roughly blitz in a food processor 500 g (1 lb 2 oz) mushrooms. Heat 2 tablespoons olive oil in a frying pan over medium heat and sauté 1 small finely chopped onion or ½ bunch spring onions for 5 minutes or until soft, sweet and translucent. Add 2 minced garlic cloves and ½ teaspoon each of salt and pepper, and sauté until fragrant. Add the mushroom in batches, a large handful at a time, stirring frequently to reduce the mushroom liquid (this will prevent the mixture being too watery). Cook for 15 minutes or until the mushroom looks thick and paste-like, then add ½ teaspoon ground nutmeg, a handful of chopped parsley and 3 tablespoons red wine vinegar. Simmer for another 10 minutes until the vinegar has evaporated. Taste and adjust the seasoning if needed.

Spoon the mixture into a clean jar, press down well and drizzle over 1 cm (½ inch) oil to cover the surface. Seal the jar and allow to cool. Store in the fridge for up to 4 weeks.

Makes 380 g (13½ oz)

MUSHROOM SALT

Grind dried mushrooms (see opposite) to a fine powder using a spice grinder or a mortar and pestle. Serve sprinkled on baked potatoes, risotto or soup.

Grind together 4 tablespoons mushroom powder, 200 g (7 oz) salt, 2 tablespoons dried thyme and 1 tablespoon ground white pepper. Mix well and store in a clean jar or airtight container, where it will last in your pantry for up to 1 year (though the flavours will be best if used within 6 months).

Makes 1 x 250 ml (8½ fl oz) jar

Mushroom duxelle

DRIED MUSHROOMS

When a mushroom is dried, it intensifies in flavour, becoming a meatier, more umami version. At the height of the mushroom season, we make a big jar of dried mushrooms to flavour stocks, soups and stews throughout the year. We've given instructions here on how to oven-dry if you don't have a dehydrator.

Preheat the oven to 130°C (265°F/Gas mark 1), or as low as your oven can go. Wipe the mushrooms clean, then slice them. Spread the sliced mushroom out on a baking tray lined with baking paper and dry in the oven for around 4 hours. If your oven is lower in temperature, it will take 6 or more hours. The mushrooms must be completely dry and crisp with no moisture left. Allow to cool completely before storing in a clean, dry airtight jar or container for up to 1 year.

To rehydrate dried mushrooms, soak them in a small amount of water for 20 minutes. Never throw away the soaking liquid! Add it to soups and stews; it's full of mushroom flavour.

MUSHROOM, RICE AND GREENS PIE

Serves 4–6

This delicious, wholesome pie is an ode to a pie Jaimee ate in the Blue Mountains, which she has never forgotten. We've made this a bottomless pie, so you don't need to blind bake, making it an excellent midweek meal. Here we've used a wholemeal olive oil pastry, making it a good choice for our dairy-free friends. The added dried herbs and salt make the pastry earthy and flavoursome. You could also use the sour cream pastry on page 185.

2 cups (450 g) mushroom
    bolognese (page 152)
3 tablespoons grated ginger
2 tablespoons soy sauce
2 cups (370 g) cooked brown rice
2 cups (200 g) thinly sliced kale
    (cabbage, silverbeet/Swiss chard
    and fennel also work well)
Olive oil, for greasing

OLIVE OIL PASTRY
250 g (9 oz) plain (all-purpose)
    flour, plus extra for dusting
120 g (4¼ oz) wholemeal (whole
    wheat) flour
1½ teaspoons sea salt
½ teaspoon bicarbonate of soda
    (baking soda)
2 tablespoons mixed dried herbs
½ cup (125 ml) olive oil
½ cup (125 ml) cold water

To make the olive oil pastry, in a food processor, whiz up the flours, salt, bicarbonate of soda and herbs. With the motor running, add the olive oil in a steady stream until the mixture resembles fine breadcrumbs. Slowly add the water until the dough comes together. Tip the dough onto a floured workbench and knead for 5 minutes. Wrap in a tea towel or beeswax wrap and rest in the fridge for at least 30 minutes.

Meanwhile, heat the mushroom bolognese, ginger and soy sauce in a saucepan over medium heat until warmed through. Transfer the mixture to a bowl and stir through the brown rice and kale.

Grease a 24 cm (9½ inch) pie dish or glass ovenproof dish and fill with the pie mixture.

To roll out the pastry, cut two large sheets of baking paper (this is a delicate pastry that needs to be rolled between the layers of paper). Start by rolling the pastry out to a 10 cm (4 inch) round. Place between the sheets of baking paper and roll the pastry out to a 30 cm (12 inch) circle.

Very carefully lift the pastry and place it over the filling and remove the baking paper. Tuck the pastry in around the filling, then bake for 20–30 minutes, until the pastry is golden brown.

TIP

If you have any pastry left over, wrap it well and freeze for up to 3 months.

FRIED MUSHROOM DUMPLINGS

Makes about 24

Making dumplings isn't as hard as it sounds. The mixture is usually incredibly simple and with a few hands on deck, folding the dumplings doesn't take long, plus it's a nice way to get everyone involved. We serve these with rice and sautéed greens, such as the garlicky kale on page 165.

We've included a dumpling dough recipe here, which we got from our friend Maddy, if you want to make everything from scratch, but you can also buy dumpling wrappers, which are a good option if you're pressed for time. We'd rather you buy the wrappers and make dumplings at home than not make them at all! This mushroom mixture is full of flavour and only uses 150 g (5½ oz) raw grated mushrooms. You could add a little raw minced (ground) pork or grated tofu as well. The chicken dumpling mix on page 92 also works wonderfully in these wrappers.

150 g (5½ oz) grated mushrooms
½ cup (50 g) very thinly sliced
   cabbage
¼ teaspoon salt
1 tablespoon soy sauce
1 tablespoon grated ginger
2 garlic cloves, minced
2 thinly sliced spring onions
   (scallions), a handful of
   snipped chives or a little
   finely diced onion
24 dumpling wrappers
Up to ½ cup (125 ml) vegetable
   or sunflower oil

BASIC DUMPLING DOUGH

1⅓ cups (200 g) plain
   (all-purpose) flour, plus extra
   for dusting
100 ml (3½ fl oz) warm water

To make the dumpling dough, place the flour in a bowl, make a well in the centre and add the warm water. Whisk to combine, then bring the mixture together into a ball and turn out onto a floured workbench. Knead for 10 minutes or until smooth and elastic – when you gently push your thumb into the dough, it should spring back. Wrap in a tea towel and leave to rest on your workbench for 20 minutes.

Divide the dough into quarters. Working with one piece at a time (and keeping the rest of the dough under the tea towel so it doesn't dry out), roll the dough into a 10 cm (4 inch) log, about 2.5 cm (1 inch) thick. Cut the log into six equal-sized pieces, then roll each piece into a ball. Gently flatten each ball and use a rolling pin to roll them into 10 cm (4 inch) round dumpling wrappers. Stack the wrappers into a pile, ensuring there is plenty of flour coating them to stop them sticking together, and repeat until all the dough is rolled out.

Place the mushroom and cabbage in a bowl and gently mix. Add the salt, soy sauce, ginger, garlic and spring onion and mix gently to avoid the mushroom releasing too much liquid. Taste the mixture and adjust where needed.

Take a dumpling wrapper and spoon a scant tablespoon of the mushroom mixture onto one side of the wrapper. You don't want to overfill the dumpling or it will explode when frying. Dip your finger in water and run it around the rim of the dumpling wrapper. Fold the wrapper in half over the filling and seal the dumpling. Repeat with the remaining mushroom mixture and wrappers.

Heat the oil in a frying pan over medium heat. Working in batches, add the dumplings so they're not touching each other, and fry for 2 or so minutes on each side – the dumplings should be a deep golden brown. Drain on paper towel.

Once all your dumplings are cooked, eat straight away!

RICE

Rice is cheap, accessible and not given a lot of thought when we buy a bag at the supermarket or order a container of rice with our takeaway. However, its production and associated issues need to be mentioned. Rice is a staple for more than half the world's population, and as the population grows, so does the demand for this carbon-intensive carbohydrate. While rice's environmental impact is much smaller than meat production, it does emit significant greenhouse gases and has an incredibly heavy water footprint, accounting for an astronomical amount of water use.

The good news is there are companies engaging in environmentally responsible farming practices, reducing their water and use of pesticides.

When purchasing rice, try and look for the following:

- Companies with more sustainable farming practices. Ethical consumer apps are a great help.
- Fairtrade rice, which ensures growers are paid fair prices.
- Rice sold in bulk packages to cut down on plastics or in bulk stores where you can fill your own jar.
- Pesticide-free rice.

When cooking rice, remember to only cook as much as you and your household are going to eat – or become well versed in what to do with leftovers. We need to remember the hidden environmental costs every time we throw edible food in the bin, even if that's only a few cups of rice. Throwing away rice also means you're throwing away huge amounts of water – both the water needed to grow rice and then the water used to cook the rice.

WASTE TIP

Opposite are our favourite ways to use up any left-over cooked rice. Please remember, the greatest of care needs to be taken when storing and reheating cooked rice to prevent harmful bacteria forming. Left-over cooked rice must be cooled quickly in airtight containers in the fridge, and then reheated quickly and thoroughly. Before you start, check online for the most up-to-date guidelines on the safe storage of cooked rice.

WHAT TO DO WITH LEFT-OVER RICE

RICE FRITTERS

Everyone loves these fritters and we do, too, because breakfast, lunch or dinner is ready in 20 minutes. This recipe doubles or triples very easily.

In a bowl, combine 1 cup (185 g) cooked rice, 1 cup (100 g) thinly sliced cabbage or fennel, very thinly sliced and massaged kale, grated zucchini (courgette) or carrot, ½ cup (15 g) chopped fresh herbs such as parsley or dill, 1 minced garlic clove, ½ teaspoon sea salt and ¼ teaspoon ground turmeric. In a separate bowl, beat 2–3 eggs and then mix into the rice mixture (soft, juicy vegetables like cabbage and zucchini will only need 2 eggs, but sturdier vegetables like kale will need the third egg to bring the mixture together).

Heat ⅓ cup (80 ml) sunflower or vegetable oil in a frying pan over medium heat. Use a ¼ cup (60 ml) measure to add six rice fritters to the hot oil. Using a spatula, gently flatten the fritters, then cook for 2–3 minutes each side, until golden, then drain on paper towel and serve with a salad. Enjoy!

Makes 6

Breakfast rice porridge

FRIED RICE

As cooked rice is one of the most wasted food items, it's important to have a handful of left-over rice dishes up your sleeve. We've both cooked average fried rice for years, but it wasn't until we made Adam Liaw's egg-fried rice recipe that we realised how excellent it could actually be. We're now teaching our teenagers this method, so they can keep themselves well fed.

Beat 3 eggs with a pinch of salt and set aside. Heat a wok over high heat and add 2 tablespoons vegetable oil. Add ½ thinly sliced onion, 2 minced garlic cloves and another generous pinch of salt and stir-fry for 30 or so seconds. Add 3–4 cups (550–770 g) left-over cooked rice (both white and brown work) and 1 tablespoon soy sauce and stir to coat the rice in the oil and soy. Once the rice begins to toast, move it to one side of the pan and pour in the beaten egg. Quickly mix the egg and stir it through the rice once it starts to cook. Top with fried spring onions (page 71), carrot kimchi (page 227) or sautéed greens.

Serves 4

BREAKFAST RICE PORRIDGE

This breakfast favourite is an excellent way to use up 1 cup (185 g) left-over rice.

Place 1 cup (185 g) brown or white rice and 1 cup (250 ml) milk of your choice in a small saucepan. Add ⅓ cup (45 g) dried fruit, 1 tablespoon honey and a pinch of citrus powder (page 204) or orange zest. If you have ½ pear or apple that needs to be used, grate it into the pan. Cook the rice pudding over low heat, stirring often, for 15–20 minutes, until thick and delicious. Divide the rice pudding between two bowls, drizzle over honey or maple syrup if needed and top with sliced fruit, toasted nuts or yoghurt.

Serves 2

PILAF

Serves 6

This Iranian rice dish can be served as either a main or side depending on what you add to it or serve it with. The method is what we are teaching here and the ingredients can be flexible, but try not to skip the saffron as it is one of the characteristic flavours of pilaf and Australia grows world-class saffron. Saffron lends its singular flavour and beautiful colour to pilafs, but if you don't have it, add a little ground turmeric instead.

350 g (12½ oz) basmati rice, rinsed
Large pinch of saffron
½ teaspoon ground cinnamon
½ teaspoon ground cardamom
½ teaspoon sugar
½ teaspoon salt
1 tablespoon zesty flavour
   orange zest
   lemon zest
   chopped preserved lemon
50 g (1¾ oz) dried fruit, soaked
   in hot water for 5 minutes
   currants
   raisins
   chopped dried apricots
   chopped dried figs
50 g (1¾ oz) toasted seeds or nuts
   sunflower seeds
   chopped almonds
   hazelnuts
   pine nuts
   pistachios
⅓ cup (80 ml) olive oil
1 onion, diced
1 garlic clove, minced
3 tablespoons melted butter,
   to serve

Place the rice in a bowl, cover with water and leave to soak while you prepare everything else.

Place the saffron in a small ramekin and cover with 2 tablespoons water. Set aside.

In a small bowl, combine the cinnamon, cardamom, sugar, salt and zesty flavour and set aside. In another bowl, mix the dried fruit and toasted seeds or nuts and set aside.

Pour 5 cups (1.25 litres) water into a saucepan, add a pinch of salt and bring to the boil. Drain the rice, add to the boiling water and cook, without stirring, for 5 minutes only (your rice won't be fully cooked at this point, but don't panic as it will finish cooking in the next step). Drain well.

In a heavy-based saucepan, heat the olive oil over medium heat and sauté the onion and garlic for 4–5 minutes, until translucent. Reduce the heat to the lowest setting possible, then spoon in a third of the par-cooked rice in a layer in the bottom of the pan. Sprinkle over half the spice mix and then half the fruit and seed mix. Add another third of par-cooked rice to make another layer and add the remaining spices and fruit and seeds. Finally, top with the remaining third of rice.

With the end of a wooden spoon, poke four holes into the rice that reach all the way to the bottom of the pan. Pour the saffron water over the top of the rice, then cover the pan with a clean tea towel followed by the lid so no steam escapes. Cook for 20 minutes.

Pour the melted butter over the rice and fluff with a fork before serving. Make sure each person gets some of the crispy crust that will have formed on the bottom of the pan – in Iranian families, this is the bit that is fought over!

OVEN-BAKED RISOTTO

Serves 4–6

FOUNDATION RECIPE

Carefully stirring a risotto is a lovely thing to do, but it does take time and focus and sometimes we have neither. This is our midweek version and it has served us well for 10 years. This is a base recipe with lemon zest, garlic, whatever green veg you have and parmesan. You can also use shredded poached chicken – just add it in the last 5 minutes of cooking.

2 tablespoons olive oil or butter
Around 140 g (5 oz) finely sliced
   alliums
   onion (about 1 small)
   leek
   shallot

1–2 garlic cloves, crushed
Zest of 1 lemon
330 g (11½ oz) arborio rice
4 cups (1 litre) stock of
   your choice
1 sprig woody herbs
   thyme
   rosemary
   sage

1 cup (100 g) vegetables
   or protein
   thinly sliced asparagus
   frozen peas
   baby spinach
   chopped green beans
   poached shredded chicken (page 95)

½ cup (50 g) grated parmesan,
   plus extra to serve
Salt and freshly cracked
   black pepper
Chopped herbs of your choice,
   to serve

Preheat the oven to 180°C (350°F/Gas mark 4).

Heat the oil or butter in a flameproof casserole dish and sauté the alliums for 4–5 minutes until soft and sweet. Add the garlic and lemon zest and sauté until fragrant. Add the rice and stir to coat well. Pour in the stock, add the woody herbs and bring the mixture to a simmer.

Cover and bake in the oven for 20 minutes. Remove the lid and stir through the vegetables or chicken and cook, covered, for a further 5 minutes. Take the risotto out of the oven and stir through the grated parmesan. Taste and season with salt and pepper if needed.

Top with extra parmesan and chopped herbs.

USE IT ALL

Left-over risotto from last night? Make arancini! Roll cold risotto into balls the size of a lime. Beat an egg in one bowl and sprinkle 1 cup (60 g) fresh breadcrumbs (page 269) in another bowl. Roll each rice ball in the egg wash and then in the breadcrumb mix. Heat ⅓ cup (80 ml) vegetable oil in a frying pan over medium heat. Working in batches if necessary, fry the arancini for 3–4 minutes, making sure all sides are golden brown. Drain on paper towel and serve.

KALE

While its virtues have been slightly overstated in recent years, kale is an excellent, nutrient-dense ingredient to use in your cooking. This dark, leafy green is part of the brassica family, although it doesn't form a head like cabbage, cauliflower and brussels sprouts. Kale provides an extraordinary amount of vitamins A, C and K, and is very high in antioxidants, anti-inflammatory nutrients and fibre.

Kale can be grown all year round, but is at its best in the cooler months when the leaves are soft and sweet. Its sturdy leaves hold up well when sautéed or braised, or used in pies and fritters. Kale can be stir-fried, dehydrated, eaten raw and even juiced.

While green smoothies aren't high on our 'must-eat' list, we regularly use kale in our meals. We turn the leaves into pesto (see opposite) or sauté them with lots of garlic for a yummy side or to top pasta. Kale is also great used in salads and slaws. Don't be afraid to eat it raw – giving the leaves a massage with a little salt or oil before adding them to a salad softens them up. You can also add chopped kale in the last few minutes of simmering a soup or stew.

It's really important to wash kale well, as it is often high in pesticide residue, which isn't great for human consumption. Fill the sink with water and add a little bicarbonate of soda (baking soda) and give the kale a massage. Rinse well and pat dry.

Treat kale like other leafy greens and roll in a slightly damp tea towel and tuck the ends in – like you're rolling a kebab. Store your bundle in a sealed container, calico bag or plastic bag in the fridge and be shocked by how long it lasts.

GOES WITH ...

Kale goes with other earthy flavours, such as mushrooms and brown rice, and it loves intense flavours like chilli, garlic, ginger, parmesan and bacon. Kale will lift with a little acid – experiment with sautéing it with lemon zest and juice, raw or cooked tomatoes, olives, capers or anchovies.

WASTE TIP

Despite their fibrous tough texture, kale stems can be eaten. Pickle them (following the quick pickled red onion recipe on page 143) and add them to your salads, or add thinly sliced stems to broths or stir-fries.

BRIGHT GREEN GARLICKY KALE

This is one of the best ways to eat kale. The high heat of a sauté softens the kale while still maintaining the structure of the leaves. This can be a very quick and simple side, or stir it through pasta with lots of olive oil, parmesan and lemon juice. We also serve it with the mushroom dumplings on page 157 and a bowl of rice, or use it as a filling for an omelette with a little goat's cheese.

Strip the leaves from 1 bunch kale and tear them into bite-sized pieces. Very thinly slice the stems. Heat 3 tablespoons olive oil in a frying pan over medium–high heat. Throw in the sliced stems and a pinch of salt. Sauté, stirring often, for 3 minutes or until the stems are bright green and starting to soften. Throw in 1–2 handfuls of kale leaves and another generous pinch of salt and stir quickly so the kale wilts but doesn't start to steam. Keep adding handfuls of kale, stirring as you go. Once all the kale is in the pan and the leaves are bright green, throw in 3 minced garlic cloves, a pinch of chilli flakes and/ or 1 teaspoon lemon zest. Sauté for 1 minute, stirring the garlic through the leaves. Check the seasoning, then remove from the heat and serve.

Serves 4 as a side

KALE PESTO

This is a wintry option for pesto, giving you something bright, green and fresh in the cool months. We use walnuts or sunflower seeds in kale pesto for extra creaminess and parmesan is a lovely match with the bitter earthy flavours.

To make kale pesto, follow the recipe on page 32.

KALE CHIPS

Give these kale chips a crack. They're a tasty salty snack and, while they're not a packet of chips, they never last long in our houses.

Preheat the oven to 180°C (350°F/Gas mark 4). Wash and pat dry ½ bunch kale leaves, then tear them into bite-sized pieces and place in a bowl. Add 1 tablespoon sunflower, olive or good-quality vegetable oil, ½ teaspoon salt and a pinch of cayenne pepper. Mix well with your hands, then spread the leaves out on a baking tray. If you're using a fan-forced oven, lay a wire rack on top of the leaves to stop them flying around. Bake for 10–15 minutes, until crisp and dry. Remove from the oven, allow to cool and store in an airtight container for 2–3 days.

KALE, SEAWEED AND SESAME SEASONING MIX

This recipe is based on furikake, the Japanese dried seasoning mix. We sprinkle it on top of rice, sautéed greens, eggs, salads, fish and tofu, giving a hit of extra flavour and added nutrients.

It's best to use a spice grinder to make this seasoning mix. Blitz ½ quantity kale chips (see above) with 2–3 pieces of dried seaweed to a powder, then pour the mixture into a bowl. Next, blitz 3 tablespoons toasted sunflower and sesame seeds to a powder, being mindful not to turn the seeds into a paste (if you do, spread it on toast and try again). Mix the powdered seeds into the powdered greens, taste and add ¼–½ teaspoon salt and a pinch of cayenne pepper. Store in a jar in the pantry and use over the next few weeks.

Makes about 1 cup

GREEN BEANS

Native to South America and introduced to Europe in the 15th century, green beans have since become a global crop. They are distinguished from other beans because they are picked while their pods are still tender and the beans inside have yet to mature. Often recipes call for topping and tailing beans, but honestly, who cares? We just take off the woody tops and leave the tails.

Don't dismiss green beans as a ubiquitous side dish; their sweet flavour lends them to all kinds of transformations. Slow cook them until they are collapsing, steam them or eat them raw. Green beans are a good source of vitamins A, C and K and folate.

Keep green beans in an airtight container in the fridge for up to 1 week. If your beans have started to dry out and look a little tired, use them for longer, slower cooking. If they have become mushy and mouldy, then they are bound for the compost.

GO WITH ...

The subtle sweetness of green beans goes with many ingredients. Garlic and ginger are perfect, as are nuts, olive oil, onions, tomatoes, olives, chillies, parmesan, butter, chives, dill and tarragon.

WASTE TIP

When green beans have seen better days, we make the slow-cooked beans opposite. It is the perfect recipe to hide a multitude of sins.

USE IT ALL

Don't chuck that last handful of green beans left in the crisper. Coat them in oil and char them in a very hot pan for 3 minutes on each side (only turn them once!). Tip onto a plate and sprinkle with a squeeze of lime, a pinch of salt and a good splash of hot sauce or 1 tablespoon harissa (page 258). A delicious snack or side dish.

BLACK PEPPER GREEN BEANS

Lots of black pepper brings heat to this side dish. Eat these beans with fried rice (page 159), grilled fish or spring onion pancakes (page 71).

Heat 2 tablespoons vegetable oil in a wok or frying pan over medium–high heat. Add a 3 cm (1¼ inch) piece of ginger, thinly sliced into matchsticks, and stir constantly for a few seconds. Add 300 g (10½ oz) green beans and ¼ teaspoon salt and keep stirring. Add 2 cloves thinly sliced garlic and 1 tablespoon coarsely cracked black pepper. Stir for a few seconds, then add 1½ tablespoons soy sauce and stir until the pan is a bit sticky. Top with 1 tablespoon sesame seeds if you like. Remove from the heat and serve.

Serves 4 as a side

USE IT ALL GREEN BEAN RELISH

This is like a piccalilli, an English-style relish pickle that was originally made as a way to use up garden vegetables. Green beans work really well in this recipe as they stay crunchy and bright, but you can also use a mix of vegetables including carrots, cauliflower, zucchini (courgette), onion, fennel and white cabbage. Eat this relish in cheese sandwiches, with boiled eggs or on burgers.

Cut 250 g (9 oz) washed green beans into 3 cm (1¼ inch) lengths and lightly blanch in boiling salted water for 1 minute. Drain and set aside.

In a measuring jug, combine 100 ml (3½ fl oz) apple cider vinegar and 50 ml (1¾ fl oz) water. In a saucepan, combine 1 tablespoon cornflour (corn starch), ½ teaspoon sea salt, ½ teaspoon ground turmeric, ¼ teaspoon cracked black pepper, a pinch of cayenne pepper, 1 teaspoon mustard seeds and 1 tablespoon caster (superfine) sugar. Add a little of the vinegar brine and whisk into a slurry. Place over low heat and slowly whisk in the remaining vinegar brine to form a thick paste. Cook for 1 minute, then remove from the heat and add the green beans. Stir to coat the beans in the paste and then pack into a clean jar or container. Store in the fridge for up to 1 month.

Makes 1 x 375 ml (12½ fl oz) jar

THE MOST DELICIOUS WAY TO COOK TIRED GREEN BEANS

Be inspired to make this dish the next time you find the beans you bought last week in the back of the fridge. The slow cooking in this recipe will give beans a new life. Pair with a rice dish, grilled fish or chicken, or alongside fritters or poached eggs.

Heat 2 tablespoons olive oil in a flameproof casserole dish over medium heat. Add 500 g (1 lb 2 oz) tired green beans and sauté for 4–5 minutes. Add 4 minced garlic cloves and stir for a few minutes. Add 400 g (14 oz) passata or a can of chopped tomatoes and ½ a teaspoon each of salt and freshly cracked black pepper, then reduce the heat to low, cover and cook for 30 minutes. Take the lid off, add ¼ bunch chopped dill and allow the tomato juices to reduce for another 15 minutes.

Serve 4–6 as a side

FERMENTED GARLICKY GREEN BEANS

Makes 1 x 500 ml (17 fl oz) jar

Making brine-fermented vegetables is a good place to begin your fermenting adventures. It's easy to do, you can use up what's around and the batch is small. Put most simply, fermentation is the process of converting sugars to lactic acid using the yeast and bacteria that's already on the produce (see page 278 for more information). It is a method of food preservation that has existed for thousands of years. This brine can be used to ferment other vegetables (see variations below) so keep it in mind the next time you have a handful of carrots and half an onion looking like they need some attention.

1 teaspoon pure salt
400 g (14 oz) green beans
4 garlic cloves, thinly sliced
Black peppercorns
Tarragon or dill sprigs (optional)

Pour 1 cup (250 ml) water into a small saucepan and add the salt. Bring to a simmer, stirring to dissolve the salt. Remove from the heat and let the brine stand until cooled to room temperature.

You can keep your beans whole or chop them into smaller lengths; just make sure they will fit in your chosen jar. Pack the beans tightly into the jar and add the garlic, a few peppercorns and herbs (if using). Pour the brine over the top, leaving a 5 mm (¼ inch) gap at the top, then seal.

Place the jar in a cool, dry spot for 2 days. This is the period of fermentation. During this time your brine will bubble and some juice may escape – simply wipe down the jar if this happens. Ferment your beans for 2–4 days depending on how sour you like them, then store in the fridge for up to 6 months.

The beans can be eaten immediately, but their flavour will become more complex with time (we suggest a week or two).

COMBINATIONS WE LIKE

- Carrots: Cut 400 g (14 oz) carrots into rounds or matchsticks and replace the tarragon and black peppercorns for 1 teaspoon cumin seeds
- Green tomatoes: Quarter 400 g (14 oz) green tomatoes and replace the tarragon and black peppercorns with 2 teaspoons caraway seeds
- Celery: Cut 400 g (14 oz) celery stalks to fit your chosen jar and replace the tarragon with 2 teaspoons fennel seeds.

GRAPES

Table grape varieties are eaten fresh and chosen for their thin skin and sweetness. They tend not to have the deep complexity of grapes that are grown for wine making. This, of course, depends on the kind of grapes you buy. White seedless grapes are bland, but have their place among picky children. Dark purple and almost black varieties are another story and worth seeking out.

Grapes contain a decent amount of vitamins C and K, as well as potassium. Cooking and preserving with grapes can bring out their very best. Try using fresh green grapes instead of sultanas in a tea cake, or add them to salads, such as the tabbouleh on page 27.

Choose grapes that are firm and attached to the branch. Grapes don't ripen off the vine, so sneak one to taste before buying to ensure they are ripe. Darker varieties have a natural bloom that dusts their skin. This protects grapes and will keep them fresh for longer. If stored in an airtight container in the fridge, grapes will last a few weeks.

It's really important to wash grapes well, as they are often high in pesticide residue. Fill the sink with water, add a little bicarbonate of soda (baking soda) and give the grapes a good wash. Rinse well and pat dry.

GO WITH …

Depending on the variety, a grape's flavour can range from merely sweet and fruity to deeply perfumed and more like a berry. We all know that grapes make a good counterpoint to the richness of cheese and this also works well with roasted meats and even pork sausages. Grapes and nuts go well together, so you should put both in a salad. Grapes also pair well with berries. A simple fruit salad of purple grapes and blueberries looks dramatic, tastes wonderful and is probably some kind of antioxidant miracle dessert.

WASTE TIP

If you have old and wrinkly grapes hanging around that no one is keen to eat fresh, try roasting them to give them a new lease on life (see opposite).

USE IT ALL

Use up that last handful of grapes in the bowl by pickling them (see opposite).

ROASTED WRINKLY GRAPES

Roasting fruits not only disguises any imperfections, it also intensifies the flavour. You can make these with grapes you've just bought, or ones that have been sitting in the back of the fridge for a few weeks. Once roasted, they are rich and tangy and sweet and salty, and an excellent addition to salads and slaws, or served with goat's cheese or roasted meats.

Preheat the oven to 200°C (400°F/Gas mark 6). Spread out 300 g (10½ oz) grapes onto a lined baking tray and coat with 2 tablespoons each of apple cider vinegar, brown sugar and olive oil. Add 1 teaspoon salt, ½ teaspoon cracked black pepper and, if you like a bit of bite, ½ teaspoon chilli flakes. Shake the pan to coat the grapes well and then roast for 15 minutes until they start to wrinkle or split (shake the pan again every 5 minutes or so to stop the grapes from sticking and to coat them in the juices). Remove from the oven, allow to cool and store in a container or jar in the fridge for up to 1 week.

Makes 300 g (10½ oz)

QUICK PICKLED GRAPES

Pickled grapes are on high rotation at Cornersmith. This is our quick at-home version; they'll make your cheese plates fancy, and are delicious thinly sliced in a bitter green salad or the raw cauliflower salad on page 103. They are also very nice with the Christmas ham, or garnishing a whiskey sour (page 18).

In a small saucepan, dissolve ½ cup (100 g) brown sugar with ⅓ cup (80 ml) apple cider vinegar and 3 tablespoons water over low heat for a few minutes. Once the sugar has dissolved, add 3 slices ginger, 1 bay leaf, ½ teaspoon peppercorns and 2 cloves. Simmer for 1–2 minutes, then turn off the heat. Place 1 cup (180 g) green or red grapes in a jar, then pour in enough hot brine to completely cover the grapes (tipping in the ginger and spices, too). Seal, allow to cool, then store in the fridge for a few days before eating. They will keep for up to 1 month.

Makes 1 cup (180 g)

TIRED GRAPE AND DATE PASTE

This grape paste can replace store-bought quince paste for your cheese platter, but it is also yummy on banana bread, scones and even porridge. You can also use it in the wholemeal slice on page 175. Feel free to replace the dates with whatever dried fruits you have: pitted prunes, apricots and raisins all work well.

In a saucepan, place 2 cups (360 g) grapes, 1 cup (160 g) chopped dates, 1 cup (250 ml) liquid (red or white wine, apple or orange juice or water all work), 2 teaspoons roughly chopped rosemary leaves and 1 tablespoon lemon or orange zest. Bring to a simmer and cook over low heat for 15 minutes. Remove from the heat and mash with a fork or potato masher until everything is broken down but still a little chunky. Add ½ cup (110 g) caster (superfine) sugar and 1 tablespoon lemon juice or a splash of vinegar. Return to low heat and simmer for 20 minutes, stirring often, until thick and glossy. Transfer to a clean jar or container and store in the fridge for up to 1 month.

Makes 1 x 300 ml (10½ fl oz) jar

Quick pickled grapes

DRIED FRUITS

Drying food was once a necessity and not just a snack option. As a way to make the most of the summer bounty, fruits, vegetables, fish and meat were dried in the hot sun and wind, preserving them for the cold, leaner months. This early preservation method allowed people to set down roots and form communities as food could be stored and eaten later in the year.

Using drying or dehydration techniques is vital if you're looking for ways to reduce your food waste, make your own snacks and avoid packaged ingredients. The idea is that you use heat and air to remove moisture and thereby inhibit the growth of moulds and yeasts that destroy food.

Drying herbs, excess fruits and vegetables and seaweed, along with making jerky, roll-ups, crackers and even granola, are simple and effective preserving techniques in a sustainable kitchen.

GO WITH ...

Dried fruits are great in lunchboxes, on a cheese board, in baked goods, porridges, rice dishes and meaty stews. Store-bought dried fruits, however, are expensive and usually imported, plus they're often full of sulphates.

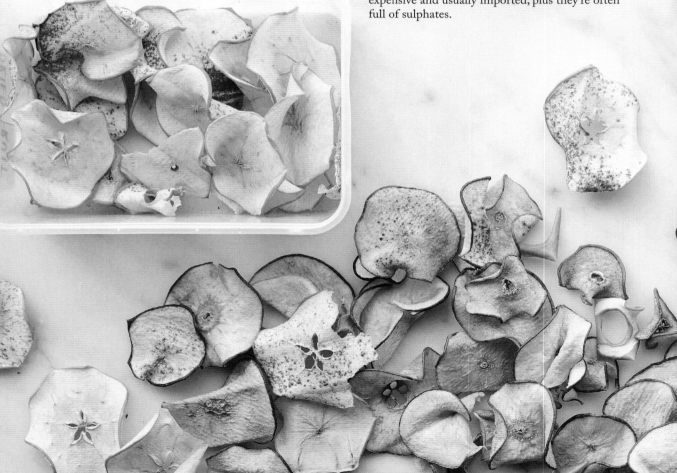

Owning a dehydrator makes drying fruit very easy, and if you've been thinking about getting one, we do recommend it. However, your oven also dries fruits very well. Here are our tips for drying fruits at home.

Preheat your oven to somewhere between 60–100°C (140–210°F/Gas mark ¼–½) (dehydrators work around the 40–50°C/105–120°F mark, meaning the dried foods are still considered raw). The lower your oven temperature is, the longer your fruit will take to dehydrate but it will retain more of its natural colour and flavour. If your oven doesn't go below 100°C, chock open the door with a wooden spoon to allow more airflow.

Wash and thinly slice your fruits. You can leave the skins on apples, pears, citrus and stone fruits, but peel mangoes, bananas and pineapples. Place the slices in a bowl of water with the juice of ½ a lemon for 2 minutes to stop the fruit going brown, and then spread the slices on a baking tray or wire rack. If you have a fan-forced oven, press the slices between two wire racks and then put the racks onto a baking tray to stop the fruit slices moving around.

The higher the water content of the fruit, the longer it will take to dry. So berries will take longer than apple slices. Keep in mind thin slices of apricot will dry faster than half an apricot. With practice, you will understand how different fruits behave in the oven and how long it takes for them to dry. It will vary from anywhere between 1 hour to 6 hours, so keep an eye on them. The fruit should be dry but still a little spongy – you don't want fruit chips! Once dry, cool the fruit completely and place in an airtight container in the pantry for a few months. You can also store your dried fruits in the fridge or even the freezer.

WHOLEMEAL DRIED FRUIT SLICE

Makes 12

This wholemeal dried fruit slice is old-fashioned afternoon-tea fare. It's nutty and sticky but not too sweet. We like it best with the dried fruit compote used here, but you can also use roasted fruits, thick jams or the grape and date paste on page 171 to spread between the layers. The compote is worth making in its own right as it's the perfect addition to steaming bowls of porridge, or it can be spooned over unsweetened yoghurt or served with custard.

1½ cups (220 g) wholemeal
   (whole wheat) flour
Pinch of salt
½ teaspoon baking powder
1 teaspoon ground ginger or
   cinnamon
1 cup (185 g) brown sugar
½ cup (50 g) rolled oats
¼ cup (40 g) sunflower seeds
170 g (6 oz) cold butter, diced,
   plus extra for greasing
1 egg

DRIED FRUIT COMPOTE

2–3 teabags, such as earl grey,
   English breakfast or orange
   pekoe
400 g (14 oz) mixed dried fruit
Zest and juice of 1 orange
1 teaspoon ground cinnamon
1 tablespoon honey
⅓ cup (80 ml) rum or whiskey
   (optional)

To make the compote, boil the kettle and steep the tea (you'll need 400 ml/13½ fl oz for this recipe). Place the mixed dried fruit in a saucepan with the orange zest and juice, cinnamon and honey. When the tea is nice and strong, pour 300 ml (10½ fl oz) into the saucepan. Simmer over low heat, stirring frequently, for 30 minutes or until the dried fruits are soft, sticky and glossy. Add the remaining tea, or add the rum or whiskey, and simmer for a few more minutes until the mixture comes together but isn't too dry.

The compote will keep in a clean jar in the fridge for up to 1 month, or heat-process it for 30 minutes (page 278) and store in the pantry for up to 2 years.

Preheat the oven to 180°C (350°F/Gas mark 4). Butter and line a 20 cm x 25 cm (8 inch x 10 inch) slice tin or baking dish.

Place the flour, salt, baking powder and ginger or cinnamon in a food processor and blitz until combined. Add the sugar, oats and sunflower seeds and blitz again. Add the butter and blitz until the mixture resembles fine breadcrumbs. Add the egg and mix until the mixture looks crumbly and a little moist.

Spoon half the mixture into the prepared tin, pressing down firmly with your hand to form a hard, flat surface. Spoon the dried fruit compote over and evenly spread to make a 5 mm (¼ inch) thick layer. Top with the other half of the mixture and lightly press with the back of a spoon. Don't worry if the compote isn't completely covered; it makes a pretty mottled top.

Bake in the oven for 20–25 minutes, until golden. Eat warm, or cool in the fridge and then cut into squares. Store in an airtight container in the fridge for up to 1 week.

CLEAR-OUT-THE-PANTRY COOKIES

Makes 24 cookies

Another life-saving recipe from our baker friend Greer. This recipe turns pantry strays into the best treat in the house, where those last bits of shredded coconut, almond meal, sesame seeds, sultanas and even spent coffee grains are used up. Don't be alarmed by the scale of the ingredients. This recipe makes enough for two batches: one to cook now and one to roll into a log and hide in the freezer.

550 g (1 lb 4 oz) plain flour, or
  half flour and half almond meal
  half flour and half desiccated
    coconut
  half flour and half bran
  half flour and half LSA

3 tablespoons pantry strays
  spent coffee grounds
  cocoa powder
  sesame seeds
  chopped sunflower seeds

1 tablespoon spice
  cinnamon
  ginger
  nutmeg
  allspice

1½ teaspoons bicarbonate
  of soda (baking soda)
1½ teaspoons baking powder
300 g (10½ oz) soft butter
250 g (12½ oz) sugar
  brown
  raw
  caster (superfine)
  or a combination of what needs
    using up

3 eggs
100 g (3½ oz) sticky sweetener
  molasses
  golden syrup
  honey
  maple syrup

⅓ cup chopped extras
  dried fruit
  nuts
  sunflower seeds
  choc chips

Preheat the oven to 170°C (325°F/Gas mark 3). Line a baking tray with baking paper.

Combine the flour, pantry strays, spice, bicarbonate of soda and baking powder in a bowl.

Using a stand mixer or electric beaters, cream the butter and sugar until light and fluffy, then add the eggs one at a time until well combined. Add the sweetener and continue to mix on medium speed, then fold the dry ingredients into the creamed butter until just combined. Fold through your choice of chopped extras.

Divide the mixture in half and set one portion aside. With the rest, roll into 50 g (1¾ oz) balls and flatten slightly, then arrange on the prepared tray with room to spread.

Bake for 12–15 minutes, until cooked through but still a little soft, then allow to cool for 5 minutes on the tray. Set aside to cool completely on a wire rack. Store in an airtight container for up to 1 week.

Roll the remaining dough into a thick log, wrap well and store in the fridge for up to 1 week or the freezer for a few months. You can slice straight off the log and bake from frozen.

A BUNCH OF CELERY

CITRUS

FROZEN PEAS

SILVERBEET

SHOPPING BASKET 6

In the depths of winter, we all want to come home to a warm meal that is not hours away from being ready. Now is when we really try and be organised, because who feels like putting together a spontaneous meal when the sky is dark at five o'clock? This basket has two base recipes that can be turned into multiple meals: a beef bone stock and sautéed silverbeet (Swiss chard). There is a guide to soup-making, and we nut out the pros and cons of the frozen pea. You'll also find plenty of ideas for how to use celery leaves, silverbeet stems and citrus peels.

CHICKPEAS

BEEF BONES

FROM THIS BASKET ...

MEALS

Silverbeet green pockets (page 182)

Silverbeet baked eggs (page 182)

Silverbeet and potato curry (page 183)

Whole-bunch-of-silverbeet soup (page 183)

Silverbeet galette (page 185)

Pasta in broth (page 187)

Minestrone (page 189)

Cheat's ramen (page 191)

Creamy mushroom soup (page 191)

Roasted tomato soup (page 191)

Pea and mint soup (page 195)

Chickpea and pea falafel (page 197)

SIDES

Sautéed silverbeet stems (page 183)

The most delicious way to cook tired celery (page 193)

Waldorf salad (page 193)

Herby pea purée (page 195)

Curried peas (page 195)

Chickpea flatbreads (page 199)

Socca (page 199)

SNACKS, SWEETS & DRINKS

Silverbeet savoury scrolls (page 182)

Homemade bhaji mix (page 199)

Hummus (page 200)

Citrus-flavoured teas (page 204)

Blood orange tarte tatin (page 209)

QUICK PRESERVING IDEAS

Quick pickled celery (page 193)

Whole fruit marmalade (page 203)

Whole lime or lemon pickle (page 203)

Preserved lemons or limes (page 207)

NOTHING GOES TO WASTE

Basic beef bone stock (page 187)

Garlicky celery leaf pesto (page 193)

Citrus zest butter (page 203)

Dried citrus peels and powders (page 204)

Preserved lemon gremolata (page 207)

SILVERBEET

With its ruffled glossy leaves in generous bunches, silverbeet is a welcome dose of green in the depths of winter. Confusingly, silverbeet is also known as Swiss chard and is sometimes misnamed as spinach. Whatever the label, its distinctive appearance and earthy bitterness are an excellent foundation for pies and tarts, soups and curries.

Silverbeet's slender stalks have all the flavour of the leaves, so learn how to thinly slice and cook them down to incorporate in your cooking. Silverbeet is a nutritional storehouse, full of vitamins A and B6, and the harder-to-come-by vitamin K, which is essential for bone health. Silverbeet is also rich in minerals, such as folate, copper, calcium, potassium and iron.

Give silverbeet a good wash and then gently shake dry. It will last longer if you keep the whole leaf intact, so wrap the leaves loosely in a tea towel and store in the crisper drawer for up to 5 days.

GOES WITH ...

Silverbeet's flavour is mildly bitter and metallic when raw, and it has a rustic sweetness when cooked. Raw or cooked silverbeet holds up well when paired with other strong flavours, such as nuts, eggs, capers, preserved lemon, garlic, ginger and nutmeg. Cream, yoghurt and cheese tend to tame any bitterness and combine so well that they create something luscious every time.

WASTE TIP

If you've used silverbeet leaves in a recipe or salad, don't throw away the stems! They make a great sautéed side (see overleaf) to serve with roasted fish, or flatbreads and falafels (page 197), and they're yummy stirred through couscous.

A BATCH OF SAUTÉED SILVERBEET

When silverbeet (Swiss chard) is going wild in the garden or crazy cheap at the market, we buy a few bunches and make a big batch of this flavoursome sautéed silverbeet. We then use it as the base of multiple meals throughout the week.

Two bunches of silverbeet will yield about 5–6 cups (650–700 g) of this sautéed base, depending on the size of your bunches, which is enough for two or three greens-based meals.

We also love this as a side with pilaf (page 161), baked fish (page 48) and potato rosti (page 131).

Wash 2 big bunches of silverbeet, then remove the leaves from the stems and set aside. Put the leaves in a large bowl and cover with boiling water, making sure the leaves are covered. Allow to sit for 5–10 minutes.

Very thinly slice the silverbeet stems, ½ onion and 1–2 celery stalks if you have them. Heat 50 ml (1¾ fl oz) olive oil in a large frying pan over medium heat and sauté the sliced vegetables with ½ teaspoon salt for 10 minutes or until the silverbeet stems are starting to soften. Add 2 crushed garlic cloves, 1 tablespoon finely diced preserved lemon (page 207) (or the zest and juice of 1 lemon), 1 teaspoon allspice or ground cinnamon and 1 teaspoon ground cumin and sauté for another 3–5 minutes. Once everything is soft and sweet and delicious, turn off the heat.

Drain the silverbeet leaves and use your hands to squeeze out as much moisture as possible. Finely chop the leaves and add them to the mixture in the pan with 1 cup (30 g) chopped herbs, such as parsley, dill or celery leaves. Mix well to make sure everything is combined and the leaves are well coated. Taste and add more seasoning if needed.

Use straight away or store in an airtight container in the fridge for 4 days.

Makes 5-6 cups (650-700 g)

SILVERBEET GREEN POCKETS

Mix 2 cups (about 300 g) of this mixture with ½ cup (50 g) crumbled feta and use to fill green pockets (page 28).

SILVERBEET BAKED EGGS

Use 2 cups (about 300 g) as a base for baked eggs (page 21). Top with a little grated haloumi.

SILVERBEET GALETTE

For a simple silverbeet pie, use 3 cups (350 g) of this mixture as a filling for a galette (page 185).

SILVERBEET AND POTATO CURRY

Use 2 cups (about 300 g) to add to the base of the curry opposite.

SILVERBEET SAVOURY SCROLLS

Spread 1 cup (150 g) over the scroll dough (page 146) and sprinkle with ½ cup (50 g) grated haloumi.

SILVERBEET AND POTATO CURRY

Once you've got a batch of sautéed silverbeet (Swiss chard) tucked away (see opposite), this curry is really quick to cook. It has a depth of flavour that you only normally get from a longer cooking time.

Dice 500 g (1 lb 2 oz) potatoes and boil for 15 minutes or until cooked through. Drain well and shake to dry. Heat 80 g (2¾ oz) ghee or ⅓ cup (80 ml) vegetable oil in a frying pan over medium heat. Add the potato, 1 tablespoon black mustard seeds, 2 teaspoons ground cardamom, 2 teaspoons garam masala, 1 teaspoon salt and 3 tablespoons grated ginger and fry for 5 minutes or until fragrant. Add 2 cups (about 300 g) sautéed silverbeet and ½ cup (75 g) frozen peas. Cook for 4–5 minutes, then add 1½ cups (375 ml) passata (page 247) or a 400 g (14 oz) can of crushed tomatoes. Reduce the heat to low, cover and simmer for 20 minutes. Turn off the heat and stir through 100 ml (3½ fl oz) cream or yoghurt. Serve with rice, coriander and lime pickle.

Serves 4

WHOLE-BUNCH-OF-SILVERBEET SOUP

You'll notice that this recipe is almost the same as the sautéed silverbeet opposite, but we've turned it into a light yet hearty rustic soup for winter nights.

Wash 1 bunch silverbeet (Swiss chard) and remove the leaves from the stems. Thinly slice the leaves and set aside. Thinly slice the stems, along with 1–2 celery stalks, and roughly chop 1 onion. Heat 2½ tablespoons olive oil in a large frying pan over medium heat and sauté the vegetables with ½ teaspoon salt for 10 minutes or until the stems are starting to soften. Add 2 crushed garlic cloves, 1 tablespoon finely diced preserved lemon (page 207), 1 teaspoon allspice or ground cinnamon, 1 teaspoon ground cumin and ½ teaspoon chilli flakes and sauté for another 5 minutes. Stir through 2 cups (330 g) cooked chickpeas (or 2 cans chickpeas, drained) and cook for 1–2 minutes, then add 4 cups (1 litre) stock and the juice of 1 lemon and simmer for 5 minutes. Add the leaves to the pan, cover and cook for 4–5 minutes. Top with herbs, yoghurt and chilli sambal (page 261).

Serves 4

SAUTÉED SILVERBEET STEMS

Make this recipe when you have silverbeet (Swiss chard) stems. Using yoghurt in this dish makes it tangy and creamy without being rich. Serve with fish, falafel or lamb skewers.

Thinly slice the stems from a bunch of silverbeet, along with 1 small onion. Heat 2½ tablespoons olive oil in a frying pan over medium heat and sauté the sliced vegetables with ½ teaspoon salt for 10 minutes or until the silverbeet stems are starting to soften. Add 2 minced garlic cloves, the zest and juice of 1 lemon, 1 teaspoon crushed fennel seeds, 1 teaspoon sumac and ½ teaspoon chilli flakes and sauté for another 5–7 minutes. Once everything is soft and sweet, turn off the heat and stir through 3–4 tablespoons yoghurt and a large handful of finely chopped dill or parsley. Season if needed and serve warm.

Serves 4 as a side

Sautéed silverbeet stems

SILVERBEET GALETTE

Serves 6–8

A galette is a savoury or sweet free-form pie that is easy to assemble, requires minimal technique and is very forgiving for those (like us!) without pastry skills. You can fill a galette with nearly any damn thing you like. We love mushrooms in autumn, tomatoes in summer and, of course, silverbeet (Swiss chard) in winter.

3 cups (350 g) sautéed silverbeet
   (page 182)
Milk or 1 egg, beaten
Olive oil, for drizzling
Chopped parsley and dill, to serve

SOUR CREAM PASTRY
1⅔ cups (250 g) plain
   (all-purpose flour),
   plus extra for dusting
1 teaspoon salt
200 g (7 oz) cold butter,
   roughly chopped
120 g (4½ oz) sour cream

To make the sour cream pastry, combine the flour and salt in a food processor, then add the butter and pulse until the mixture resembles sand. Add the sour cream and pulse until the mixture forms a dough ball. Wrap in plastic wrap and set aside in the fridge for at least 30 minutes.

Preheat the oven to 180°C (350°F/Gas mark 4). Roll out the dough on a lightly floured workbench to a 40 cm (16 inch) circle. Transfer the dough circle to a large lined baking tray.

Spread the sautéed silverbeet over the dough, leaving a 5 cm (2 inch) border. Fold the edges over to partially enclose the filling, overlapping the dough as needed. Brush the dough with milk or beaten egg, then bake the galette for 35–45 minutes or until golden.

Drizzle olive oil over the top, finish with chopped herbs and serve.

COMBINATIONS WE LIKE

- Potato, onion and dill: par-cook 500 g (1 lb 2 oz) potatoes, then drain and slice into rounds. Sauté 2 sliced onions, 2–3 crushed garlic cloves and a little salt and pepper in olive oil for 10–12 minutes until browned, then spread onto the dough and cover with a layer of potato. Bake, then top the cooked galette with chopped dill.

- Caramelised onion and goat's cheese: Spread 2 cups (400 g) of the caramelised onions on page 143 over the dough. Scatter 50 g (1¾ oz) goat's cheese over the top, season with black pepper and bake. Top the cooked galette with fresh herbs or rocket (arugula).

- Tomato party: Quarter 6 tomatoes, sprinkle with salt and leave to drain for at least 1 hour. Sauté 2 chopped onions and 6 crushed garlic cloves in olive oil for 10–12 minutes, then add the tomato and cook for 30 minutes or until reduced. Spread over the dough and top with a few fresh tomato slices. Bake, then top with chopped basil.

- Apricot: Bake about 12 apricots with their stones removed using the technique for roasting pears on page 235. Spread ½ cup (50 g) toasted flaked almonds or a layer of jam over the pastry and arrange the apricots on top. Sprinkle with raw sugar and bake.

BEEF BONES

There is no getting around the fact that those of us who eat meat need to reduce our consumption. The beef industry is one of the most costly to the environment. For this reason, and because we generally approach meat as an accompaniment to a main meal, we only use beef in small amounts.

When we do eat beef, it is always pasture raised, and we make all efforts to appreciate the whole animal, even the parts that are so often discarded. Bones are a valued source of nutrition and flavour. Understanding how to use bones to make stock is an essential skill for the home cook. To the French, a good stock is the foundation of sauces, stews and soups. Making a batch of stock on a Sunday makes cooking for the rest of the week much easier, as you will already be half way to making risottos, soups and stews.

Bones are made of calcium. The flavour of stock comes from the fat, tendons and connective tissue found close to the bones. This is also where the nutrition comes from. These parts of the animal are rich in collagen, and when cooked convert to gelatine. Gelatine is nearly pure protein. It is good for hair, nails and skin, plus it aids digestion and is soothing to the gut.

Beef bones are not usually on display at the supermarket, so it's best to visit a good butcher who will definitely have plenty of bones.

GO WITH ...

Beef bones don't offer quite the same flavour as beef. They are more subtle. However, the bones are the very constitution of the animal – the exercise it did and the food it ate – so the flavours that pair with beef will also pair with the bones. The flavour is a little sweet, a little salty, a little metallic and, of course, meaty. Your stock will go with onions, carrot, celery and all woody herbs, as well as warm flavours, such as ginger, garlic, parsley, cloves, black pepper, allspice and star anise.

BASIC BEEF BONE STOCK

This is our shortish recipe for a bone stock. We don't often have time to make a 24-hour bone broth, so this recipe is a good compromise that sets you up for a promising week of meals (see below for suggestions). Browning the bones is an essential step. Like all browning techniques, such as caramelising onions, the result is a more intense and fuller flavour than simple boiling can give. You may need to cook this stock in two saucepans if you don't have a big enough stockpot.

Preheat the oven to 200°C (400°F/Gas mark 6). Place 2 kg (4 lb 8 oz) pasture-raised beef bones in two roasting tins and roast for 30–45 minutes, until browned. Set aside to cool a little.

Place 10 garlic cloves, 3 unpeeled roughly chopped onions, 3 roughly chopped carrots and/or celery stalks, 6 fresh bay leaves, 1 star anise, 3 tablespoons apple cider vinegar and 6 litres water in a large stockpot. Add the browned bones, then place over medium–high heat and bring to the boil. Reduce the heat to its lowest setting and simmer for 4 hours, regularly skimming the scum from the surface.

Allow the stock to cool slightly, then strain through a sieve into a large bowl. Divide the stock among smaller containers and set aside to cool – the fat will rise to the top and seal the stock. Keep in the fridge for up to 1 week or in the freezer for up to 3 months.

Makes 12 cups (3 litres)

CHEAT'S RAMEN

Use 4 cups (1 litre) stock to make ramen (page 191).

MINESTRONE

Use 4 cups (1 litre) stock to make minestrone (page 189).

HEARTY ROAST VEGETABLE SOUP

Use 4 cups (1 litre) stock to make the soup on page 214.

OVEN-BAKED RISOTTO

Use 4 cups (1 litre) stock to make risotto (page 163).

Basic beef bone stock

PASTA IN BROTH

This is what we cook when we can't face cooking another meal. It's comforting, warming and nourishing, and requires the least amount of effort possible.

In a saucepan, bring 6 cups (1.5 litres) stock to the boil, then taste and season as needed. Add 3 cups (200 g) small-shaped pasta and cook following the packet instructions until al dente. In the last few minutes of cooking, add 1 cup (155 g) frozen peas (or whichever vegetables you like: broccoli, cauliflower, asparagus and spinach all work well). Once the peas and pasta are cooked, add 1 tablespoon butter and serve with grated parmesan and freshly cracked black pepper.

Serves 4

MINESTRONE

Serves 4–6

If you've got stock and passata on hand, you've pretty much got the base of minestrone. This dish is often on our tables in winter, and really should be called use-it-all soup rather than minestrone.

It's an easy one to make when you get home from work at 6pm and want a home-cooked meal on the table. You can definitely use store-bought stock and passata, but if you have the homemade versions it will taste even better.

Make sure you're really happy with the flavour of your tomatoey broth before you add the vegetables and pasta. If the broth is lacking flavour, try adding some sugar, Worcestershire sauce or minced garlic. Once you have the base right, you can assemble the soup.

4 cups (1 litre) basic beef bone stock (page 187) or stock of your choice
2 cups (500 ml) passata (page 247)
1 parmesan rind (optional)
Salt
2 teaspoons dried herbs, such as oregano or thyme
½ teaspoon sugar, 1 tablespoon Worcestershire sauce and/or 1 minced clove garlic (optional)
2 cups (350 g) cooked pasta of your choice (or use cooked or canned chickpeas/garbanzo beans if you're gluten free)
2 cups chopped mixed vegetables
  diced potato
  chopped carrot
  cauliflower florets
  broccoli florets
  frozen peas
  chopped green beans
  thinly sliced silverbeet (Swiss chard) or kale
Pesto (page 263), to serve
Shaved parmesan, to serve
Good-quality olive oil, to serve

Place the stock and passata in a stockpot and throw in a parmesan rind if you have one. Bring to a simmer, then taste and season with salt and dried herbs. If you feel your broth needs a lift, add the sugar, Worcestershire sauce and/or minced garlic.

Cook your pasta in a large saucepan of salted boiling water. This is a good opportunity to use up any ends of packets of pasta – you'll need about 2 cups (350 g) cooked pasta all up.

Bring another saucepan of salted water to the boil and blanch your vegetables until firm but cooked. (Note that some vegetables will cook faster than others so add your hard vegetables, such as carrot and potato, first.) Add the cooked vegetables and pasta to the broth and bring back to simmering point.

Divide the minestrone among bowls and serve with a tablespoon of pesto spooned over the top of each bowl, a little shaved parmesan and a drizzle of your best olive oil.

LESSONS IN SOUP MAKING

Knowing how to make a good nourishing soup is a vital life skill, and in a sustainable kitchen it's an excellent way to use up vegetables and herbs. But there's more to understand than just chucking all the old things into a pot with store-bought stock.

Start by looking at what you have and deciding what needs to be used first. In the cooler months, all the root vegetables are friends and they pair well with their rooty pals ginger, turmeric and garlic. Pumpkin works well, too (check out page 214 for a hearty roast veg soup). In the warmer months, green soups with spinach, leek, fennel, peas and green herbs are lovely, and you can add a potato if you want to make them thicker and heartier. When it's really warm, think about cold soups to suit the weather. Try tomato gazpacho, cucumber soup or the pea and mint soup on page 195 served chilled.

STOCK

You can make soup with water, but it's going to taste so much better with stock, especially homemade. You only need 4 cups (1 litre) of stock to serve four, so start small and manageable. Use the scraps and bones from your roast chicken (page 97) or veggie scraps (page 220), or make a batch of the beef bone stock on page 187 or the fish stock on page 51. If your stock is good, even just adding a few cups of frozen peas and sautéed leek and garlic will make a delicious warming meal. Add lots of herbs and some lemon zest and dinner is ready.

You can also check out the spicy kitchen scrap paste recipe on page 239 – a much better version of stock cubes, with zero waste. Add 2 tablespoons stock paste to 4 cups (1 litre) water.

CREAMY SOUPS

Dairy is best added once your soup is off the heat. If you're adding cream, make sure it's warm to avoid curdling. A tablespoon of natural yoghurt or sour cream stirred through a spinach or spicy lentil soup will brighten the flavour and add creaminess. To add creaminess without dairy, add grated cooked potato, crushed cooked white beans or purée a cup of the vegetables from the soup, then add them back in.

PURÉED OR HEARTY SOUPS

Slowly sweat chopped onion, carrot, fennel, celery, shallots, etc. in oil or butter until soft, sweet and flavoursome. Add in woody herbs, garlic, ginger or your choice of spices and sauté until fragrant.

Add your vegetables. We like to pre-roast pumpkin, sweet potato, turnip, parsnip and beetroot (beets) with a little oil and salt and pepper to increase their flavour and sweetness. It also means you'll need less stock as your vegetables are already cooked. Add your stock and simmer – don't boil – until the vegetables are full of flavour and cooked through. Check the seasoning, then serve as is or purée.

BROTHY SOUPS

For clear brothy soups with clean fresh flavours, there is no need to sauté your ingredients. Add raw or pre-blanched vegetables to super-tasty stock in the order of time it takes them to cook (a pea will only take a few minutes to cook, whereas a cube of potato will take a bit longer).

Parmesan rinds, a good tomato paste, a minced anchovy or finely diced preserved lemon will add umami, as will a little splash of fish sauce, tamari, soy sauce or a tablespoon of miso.

Pasta, noodles, rice and starchy vegetables are more flavoursome cooked in broth, but they will make your soup cloudy. If you want a clear soup, par-cook potatoes and pasta in salted boiling water and then add to the stock for the last 5 minutes of cooking.

TIPS

Simmer, never boil, your soups.

Save your salt seasoning until the end of cooking.

Add a little acid at the end of cooking, just before serving. A squeeze of lemon or lime juice or a little splash of your best apple cider vinegar will brighten all the flavours.

CHEAT'S RAMEN

This is not a traditional ramen that takes three days to cook. It's quick, full of flavour and nutritious, and definitely beats the 2-minute microwave version.

Heat 1 tablespoon vegetable oil in a saucepan over medium heat and carefully sauté 3 chopped garlic cloves and 1 tablespoon grated ginger for 30 seconds. Add 4 cups (1 litre) beef broth, 3 dried mushrooms (rehydrated in 1 cup/250 ml water, then sliced; add the soaking liquid too), 1 tablespoon soy sauce, 1 tablespoon fish sauce, the juice of half a lemon or lime and an optional pinch of cayenne pepper and mix well. Simmer for 10 minutes, taste and adjust flavourings if needed, then add 300 g (10½ oz) cooked ramen noodles and 2–3 cups (200–300 g) thinly sliced vegetables, such as spinach and carrots (corn kernels also work well). Simmer for 3 minutes, then divide the ramen among bowls and top with halved hard-boiled eggs, kimchi, sesame seeds and nori.

Serves 3–4

CREAMY MUSHROOM SOUP

We serve this soup in our mushroom cooking classes and the crowd goes wild. This deluxe soup should be made at the height of mushroom season and needs 6 cups (1.5 litres) of your best homemade stock. Use button, field, pine or Swiss brown mushrooms.

Melt 50 g (1¾ oz) butter in a large saucepan and sauté 1 chopped onion and 4 chopped garlic cloves over low heat for 3–5 minutes. Stir in 3 tablespoons plain (all-purpose) flour, then add 100 ml (3½ fl oz) of the stock and stir to make a paste. Continue to stir while slowly adding the remaining stock, taking care to avoid lumps, then simmer for 20 minutes.

Meanwhile, melt 100 g (3½ oz) butter in a frying pan over medium heat, add 600 g (1 lb 5 oz) sliced mushrooms and a handful of chopped tarragon and sauté for 10 minutes or until golden, then set aside. Whisk 2 egg yolks and 1 cup (250 ml) cream in a jug until blended. While whisking, slowly add 1 cup (250 ml) of the simmering stock to the cream mixture, and then add the combined cream mixture back into the soup and turn the heat to low (don't let the soup simmer or the egg will curdle). Add the cooked mushrooms and stir to combine. Grate a little nutmeg into the soup and garnish with tarragon. Taste and add salt if needed (if you are using store-bought stock they tend to be very salty).

Serves 4–6

ROASTED TOMATO SOUP

Make this delicious soup with the roasted tomato sauce on page 247. Serve with fried cheese sandwiches and make everyone's dreams come true.

Place 3 cups (750 ml) roasted tomato sauce in a large saucepan with 2 cups (500 ml) stock and bring to a simmer. Season with salt and pepper, and add a splash of red wine vinegar if it's a little sweet or a pinch of sugar if it's a little acidic, then cook for 5 minutes. Spoon into mugs and top with basil, a spoonful of pesto (page 263), parmesan shavings, cracked pepper and a drizzle of olive oil.

Serves 3–4

A BUNCH OF CELERY

Traditionally, celery was used medicinally to treat high blood pressure, anxiety and circulation problems, while in medieval times it was renowned as an aphrodisiac – a lust-provoking celery soup was often on the medieval kitchen table.

Celery's clean and refreshing flavour make it an excellent raw snack for crudités to serve with dips and cheeses. It's most commonly used as a base flavour and texture for soups, stocks and stews, but it shouldn't be forgotten as a standalone vegetable, as it maintains its texture and absorbs flavour beautifully when cooked. Celery also makes a wonderful pickle and ferment.

As celery is 95 per cent water, it's not the nutritional powerhouse Instagram would have you believe. It does, however, contain a good amount of fibre, vitamin K and potassium.

Nutritionally, celery is best eaten within 5–7 days, but if stored correctly it will last longer. Wash celery well and wrap tightly in a bag or large beeswax wrap and it will keep for at least 10 days. Or if you have a little more time, chop off the leaves and base and store the stalks in a little water in an airtight container in the fridge for up to 2 weeks, changing the water every few days. Keep the base in the fridge or freezer for stocks, then wrap the leaves tightly in a damp cloth and store in the fridge for salads and pestos or to garnish soups and stews.

GOES WITH …

Celery is crunchy and salty fresh, so it matches well with creamy ingredients, such as nut butters, hummus, ricotta, blue and cream cheeses. It works well braised in butter or olive oil or in a creamy potato soup. The lightness and tanginess of raw celery works in salads with potatoes, apples or crunchy pears. Celery also stir-fries nicely with lemon zest, garlic, ginger and chilli.

USE IT ALL

Never waste your celery leaves! They have a peppery flavour that makes a great pesto (see opposite). You can also finely chop them and use in place of parsley. Add to tabbouleh (page 27), chickpea (garbanzo bean) or potato salads, or use them in stocks and in stir-fries.

WASTE TIP

After you've used a few stalks in a soup or bolognese, the rest of the celery often sits in the fridge for a week or more, getting tired and sad. Don't throw away these tired stalks – instead braise them in butter (see opposite) and you have a quick and delicious side dish.

THE MOST DELICIOUS WAY TO COOK TIRED CELERY

This dish is simple, hearty and delicious and an excellent way to use up any extra (or tired-looking) celery stalks. Serve this with a roast or toss through warm chickpeas (garbanzo beans) with lots of herbs and lemon zest for a wintry salad.

Cut 6 celery stalks on an angle into 3–4 cm (1¼–1½ inch) pieces (removing the strings if they are very stringy). Melt 1 tablespoon butter in a frying pan over medium heat and add the celery and a pinch of black pepper. Cook for about 5 minutes or until the celery is starting to soften. Add ½ cup (125 ml) beef, chicken or vegetable stock and cover the pan. Reduce the heat to low and cook for 5–10 minutes, until the stock reduces and thickens. Taste and add extra salt if needed.

Sprinkle with chopped parsley or celery leaves and toasted nuts or seeds.

Serves 2–3 as a side

WALDORF SALAD

This is our take on the classic Waldorf salad.

Thinly slice 2–3 silverbeet (Swiss chard) leaves (reserve the stems for another use; see page 183). Using a mandoline, shave ¼ fennel bulb and thinly slice 2 celery stalks. Combine the ingredients in a bowl. Cut the most delicious apple you have into batons and toss through the vegetables. Squeeze over some lemon juice and mix well to stop everything going brown. Add a small handful of chopped dill and gently mix. Make a dressing by combining 2 tablespoons olive oil, 1 tablespoon each vegetable oil, apple cider vinegar and natural yoghurt, and a good pinch of salt, pepper and sugar in a jar. Shake well, then toss through the salad. Top the salad with toasted walnuts or sunflower seeds and serve.

Serves 4

QUICK PICKLED CELERY

While your celery is still fresh and crunchy, make a jar of pickled celery to use in any green salad.

Place 1 cup (250 ml) boiling water, 1 cup (250 ml) white wine or apple cider vinegar, ⅓ cup (80 g) caster (superfine) sugar and 1 teaspoon salt in a heatproof jug. Whisk to dissolve the sugar, then add the peel of ½ lemon, 1 teaspoon black peppercorns, 1–2 bay leaves and 1 garlic clove. Thinly slice ½ bunch celery and place in a clean jar. Cover with the vinegar brine, then seal and store in the fridge for 3–4 weeks.

GARLICKY CELERY LEAF PESTO

Perfect for spreading on toast with a fried egg for breakfast, or stirring through hot buttery potatoes.

Place 1–2 cups (20–40 g) celery leaves, 40 g (1½ oz) raw cashews, 2 garlic cloves, ½ cup (50 g) grated parmesan (optional) and a pinch or two of salt in a food processor and blitz to a paste. With the motor running, add 100–150 ml (3½–5 fl oz) olive oil until well combined. Transfer to a jar and store in the fridge for up to 10 days.

Makes 1 cup (250 g)

FROZEN PEAS

We both tend towards the 'fresh is best' school of thought, but admit that we often have a bag of frozen peas or raspberries in the freezer. While writing this book we discussed at length if there was a place for frozen food in a sustainable kitchen, and here's what we came up with.

The frozen food aisle at the supermarket is a terrifying place, heaving with highly processed, overly packaged foods that promise quick fixes for dinner without mentioning the huge health and environmental implications.

When it comes to packaged food, we look for products with minimal packaging and check food labels to ensure that ingredients are as locally sourced as possible with no nasty additives, but, when it comes to frozen vegetables, things can get confusing.

While they are convenient, imported frozen vegetables and fruits are transported long distances and, therefore, rely on enormous amounts of fuel for production and electricity for storage. This is not always the case for locally grown frozen fruit and vegetables. Freezing fruit and vegetables for later sale is a lesser evil than seeing unsold produce end up in landfill, which is often the case. Frozen food might also be the only practical option for communities that do not have access to fresh fruit and vegetables. They might also be the only practical option for those of us

on tight budgets or coming home late in the day, but still needing to feed a family. Our conclusion is this: do your best, find out more, choose fresh when you can and when you can't, be conscious of packaging, buying local and avoiding additives.

Frozen peas are part of the legume family and are surprisingly high in protein and vitamin K. They're an excellent way to get a serving of green vegetables into your day when the fridge is empty. A cup of peas stirred through pasta cooked in broth is simple and nutritious, and much faster than waiting for takeaway.

Tip: Thaw your frozen peas before cooking by placing them in a colander in the sink for 10 minutes.

GO WITH ...

Peas love soft herbs, such as mint, dill, parsley and sage, or woody herbs, such as thyme and rosemary. They also go well with intense flavours, such as anise, so also consider tarragon or fennel. When it comes to spices, the curried flavours of cumin, ginger and curry leaves are an excellent pairing with peas. Sweet peas also need a little acid, so use lemon, white wine or garlic. Other green vegetables such as broccoli and asparagus are good mates with peas, or make simple pairings with potatoes, carrots, butter and salt.

HERBY PEA PURÉE

For easy, thrifty midweek meals, make this pea purée. It's a staple in both our houses as an alternative to pesto, and it's great on toast or baked potatoes, with pasta or warm potato salad, or in soups or a pea and ham toastie.

Heat 1 tablespoon olive oil in a frying pan and sauté 1 small chopped onion for 4–5 minutes, until soft and sweet. Add 1 crushed garlic clove, 1 tablespoon lemon zest, 3 tablespoons chopped herbs such as dill, parsley, celery leaves or mint, and 1 teaspoon dried thyme or oregano. Sauté for 1 minute until fragrant, then add 2 cups (310 g) thawed frozen peas and mix well. Pour in 200 ml (7 fl oz) beef bone stock (page 187) or good vegetable stock (page 220) and a pinch of salt and pepper. Simmer over low heat for 10 minutes. Transfer the pea mixture to a food processor or use a stick blender and blend to a rough purée. Store in a jar or airtight container in the fridge for 3–4 days.

Makes 400 g (14 oz)

CURRIED PEAS

This dish may sound daggy but it is true comfort food. Serve as a side with a stew and mash, with curry, with fish cakes or with rice for a simple lunch.

In a saucepan over medium heat, sauté a finely diced onion in 2 tablespoons olive oil until soft and sweet. Add 2 teaspoons curry powder, 1 teaspoon ground cumin, 1 teaspoon ground coriander, ½ teaspoon mustard seeds, 1 minced garlic clove and ½ teaspoon salt and sauté for 1 minute. Add 2 cups (280 g) thawed peas and sauté again for 3 minutes, then add ½ cup (125 ml) stock and simmer for about 5 minutes, until the stock has absorbed into the peas. Stir through 2 teaspoons freshly grated ginger before serving.

Serves 4 as a side

PEA AND MINT SOUP

Mint really helps peas to be their best self. It's a classic combination and makes for a bright soup. Serve warm or chilled.

Heat 2 tablespoons butter or olive oil in a large saucepan. Add 1 diced onion and sauté, stirring, for 5 minutes or until translucent. Add 500 g (1 lb 2 oz) thawed peas and sauté for 3–5 minutes. Pour in 3 cups (750 ml) chicken or vegetable stock and simmer over medium heat for 7–10 minutes. Reduce the heat, add 1 teaspoon pepper (and salt if needed), then stir through 1 bunch picked mint leaves. Blend with a stick blender or in a food processer. Check for seasoning and serve with buttered toast.

Serves 4

CHICKPEA AND PEA FALAFEL

Makes about 15

The frozen pea is not a traditional addition to falafel, but these are delicious. Crunchy and green, they'll disappear as soon as they hit the table. The beauty of falafels is that you use chickpeas that are soaked but not cooked, making things much quicker. At a pinch, you could use canned chickpeas, but the result will be a mushier falafel. Serve with hummus (page 200–1), flatbreads (page 199) and a few of the many vegetable sides in this book.

¾ cup (135 g) dried chickpeas (garbanzo beans), soaked in cold water overnight, drained and rinsed
4 garlic cloves
½ red or brown onion, roughly chopped
½ bunch parsley or coriander (cilantro)
1½ teaspoons ground cumin
½ teaspoon ground cinnamon
½ teaspoon chilli flakes
½ teaspoon freshly cracked black pepper
1 teaspoon salt
2 tablespoons plain (all-purpose) flour
¾ cup (110 g) thawed peas
1 teaspoon baking powder
35 g (1¼ oz) sesame seeds
1 cup (250 ml) vegetable oil

Place half the chickpeas, the garlic cloves, onion, parsley or coriander (cilantro), cumin, cinnamon, chilli flakes, black pepper, salt and flour in a food processor and blend until smooth. Add the remaining chickpeas, the peas and baking powder, then pulse or process on low speed until roughly combined (you want to keep some texture). Tip the mixture into a bowl and refrigerate for 30 minutes.

Form your falafels into 15 flattish balls about 5 cm (2 inch) in diameter. To ensure they hold together, firmly squeeze the balls when forming the falafel so the mixture becomes dense. Roll the falafel in the sesame seeds and set aside.

Heat the vegetable oil in a large deep frying pan over medium heat and fry the falafels in batches for 2 minutes each side until golden brown.

Serve with hummus, flatbreads, salad and pickles.

CHICKPEAS

Originating in the Middle East, chickpeas (garbanzo beans) are a staple of Middle Eastern, Indian, Italian, French and Spanish cooking. Across all of these cultures, the chickpea is prized for its nutty flavour and as a great source of protein.

Chickpeas are a crop that we should be eating more often, as they increase soil health and grow with resilience in drier climates. With its high content of soluble fibre and protein, a meal that includes chickpeas can fuel you for many hours. Chickpeas are also high in calcium.

Fresh chickpeas grow in pods and are bright green. However, they are hard to get hold of and most of us will only ever know a dried chickpea. Like all dried pulses, chickpeas need to be soaked and, in most cases, boiled before eating. Buy chickpeas at a bulk store, then keep them in your pantry for years.

Sometimes called besan, chickpea flour is a delicious gluten-free alternative to wheat flour and can be used to make the flatbreads on the opposite page.

GO WITH ...

Chickpeas go with nearly everything. They are great with fresh herbs, such as parsley, coriander (cilantro), dill and mint, and pair nicely with silverbeet (Swiss chard), spinach, tomatoes, chillies and olives. Chickpeas love almonds, pine nuts, sesame seeds and hazelnuts, along with stronger flavours such as garlic, preserved lemon, sumac, cumin and paprika. Serve them with grilled meats as a complementary protein.

PREPARATION

Soak chickpeas overnight in a large bowl of water with a pinch of salt or a squeeze of lemon. The next day, strain the soaking water and rinse the chickpeas. To cook chickpeas, add 3 cups (750 ml) water to 1 cup (200 g) soaked chickpeas and simmer over medium heat for 20 minutes or until tender. Chickpeas will more than double in size once they've been soaked. Roughly speaking, 1 cup (185 g) dried chickpeas will yield just under 3 cups (430 g) of soaked and cooked chickpeas.

CHICKPEA FLATBREADS

This is the easiest flatbread that is possible to make. It's a riff on Niki Segnit's recipe from *Lateral Cooking*. Make it even when you think you don't have the time.

Combine 125 g (4 oz) plain (all-purpose) flour, 125 g (4 oz) chickpea flour (besan), 1 teaspoon salt, 1 tablespoon sesame seeds, 120–150 ml (3¾ fl oz– 5 fl oz) warm water and 2 tablespoons olive oil in a large bowl. Bring the ingredients together to form a dough, then cut into 6–8 equal-sized pieces and roll each piece out on a lightly floured workbench to a 13 cm (5 inch) circle. Cook each flatbread in a hot, dry frying pan over medium–high heat for 1 minute each side. Serve with the silverbeet and potato curry (page 183) for dinner or with falafel (page 197), hummus (page 200–1) and salad for lunch.

Makes 6–8

SOCCA

In Nice, France, where this flatbread originates, they eat it plain with a little pepper and a glass of rose. This is how we like to eat it, too, but more often we serve it as a quick flatbread with a pile of leafy salad on top. Traditionally, socca is baked but our version is more like a crêpe.

Sift 1 cup (120 g) chickpea flour (besan) and a generous pinch of salt into a bowl. Whisk 200 ml (7 fl oz) water into the flour and mix until there are no lumps. Whisk in another 100 ml (3½ fl oz) water and 2 tablespoons olive oil – the batter should be runny. Heat 1 tablespoon olive oil in a frying pan over medium heat. Transfer the socca batter to a jug or use a ladle and pour about 150 ml (5 fl oz) batter into the pan. Move the pan around so the batter spreads to the edges. Cook the batter for 3–4 minutes, until it becomes firm and the bottom turns golden brown and crisp. Carefully flip using the largest spatula you own, then cook the other side for 2–3 minutes, until it also becomes golden brown and crisp. Remove from the pan, cut into wedges, and serve.

Makes 4–6

HOMEMADE BHAJI MIX

Alex is addicted to bhaji mix and if there's a packet near her she has no control. Determined to make her own, she spent many afternoons trying to nail it. Here's the result, which uses minimal ingredients, but still hits the spot. It's so good with beer!

Preheat the oven to 200°C (350°F/Gas mark 4). Place 1½ cups (215 g) cooked, drained and dried chickpeas (garbanzo beans) and ½ cup (75 g) thawed frozen peas in a bowl with 1½ tablespoons vegetable or sunflower oil, 1½ teaspoons salt, 2–3 teaspoons curry powder and a good pinch of cayenne pepper (if you want a spicy version). Mix well, then spread the mixture on a baking tray in an even layer and roast for 8–10 minutes. Remove from the oven, add ½ cup (80 g) mixed nuts and roast for a further 5–7 minutes, until the chickpeas and green peas are crisp. Add ⅓ cup (60 g) raisins, sultanas or currants and give the tray a gentle shake, then return to the oven for another 3–5 minutes. Allow to cool completely, then taste and add more salt if needed.

This is best eaten straight away, but you can store it in an airtight container for 1–2 days. If it loses its crunch, pop it into a hot oven for a quick refresh.

Makes 2 cups (180 g)

HUMMUS

Hummus is found in supermarkets the world over, sitting alongside all the other dips, and it's a bit ho-hum. But hummus is serious business: at its best, it transcends being merely a dip to something much more central to a meal.

In Arabic, hummus simply means chickpeas (garbanzo beans), as they are the only constant ingredient in a dish that can have many, many iterations. Egypt, Lebanon, Jordan, Syria, Palestine, Israel and Greece all lay claim to hummus, with each cuisine making it their own by serving it warmed or at room temperature, adding pine nuts or yoghurt, roasted chickpeas or lemon.

Our version is creamy and fluffy, and we serve it at room temperature with a glug of olive oil. A few left-over vegetables or herbs can be added to make hummus with distinct flavours and vibrant colours. Follow the basic recipe opposite and use our suggested combinations as a guide.

BASIC HUMMUS

CARROT HUMMUS

150 g (5½ oz) dried chickpeas (garbanzo beans), soaked in cold water overnight (you'll need 300–350 g/ 10½–12 oz soaked and cooked, or canned, chickpeas)
2 garlic cloves, chopped
1 teaspoon salt
3 tablespoons lemon juice
¼ teaspoon bicarbonate of soda (baking soda)
½ cup (135 g) hulled tahini
1 tablespoon olive oil

Drain the chickpeas, place them in a large saucepan and cover with cold water. Bring to the boil, then reduce the heat to a simmer and cook for 20 minutes or until tender. Drain and set aside to cool.

Place the chickpeas, garlic and salt in a food processor and blend to a coarse paste. With the motor running, add the lemon juice and bicarbonate of soda, then add the tahini, olive oil and ½ cup (125 ml) water. Blend for 2–3 minutes until you have a smooth hummus (you may need to add a little more water to get a really smooth consistency). Let the hummus sit for at least 15 minutes before serving.

Hummus will keep refrigerated for 3–4 days. Always serve it at room temperature.

COMBINATIONS WE LIKE

- Carrot hummus: Add ¼ cup (50 g) chopped roasted carrot with the chickpeas

- Green hummus: Add a large handful of mixed herbs, such as parsley and coriander (cilantro), with the chickpeas

- Beetroot hummus: Add ¼ cup (50 g) chopped roasted beetroot (beets) with the chickpeas

- Preserved lemon: Add 2 tablespoons chopped preserved lemon (page 207) and 1 teaspoon cumin with the chickpeas

- Pile the spiced mince on page 265 on top of hummus with a big handful of herbs and serve with flatbreads for a simple lunch or dinner.

GREEN HUMMUS

BEETROOT HUMMUS

CITRUS

The genus citrus includes lemons, oranges, limes, grapefruits, cumquats, mandarins and the Australian native finger lime, along with many more. Originating in South East Asia, citrus cultivation has spread across the world to become a key part of nearly everyone's cooking. In this section we focus on lemons and oranges as they are by far the most commonly bought citrus, but they are anything but humble and both bring brightness to winter.

Nearly every part of the citrus fruit is useful. Sadly, most citrus skins get thrown in the bin. This is a waste of so much flavour! The little cells contain aromatic oils that are less acidic than the juice and very concentrated. Before you juice any citrus, take the extra two minutes to zest or peel them. See page 204 for lots of tips on how the zest and peels can be used and how to preserve their flavour for later use. When it comes to peeling citrus, it's important to avoid as much of the white pith as possible. We recommend removing just the coloured skin using a vegetable peeler. This means you'll be highlighting the flavour of the citrus rather than its bitterness.

Citrus fruits have a high concentration of vitamin C, which benefits our immune and cardiovascular systems. One orange contains all our vitamin C requirements for one day, making them the perfect package in winter. Citrus is also high in magnesium, potassium and soluble fibre, which is good for cholesterol levels.

Citrus fruit is fine to leave in the fruit bowl, but they can dry out after a week or so. If you have more than a week's worth of citrus, store them in a bag or airtight container in the fridge.

GOES WITH...

Citrus juice, zest and even the leaves can all be used in cooking. The juice and zest contain the compound citral, which is what we recognise as uniquely citrusy. This flavour pairs beautifully with fennel, brussels sprouts, dark leafy greens, carrot, pumpkin and beetroot. This aromatic scent also has affinities with dill, ginger, juniper, goat's cheese, chocolate, lavender and, of course, fish. It really is the flavour companion in the kitchen.

USE IT ALL

Citrus peels can be frozen in an airtight container or jar and then used in gin and tonics and negronis, or added to soups and stews that call for citrus zest. Try adding strips of lemon peel to a spinach and potato soup or a vegetable and chicken broth, or add orange peels to a slow-cooked lamb dish with rosemary or a spiced chickpea (garbanzo bean) stew. Or see page 204 for many more ways with citrus peels.

WASTE TIP

If you've got any oranges, lemons or limes that are starting to wrinkle, the marmalade opposite is a delicious way to transform them. You need to boil the citrus whole, so if you've got an excess you could boil enough for this and the whole lime or lemon pickle and make an afternoon of it.

WHOLE FRUIT MARMALADE

This recipe is scaled down and uses just three pieces of fruit (about 500 g/1 lb 2 oz). You can use just one variety of citrus, or a combination of lemons, limes, grapefruit and oranges.

Give the citrus a good scrub, place it in a good-sized saucepan and cover with 6 cups (1.5 litres) water. You need to boil the citrus until it is tender and the skins can be easily pierced. Don't rush this step – if you don't soften the skin, you'll end up with chewy bits in your marmalade! Oranges and grapefruit may take up to 2 hours, while lemons and limes should be closer to 1 hour.

Once the fruit is soft, remove from the pan and set aside until cool enough to handle, reserving the cooking liquid in a measuring jug. Cut the fruit in half and remove the pips, then thinly slice into long strips. Put the fruit strips and all their juices in a wide-mouthed pan with 850 ml (28½ fl oz) of the cooking water (adding extra fresh water if you don't have enough), 3 cups (690 g) caster (superfine) sugar, a pinch of salt, and any flavours of your choice, such as a sprig of thyme or rosemary, some lemon zest, 2–3 tablespoons freshly grated ginger, or warm spices, such as cinnamon or clove. Stir until the sugar is dissolved, then bring to the boil and cook for 20–25 minutes until the marmalade is set.

Allow the marmalade to sit for 5–10 minutes, then bottle into sterilised jars (page 278) and store in the fridge for up to 3 months.

Makes about 4 cups (1.2 kg)

WHOLE LIME OR LEMON PICKLE

This is a short-cut version of our Cornersmith lime pickle and a nice way to turn a few pieces of citrus into a quick Indian-style condiment to eat with curries. The original version needs a few weeks of careful attention, but the result is incredible. This is the next best thing, making a tangy, spicy pickle in under an hour.

Place 250–300 g (9–10½ oz) limes or lemons in a saucepan of water and bring to the boil. Boil for 30–40 minutes, until the citrus starts to soften. Drain the fruit and allow to cool, then chop into 1–2 cm (½–¾ inch) pieces, removing any pips as you go.

Return the chopped lime or lemon to the saucepan, along with 3 tablespoons white wine vinegar, 3 tablespoons water, 2 tablespoons caster (superfine) or raw sugar, ¾ teaspoon salt, ¼ teaspoon ground turmeric, 1 teaspoon mustard seeds, ½ teaspoon chilli flakes, 1 teaspoon cumin seeds and 1 tablespoon grated ginger. Reduce the heat to low and stir to dissolve the sugar. Simmer for 15 minutes or until the mixture is glossy and starting to thicken. Taste and adjust the seasoning if needed.

Spoon into a clean jar, pressing down so the pieces of lime or lemon are covered in the thickened sauce. You can enjoy this straight away but it will be better if it sits in the fridge for a week before you eat it. Once opened, the pickle will last for at least 1 month.

Makes 200 g (7 oz)

CITRUS ZEST BUTTER

We're obsessed with this citrus butter and are so happy when it's in the fridge. It makes everything delicious. We find that orange or lemon zest works best, but lime is nice, too. Try pan-frying fish with it, spread it on toast or use it in baking. It's also great stirred through couscous and, of course, on crêpes or pancakes. Jaimee's lucky little piggies get French toast fried in orange butter for breakfast before school! The options are endless.

Combine 2 tablespoons orange zest with 90 g (3 oz) slightly softened butter, plus a generous pinch of salt. Mix well, then transfer to a jar and store in the fridge.

Makes about 100 g (3½ oz)

WHAT TO DO WITH LEFT-OVER CITRUS PEELS

DRIED CITRUS PEELS AND POWDERS

Dried citrus peels and powders will keep in a sealed jar for up to 6 months, although the flavour and aroma will be best within 3 months.

Dry fresh peels in a dehydrator or a 60–80°C (140–175°C/Gas mark ¼) oven for 1–2 hours or until completely dry (if using a fan-forced oven, place a wire rack on top of the peels to stop them flying around). Store in an airtight jar, or place in a spice grinder and grind to a powder.

USES FOR CITRUS POWDER

- Use orange and lemon citrus powders as you would ground cinnamon in sweet baking.
- Add lime or lemon citrus powders to guacamole.
- Flavour icing with 1 tablespoon lemon or mandarin citrus powder.
- Make a flavoured salt (page 229).
- Add 1–2 teaspoons to salad dressings.
- Add a few teaspoons of orange citrus powder when roasting fennel, or lemon citrus powder when roasting chicken or vegetables.

FRESH CITRUS PEELS

Keep fresh peels in the fridge for up to 1 week.

- Make a citrus skin syrup for the perfect bitter non-alcoholic aperitif. Place 1 cup (120 g) citrus peels, 1½ cups (375 ml) water, ¾ cup (165 g) caster (superfine) sugar, 2 star anise and 4 allspice berries in a saucepan. Bring to the boil, then reduce the heat to a simmer and cook for 10 minutes. Allow to cool for 10–15 minutes. Strain through a sieve into a clean jar, then keep in the fridge for at least 1 month. Stir 1 tablespoon into a glass of sparkling water.

- Add citrus peels to a full bottle of white wine vinegar or apple cider vinegar to make a beautiful flavoured vinegar. Let it sit on your bench for about 6 weeks or until the flavour is singing (keep adding to it over this time), then strain and return the citrusy vinegar back into the bottle. Use as a base for dressings in green salads or grain-based dishes.

CITRUS-FLAVOURED TEAS

We make versions of this tea to serve in our classes. Sometimes it is the star of the show and it's all anyone wants to talk about. It's incredibly simple – use what's in season and in your fruit bowl.

Place the peels of 1–2 oranges and herbs or spices of your choice – we like to use 2 star anise, a few sprigs of thyme, a sprig of rosemary, 2 fresh bay leaves or 1 cinnamon stick – in a saucepan and cover with 4 cups (1 litre) water. Bring to the boil and simmer for 5 minutes. Turn off the heat and allow to cool for 10 minutes. Add 1–2 tablespoons honey and stir to dissolve. Allow to sit for another 5 minutes, then strain. You can serve this straight away, bring back to the boil to serve hot or allow to cool completely and serve over ice. The tea will keep in the fridge for up to 1 week.

Makes 4 cups (1 litre)

CITRUS ZEST

Citrus can also be zested instead of peeled, and then dried or frozen so that you always have it on hand, even when it's not in season.

To freeze citrus zest, you can opt for the lazy version, which is to freeze it in a jar and keep adding to it every time you have excess zest. The best version (and one that avoids the zest clumping together) is to spread the zest on a tray and freeze it. Once frozen, transfer the zest to a jar where it will keep for 6 months. There's no need to thaw the zest before using it.

To dehydrate citrus zest, preheat the oven to its lowest setting and turn off the fan. Spread the zest out on a baking tray, then place in the oven and leave to dry until there is no moisture left, checking every 15 minutes to ensure the zest doesn't burn. Allow to cool completely, then store in a jar in the pantry.

CITRUS SALT

DRIED LEMON PEEL

DRIED ZEST

LEMON JAM

MARMALADE

PRESERVED LEMON

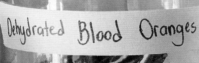

Dehydrated Blood Oranges

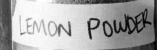

LEMON POWDER

GRAPEFRUIT PEEL

ORANGE BUTTER

PRESERVED LEMONS OR LIMES

This recipe is in our other cookbooks, but you just can't have a pantry without preserved lemons! Plus, they are so expensive to buy. You will need 1 kg (2 lb 4 oz) lemons or limes for this (you may need extra for juicing if your citrus is dry) and 200 g (7 oz) pure salt.

Cut the lemons or limes into quarters (or halves if they're very small). Put 20 g (¾ oz) salt into the bottom of 2 sterilised jars (page 278) and top with a few layers of lemon or lime, pressing down on the skins as you go to release the juices. Sprinkle with another 20 g (¾ oz) salt, then add another layer of fruit. Slide 1 teaspoon black peppercorns, 1–2 bay leaves and a pinch of chilli flakes down the side of each jar. Repeat the layering with the fruit and salt until the jar is almost full (leave a 1 cm/½ inch gap at the top), remembering to keep pushing down as you go – the fruit needs to be entirely covered in juice. If your fruit hasn't released enough of its own juices, squeeze a few extra lemons or limes and pour the juice over to cover.

Wipe the rim of the jar with paper towel to remove excess salt, then seal and let it sit in a cool, dark place for 6 weeks.

You know your lemons or limes are preserved when the salt has completely dissolved into a gel-like liquid. Once opened, store in the fridge for up to 1 year.

Makes 2 x 500 ml (17 fl oz) jars

USES FOR PRESERVED LEMON

Use thinly sliced preserved lemon to flavour and freshen a clear chicken soup (see page 190 for lessons in soup-making).

Add a few teaspoons of very thinly sliced preserved lemon, a pinch of chilli flakes and a glug of olive oil to mashed avocado.

Make a preserved lemon dressing: Combine 1 tablespoon apple cider vinegar, 2 tablespoons extra virgin olive oil, 1 tablespoon finely diced preserved lemon peel, ½ teaspoon ground cumin, ½ teaspoon sugar or honey, a good crack of black pepper and a small pinch of salt.

Make a yoghurt raita with finely diced cucumber, finely diced tomato, minced garlic and finely chopped preserved lemon.

Add a tablespoon of finely chopped preserved lemon to green sauces (page 32–33), mayonnaise (page 19) or hummus (page 200–1).

Stir thinly sliced preserved lemon through a potato salad with hard-boiled eggs and lots of fresh herbs.

Add to the green pockets on page 28 or the galette on page 185.

PRESERVED LEMON GREMOLATA

This takes 5 minutes to make and adds so much flavour to numerous dishes. Serve on lamb stew or barbecued fish, stir through roasted beetroots (beets) with lots of olive oil or hot, cooked chickpeas (garbanzo beans), rice or couscous, or add a few teaspoons to wilted greens.

In a bowl, combine ½ bunch roughly chopped parsley, mint or dill with a heaped ¼ cup (40 g) finely diced preserved lemon skin, 1½ tablespoons olive oil, ½ teaspoon caster (superfine) sugar, ¼ teaspoon fennel seeds and ¼ teaspoon pepper. You can also add ½ teaspoon chilli flakes and 1 tablespoon grated ginger or garlic if you like. Mix together, taste, add a pinch of salt if needed and let it sit for 10 minutes before serving. It will keep in an airtight container for up to 5 days in the fridge. This recipe scales up well if you're feeding a crowd.

Makes 75 g (2½ oz)

BLOOD ORANGE TARTE TATIN

Serves 6–8

This is a simple and delicious tarte tatin (really an upside-down galette) that can be made with all sorts of fruit. Try it with slices of apple or pear, poached quince or rhubarb. Here, we've used thin slices of blood orange to make a very impressive-looking dessert that's surprisingly easy. The pastry is our very straightforward sour cream pastry that can be made in the food processor. You can also make or buy puff pastry instead.

4–5 blood oranges
1 tablespoon unsalted butter
½ teaspoon cardamom seeds
3 tablespoons caster (superfine)
    sugar
1 quantity sour cream pastry
    (page 185)
Splash of milk or 1 beaten egg
Ice cream, cream or custard,
    to serve

Preheat the oven to 180°C (350°F/Gas mark 4).

Peel and thinly slice three or four of the blood oranges into rounds, removing any pips.

Juice the remaining blood orange to yield 3 tablespoons juice. Pour the juice into a 30 cm (12 inch) ovenproof frying pan and add the butter, cardamom seeds and sugar. Warm gently over low heat, stirring to dissolve the sugar, then arrange the orange slices on top of the caramel in the prettiest way that you can. Turn off the heat.

Roll the pastry out on a lightly floured workbench to a circle large enough to cover the dish. Gently place the pastry over the orange slices, tucking the edges down inside the dish. Prick the pastry all over with a fork and brush with milk or beaten egg.

Bake in the oven for 30 minutes or until the pastry is golden brown and the caramel is bubbling at the edge. Remove from the oven and let sit for 5–10 minutes.

Invert the tarte tatin onto a serving dish and serve with ice cream, cream or custard.

COMBINATIONS WE LIKE

- Apple or pear: Use 3–4 thinly sliced apples or pears and replace the blood orange juice with 3 tablespoons lemon juice. Add ½ teaspoon freshly grated nutmeg instead of the ground cardamom.
- Lemon: Replace the blood orange slices and juice with lemon. Replace the cardamom with 2–3 fresh bay leaves and 1 tablespoon chopped thyme.
- Peach: Slice 4–5 peaches into fat wedges. Use lemon juice instead of orange and replace the cardamom with the chopped leaves from 1 rosemary sprig.

WOODY HERBS

GINGER

DRIED BEANS

BANANAS

A WHOLE PUMPKIN

PEARS

CARROTS

SHOPPING BASKET 7

Winter has an abundance of fruit and vegetables. It's time for the deep, earthy flavours and surprising sweetness of pumpkin (squash) and beetroot (beets): hearty vegetables that are filling and nourishing. All of the recipes and tips in this basket can be vegetarian, although we do sneak in a little bacon here and there for extra seasoning, but leave it out if you prefer. Make a big batch of the roasted root vegetables on page 214 to set yourself up for a week of simple and warming meals.

A BUNCH OF BEETROOT

BACON

FROM THIS BASKET ...

MEALS

Winter vegetable salad (page 213)

All-purpose roasted winter vegetables (page 214)

Hearty roast vegetable soup (page 214)

Curried vegetable pocket pies (page 216)

Pumpkin and sage sauce for pasta, lasagne and ravioli (page 220)

Beetroot and barley risotto (page 223)

The best baked beans (page 233)

SIDES

Whole beetroot salad (page 225)

Carrot salad with carrot tops (page 227)

Mexican-style beans and refried beans (page 233)

Savoury-roasted pears (page 235)

SNACKS, SWEETS & DRINKS

Seeded pumpkin soda bread (page 219)

Spicy pepitas (page 220)

Beetroot chocolate brownies (page 223)

Healing herbal tea (page 229)

Honey caramel roasted pears (page 235)

Banana whip: the quickest ice cream ever (page 237)

Banana chips (page 237)

Ginger cookies (page 239)

Use it all loaf (page 240)

QUICK PRESERVING IDEAS

Vietnamese-style pickles using one carrot (page 227)

Carrot kimchi (page 227)

Flavoured herb vinegar (page 229)

Quick banana and coconut chutney (page 237)

Quick pickled ginger (page 239)

NOTHING GOES TO WASTE

Pumpkin skin and vegetable-scrap stock (page 220)

Beetroot stem salsa (page 223)

Herby salt (page 229)

Pear butter (page 235)

Black banana jam (page 237)

Spicy kitchen scrap paste (page 239)

A WHOLE PUMPKIN

Pumpkin (squash) is the largest and longest-growing member of the squash family. According to Stephanie Alexander's *The Cook's Companion*, its name is derived from the Greek word *pepon*, meaning 'cooked by the sun'. This slow growth under the sun means that pumpkin can bring the taste of summer to the winter months. The natural sweetness of pumpkin makes it one of the most popular vegetables and its versatility is almost unmatched.

We tend to use Kent and butternut pumpkins most often. They are sweet, with dense flesh that makes them great for roasting or puréeing. Both varieties come in at around 2–3 kg (4 lb 8 oz–6 lb 12 oz), but don't be afraid of this size – we are going to show you how to use it all!

An uncut pumpkin can be stored in the pantry (or used as a doorstop) for many moons. You can store cut pumpkin covered in beeswax wrap in the fridge for at least a week or two.

Like all orange-fleshed fruits and vegetables, pumpkin is high in beta-carotene, which converts to vitamin A. It is also rich in vitamin C and is a source of vitamin E, folate and iron.

GOES WITH …

Pumpkin's sweet flavour can be enhanced with added sweeteners and spices, such as chestnut, maple syrup and honey, and nutmeg, cinnamon, clove and ginger. For savoury dishes, pumpkin's sweetness is the perfect foil for rich flavours such as blue cheese and bacon. Earthy herbs including sage, rosemary and thyme are classic pairings, along with many types of nuts – we particularly like pumpkin with walnuts, pine nuts and cashews.

WASTE TIP

Don't forget you can put washed pumpkin skins in your vegetable stocks! See our pumpkin skin and vegetable-scrap stock recipe on page 220.

ALL-PURPOSE ROASTED WINTER VEGETABLES

Making a big batch of roasted winter vegetables means that you've got the base for a few meals ready to go. We use this base for soups and vegetable pockets or as a simple side with a piece of fish or meat. If you have leftovers, see our tips below for more ideas.

2 kg (4 lb 8 oz) raw mixed winter vegetables will give you just over 1 kg (2 lb 4 oz) roasted vegetables. This makes enough for a batch of roasted vegetable soup (opposite) and also the curried vegetable pocket pies (see page 216). You can use a mix of beetroot (beets), pumpkin (squash), carrot, sweet potato, parsnip, kohlrabi or potato.

Cut faster-cooking vegetables, such as pumpkin and sweet potato, into 3 cm (1¼ inch) pieces, then cut your root vegetables into 1–2 cm (½–¾ inch) pieces. You can leave the skin on everything; just make sure you wash them well. Spread the vegetables over two baking trays and pour 50 ml (1¾ fl oz) olive oil, 1 teaspoon salt, ½ teaspoon black pepper, ½ teaspoon ground ginger and 2 teaspoons dried thyme, oregano or rosemary over the top. Mix well with your hands. Roast in a preheated 180°C (350°F/ Gas mark 4) oven for 30–45 minutes, until the vegetables are soft and sweet but not falling apart.

POCKET PIES

Stir curry powder into 400 g (14 oz) roasted vegetables and wrap in pastry to make the curried pocket pies on page 216.

FISH CAKES

Mash 400 g (14 oz) roasted vegetables with a little milk to make a wintry version of the fish cakes on page 53.

WINTER VEGETABLE SALAD

Mix 1 cup roasted vegetables with 1 cup cooked grains, such as buckwheat, farro or brown rice, and a handful of roughly chopped parsley. Dress with 1 tablespoon olive oil, 1 tablespoon lemon juice and ¼ teaspoon salt and pepper.

All-purpose roasted winter vegetables

HEARTY ROAST VEGETABLE SOUP

If you have already roasted your vegetables, you can have this soup on the table in 10 minutes. While dinner hasn't exactly cooked itself, it's pretty close.

Heat 50 ml (1¾ fl oz) olive oil in a large saucepan over medium heat and sauté 1 chopped onion for 4–5 minutes or until soft and sweet. Add 2 chopped garlic cloves and 1 finely chopped rasher of bacon. Cook until fragrant and your bacon is beginning to brown, then add 4 cups (1 litre) stock of your choice and bring to a simmer. Add 500 g (1 lb 2 oz) of the roasted vegetables, along with 1 cup (75 g) cooked or canned beans (cannellini, adzuki or kidney). Simmer for 10 minutes over low heat, then add the zest and juice of 1 lemon. Taste and season if needed. Serve with grated parmesan and chopped parsley scattered over the top and the soda bread on page 219.

Serves 4

CURRIED VEGETABLE POCKET PIES

Makes 12

Neither of us are natural bakers, but there are a few staples in our repertoire that we couldn't live without. These pocket pies are so easy to make: the pastry is made with only four ingredients in a food processor and the filling is pre-roasted, so it's really just a matter of assembling. You can make the pastry on the weekend – it will keep, well wrapped, in the fridge for 2–3 days or in the freezer for up to 3 months. Serve with a simple salad for dinner and pop leftovers in lunchboxes the next day.

2–3 teaspoons all-purpose
curry powder
400 g (14 oz) all-purpose roasted
winter vegetables (see page 214)
Milk, for brushing

BASIC PASTRY

345 g (12 oz) plain (all-purpose)
flour, plus extra for dusting
½ teaspoon salt
250 g (9 oz) cold unsalted butter,
diced
½ cup (125 ml) iced water

To make the pastry, place the flour and salt in a food processor and pulse until combined. Add the butter and pulse until the mixture resembles breadcrumbs. With the motor running, slowly pour in the iced water and pulse until the mixture forms a ball.

Turn the dough ball out onto a floured workbench and lightly knead. Flatten into a disc, then wrap and rest in the fridge for 30 minutes.

Preheat the oven to 200°C (400°F/Gas mark 6).

Roll out the dough on your lightly floured workbench until 5 mm (¼ inch) thick. Using a small cereal bowl or similar, cut out 15 cm (6 inch) circles (or your preferred size). Reroll any dough offcuts to make 12 circles.

Stir the curry powder through the roasted vegetables, then place a couple of heaped tablespoons of the mixture on one side of each dough circle. Be generous, but make sure that you don't overfill your pockets or the dough may tear. Using your finger, dab the edge of the dough circles with water, then fold the circles in half and seal – you can also do fancy pleats or use a fork to seal the edges.

Brush the pockets with milk, then transfer to a baking tray and bake for 10–15 minutes, then flip over and cook for another 10 minutes.

Serve the pockets with a salad for dinner, or allow to cool and store in the fridge for a few days.

COMBINATIONS WE LIKE

You can really put anything in these pockets; just make sure you add the filling cold to avoid soggy pastry.

- Try the baked beans on page 233 with a little grated cheese
- The lentil stew on page 137
- Mushroom bolognese (page 152)
- Curried peas (page 195).

SEEDED PUMPKIN SODA BREAD

Makes 1 loaf

FOUNDATION RECIPE

As home cooks, we are both a little late to breadmaking. We had already developed our specialties – preserving and fermenting – and these things, along with cooking dinner, seemed like enough. But this soda bread changed both our minds. It was our entry-level bread and now it's your entry-level bread. We love that there are minimal ingredients and that it can be made and baked within an hour. This means that it's possible to do on a weeknight. Quick and affordable, this bread is also flexible: add grated carrot, beetroot or potato, or even just the potato peels if you like (page 129).

Irish soda bread was traditionally made with soured milk. In this recipe, we sour the milk with lemon juice. The acidity of the soured milk reacts with the bicarbonate of soda to leaven the bread. If you would like an even lighter loaf, we suggest using all unbleached white flour instead of half white, half wholemeal (whole wheat) flour.

Squeeze of lemon juice
300 ml (10½ fl oz) full-cream (whole) milk, plus extra if needed and for brushing
4 tablespoons mixed seeds
  sunflower seeds
  linseeds
  sesame seeds
  poppy seeds
1⅔ cups (250 g) unbleached plain (all-purpose) flour, plus extra for dusting
1⅔ cups (250 g) plain wholemeal (whole wheat) flour
2 teaspoons bicarbonate of soda (baking soda)
1 teaspoon salt
200 g (7 oz) grated vegetables
  pumpkin (squash)
  sweet potato
  carrot
  beetroot (beets)
  zucchini (courgette), squeezed dry

First, squeeze a little lemon juice into the milk to make it curdle, then set aside.

Preheat the oven to 200°C (400°F/Gas mark 6). Place an oven rack in the centre of the oven.

Combine the seeds in a small bowl and set aside.

Sift the flours, bicarbonate of soda and salt into a large mixing bowl. Stir in 3 tablespoons of the seeds and the grated vegetables. Make a well in the flour mixture, pour in the curdled milk and stir until the dough just comes together. If the dough is too dry, add an extra splash of milk.

Tip the dough onto a lightly floured workbench and lightly knead, just pulling the dough together, for no more than 1 minute – you need to get it into the oven while the bicarbonate of soda is still active.

Place the dough on a lightly floured baking sheet and mark it with a deep cross across the top, cutting two-thirds of the way through the loaf with a serrated knife. Brush the dough with milk and sprinkle over the remaining seeds, making sure they make it down into the cracks.

Bake for 45 minutes, until the bread has a golden crust on the top and bottom (you may want to move the oven rack up for the last 15 minutes of cooking if you need more colour on the top of the loaf).

Cool on a wire rack, then slice and serve.

SPICY PEPITAS

Don't throw away your pepitas (pumpkin seeds)! This recipe shows you how to make your own spicy toasted pepitas. You can also make this with store-bought pepitas (just skip the first oven-drying step).

Scoop the seeds out of your pumpkin (squash) and remove the attached stringy flesh. Rinse the pepitas in a strainer, then place in a bowl of water. Pick out any pumpkin goop and strain again. Preheat the oven to 100–120°C (210–250°F/Gas mark ½), spread the pepitas on a baking tray and place in the oven to dry for 15 minutes. Remove from the oven and drizzle over a little oil of your choice, 1 teaspoon salt, 1 teaspoon paprika, 1 teaspoon ground cumin and a pinch of cayenne pepper, and stir to combine. Increase the oven temperature to 160°C (315°F/Gas mark 2–3) and bake the pepitas for a further 15 minutes or until golden. Set aside to cool, then store in an airtight container in the pantry for up to 2 weeks. Sprinkle over soups, salads or risottos.

PUMPKIN SKIN AND VEGETABLE-SCRAP STOCK

This a richly flavoured vegetable stock that uses up the tops, skins and stalks of winter vegetables or the last few vegetables in the crisper. Save up your scraps in a container in the fridge until you have enough.

Place 1 kg (2 lb 4 oz) mixed vegetables and scraps (such as carrots, celery, leeks and their tops, halved onions, pumpkin skins and mushroom stalks) in a large stockpot with ½ head smashed garlic, 1 bunch tired herbs such as thyme, parsley or a few bay leaves, and 2 teaspoons black peppercorns. Cover with 8 cups (2 litres) water and slowly bring to the boil. Reduce the heat to low and simmer for 30 minutes. Turn off the heat, add 1 teaspoon salt and allow to sit for another 30 minutes. Strain and store in the fridge for 1 week or the freezer for 3 months.

Makes about 6 cups (1.5 litres)

PUMPKIN AND SAGE SAUCE FOR PASTA, LASAGNE OR RAVIOLI

This one is for the pumpkin lovers, and you'll make a serious dent in that whole pumpkin you bought. We have gone with the classic Italian combination of pumpkin and sage to make a sauce that can be used in any pasta dish.

Grate 600 g (1 lb 5 oz) peeled pumpkin (squash) and set aside. Heat 1 tablespoon olive oil and 1 tablespoon butter in a saucepan over medium heat. Sauté 1 diced onion, 4 minced garlic cloves, 10 sage leaves picked from their woody stems and 1 teaspoon chilli flakes for 4–5 minutes or until the onion is translucent. You can also add 1–2 chopped bacon rashers at this stage if you like. Add the pumpkin, ½ cup (125 ml) stock of your choice and ½ cup (125 ml) cream (or use all stock). Reduce the heat to low and cook, stirring occasionally so the ingredients don't stick to the bottom of the pan, for about 15 minutes. Season with salt and black pepper to taste and ¼ cup (25 g) grated parmesan. Use as a pasta sauce, or add to a lasagne or ravioli.

Makes about 3 cups (750 ml)

BACON

Salty, fatty, sweet and smoky – it's no wonder that bacon makes everything so delicious. A cured meat made from pork belly, its flavour adds a little extra oomph to even the simplest ingredients. When we cook beans we use bacon like a seasoning – just one rasher of bacon can go a long way.

Our approach to eating any meat is to only buy from trusted suppliers, who take into account animal welfare and sustainable farming practices with minimal environmental impact. The standard conditions for most pig-raising and slaughtering are brutal. We're committed to only buying and eating true free-range pork, which often means it can be difficult to find. We highly recommend doing some research to find out where in your area sells true free-range pork, and don't believe the supermarket labels!

When bacon is in our kitchens it's a real treat. Alex's daughter cheers when she sees it in the fridge. As good-quality meat is more expensive, it means we have to make the most of each rasher of bacon and make it last. Celebration breakfasts might see a big plate of bacon on the table, but other than that, bacon is used to intensify flavour and create extra-tasty soups, stews and hearty meals in winter.

There is lots of great information available about eating meat ethically, so arm yourself with knowledge before you hit the shops.

A BUNCH OF BEETROOT

We love whole bunches of beetroot (beets), not only for their sweet, earthy flavour and incredible nutrients but because you can do so much with each part of the vegetable – true top-to-tail eating.

The shops mostly sell deep red beetroot, but beetroot also come in yellow, purple, white and striped. When choosing beetroot, look for a rich, vibrant colour, firm roots and bright, fresh-looking tops attached. A very hairy tail is a sign of age and toughness.

Beetroot has a good mix of the minerals iron, calcium and magnesium. It is also high in fibre, folate and anti-inflammatory antioxidants.

To store whole bunches of beetroot, separate the roots from the stems and leaves. Wrap the leaves and stems in a damp cloth and store in a bag in the fridge for up to 1 week. The roots will stay fresh for 10 days if you trim the stems a few centimetres above the roots, wrap in a cloth and keep in the crisper drawer.

GOES WITH …

Because beetroot are mellow, they go with sharper flavours, such as red wine vinegar, garlic, horseradish, ginger, orange or lemon zest, and salty cheeses, such as feta and goat's cheese. Beetroot also work well with dill, pears, nuts and chocolate.

WASTE TIP

Don't throw away the stems! Use them to make the salsa opposite, or pickle them (see page 143) and toss them through salads or serve with meats.

USE IT ALL

Make beetroot leaf chips by following the kale chip recipe on page 165.

Beetroot stem salsa

BEETROOT AND BARLEY RISOTTO

Barley has a nuttiness that perfectly complements the earthiness of beetroot. Together, they create something rich and wholesome. Barley isn't as high maintenance as arborio rice, so you can walk away between absorption stages and the world won't come to an end. You can also use the same amount of grated raw pumpkin (squash) instead of beetroot.

Bring 4 cups (1 litre) stock to a low simmer in a saucepan. In another saucepan over medium heat, melt 2 tablespoons butter and add 1 diced onion, 3 diced garlic cloves and 4 thinly sliced sage leaves. Sauté until soft, then add 1 grated beetroot (beet) and 3 tablespoons red wine (or leave the wine out if you don't have a bottle open), and sauté for another minute or so. Stir through ½ cup (100 g) barley, then pour in 1 cup (250 ml) hot stock, reduce the heat to low and stir until all the liquid is absorbed. Keep adding the stock, 1 cup (250 ml) at a time, until completely absorbed. Add ⅓ cup (35 g) grated parmesan and stir to just combine. Divide among bowls and serve with a few chopped walnuts on top.

Serves 3–4

BEETROOT STEM SALSA

Enjoy this salsa on toast with eggs or goat's cheese, tossed through a beetroot salad (see page 225) or serve with grilled lamb.

Heat 2 tablespoons olive oil in a frying pan over low heat, add 1 finely chopped red onion, 2 cups (210 g) thinly sliced beetroot (beet) stems, a handful of chopped dill leaves and stems and a pinch of chilli flakes and sauté for 10 minutes. Add something salty, such as 1 tablespoon capers or finely diced dill pickles (gherkins), chopped olives or preserved lemon, then add a little extra salt, a splash of vinegar and more dill. Cook for 5 minutes or until soft and sweet.

Makes about 2 cups

BEETROOT CHOCOLATE BROWNIES

These brownies are one of our bestsellers at the Cornersmith cafe. Beetroot and chocolate are such a beautiful combination, making the perfect earthy, rich and velvety brownie.

Trim and wash 350 g (12½ oz) beetroot (beets), then place in a saucepan of boiling water and cook until a knife slips easily through. Drain the beetroot, allow to cool a little and then slip off their skins. Grate and set aside. Preheat the oven to 160°C (315°F/Gas mark 2–3). Melt 125 g (4½ oz) chocolate buttons in a heatproof bowl set over a saucepan of simmering water. Carefully remove the bowl from the heat and set the chocolate aside to cool a little.

Break 4 eggs into a large bowl and whisk in 250 g (9 oz) brown sugar. Add the beetroot, 1 tablespoon cocoa powder and ½ teaspoon ground cinnamon. Fold through 2½ cups (250 g) almond meal. Pour ½ cup (125 ml) olive oil into the cooled chocolate, then fold this mixture into the batter. Line a 20 cm x 25 cm (8 inch x 10 inch) baking tin with baking paper and pour the mixture into the tin. Bake for 50–60 minutes, then set aside to cool completely before cutting into pieces. Set in the fridge overnight or at least for a few hours. To slice, use a hot knife to help achieve a clean cut. The brownies will keep in an airtight container in the fridge for up to 1 week.

Makes 8–12

WHOLE BEETROOT SALAD

Serves 4–6 as a side

This wintry salad makes use of all the flavours and textures of the whole beetroot. Here, the beetroot bulbs are roasted to intensify their natural sweetness, while the stems are turned into a tangy salsa and the leaves are very thinly sliced to add crunch and lighten things up. This beautiful earthy salad is always a winner in the cooler months.

1 bunch whole beetroot (beets)
2–3 tablespoons olive oil, plus extra
   for drizzling
Salt
2 tablespoons red wine vinegar
1–2 tablespoons grated horseradish
   (depending on how much bite
   you like)
2–3 tablespoons beetroot stem
   salsa (see page 223)
Handful beetroot leaves,
   thinly sliced
Handful chopped soft herbs,
   to serve
Spicy pepitas (see page 220),
   to serve
Freshly cracked black pepper

Preheat the oven to 180°C (350°F/Gas mark 4).

Remove the beetroot leaves from their stems, then wash well and dry. Use the small tender leaves whole, and thinly slice the medium-sized leaves. (Any big tough leaves can be turned into chips following the instructions on page 165.) Separate the stems from the roots, wash the stems well and then allow to dry and use them to make the beetroot stem salsa on page 223.

Place the whole beetroot in a baking dish so they fit snugly. Add a few tablespoons of water and tightly cover with foil. Bake for about 1 hour, until the beetroot are soft enough to pierce with a knife but not mushy. Remove from the oven and allow to cool for 15 minutes. (If you're pressed for time, peel the beetroot, then cut into wedges, drizzle with olive oil and sprinkle with salt. Roast in a preheated 200°C/400°F/Gas mark 6 oven for 20 minutes or until tender. They often lose some of their juices with this method but they're still very tasty and it saves a lot of cooking time.)

Once cool enough to handle, the beetroot skins should easily slip off using your hands. Cut the beetroot into wedges and place in a large bowl. Add the olive oil, red wine vinegar, horseradish, beetroot stem salsa and ¼ teaspoon salt, then gently fold through the beetroot leaves.

Tip the salad into a shallow serving bowl, top with the herbs, pepitas and plenty of black pepper, and serve.

CARROTS

In Australia we buy more carrots than any other vegetable! Healthy and easy to prepare, carrots have been an affordable staple in shopping baskets for decades. While they're easily bought, they are also easily forgotten, becoming sad and wrinkly fingers at the bottom of our crispers.

We believe the carrot needs to be remembered and celebrated. With its sweet taste and notes of parsley and lemon, it is an incredibly versatile ingredient in the kitchen. Love carrots for what they are: humble, easy and a great all-rounder. They are also very good for you – as Mother always says, 'Carrots are good for your eyes'. And it's true: the beta-carotene in carrots converts to vitamin A, which is essential for healthy sight, and especially night vision.

Store carrots unwashed in the fridge; washing them before refrigeration speeds up the deterioration process. Carrots start to go limp when exposed to air, so wrap them tightly or store them in an airtight container. They should last a good 2 weeks or more if properly cared for.

GO WITH ...

The woodiness of carrots lends itself to similar flavours, such as nuts and strong spices (cumin, coriander, fennel and ginger). Vegetables and fruits that pair well with carrots include celery, cabbage, apple, orange and olives. You can enhance their natural sweetness with honey, maple syrup or brown sugar, and they're wonderful used in baking with dried fruits.

WASTE TIP

Like potatoes, our recommendation is to stop peeling your carrots! But if you do have carrot peels, here are our top tips:

- Add them to the spicy kitchen scrap paste (page 239), along with any carrot tops
- Turn them into chips following the recipe on page 129. Sprinkle with ground cumin or coriander and salt before baking.

VIETNAMESE-STYLE PICKLES USING ONE CARROT

If you've got one tired carrot left in the fridge, make a batch of these fridge pickles, which are based on the Vietnamese pickles used in banh mi. They can be ready in 10 minutes and are perfect in salad rolls, fried rice, noodles and rice paper rolls.

Cut a carrot into matchsticks and pop it into a bowl. If you have a lonely radish, a bit of cabbage or the end of a knob of ginger, thinly slice them and add to the bowl. Sprinkle with 1 teaspoon salt and 1 tablespoon sugar and mix with your hands. Let the mixture sit for 5 minutes, then cover with ½ cup (125 ml) boiling water and ½ cup (125 ml) vinegar (white wine or rice wine). Leave for 20 minutes and then enjoy. These pickles will be fine for a few weeks in the fridge, if they last that long!

Vietnamese-style pickles using one carrot

CARROT KIMCHI

Kimchi is a living tradition, and kimchi recipes embrace produce that is both native and introduced to South Korea, resulting in a huge spectrum of this national condiment. This carrot kimchi is sweet and mild, so it might convert even those who are not fermenting enthusiasts.

Grate 500 g (1 lb 2 oz) carrots and cover with water and 2 teaspoons pure salt. Leave on the bench overnight. The next day, strain and rinse the grated carrot a few times in cold water. Place in a large bowl and add a small thinly sliced leek, 1 teaspoon chilli flakes, 1 tablespoon sesame seeds, 1 tablespoon minced garlic and 1 tablespoon minced ginger. Pack the mixture into a clean jar, pressing down as you go and making sure the water that's released is 1 cm (½ inch) above the carrot at the top of the jar. Seal and leave to ferment at room temperature (out of direct sunlight) for 2–4 days, then transfer to the fridge for another 4 days. After this time, your carrot kimchi will be ready to eat. Store in the fridge for up to 6 months. (See page 278 for more fermenting tips.)

Makes 400 g (14 oz)

CARROT SALAD WITH CARROT TOPS

It's rumoured that carrot tops are poisonous, but that is not the case. We can vouch for that after years of eating Alex's carrot-top pesto, tossing them through salads, sautéing them with other greens, adding them to our spicy kitchen scrap paste (see page 239) and stocks, and using them in place of parsley if we've run out. They are packed full of flavour and nutrients, so don't let them wind up in the compost!

Preheat the oven to 180°C (350°F/Gas mark 4). Remove the tops from 1 bunch baby carrots, then toss the carrots with olive oil, spread out on a baking tray and roast for 20 minutes or until lightly caramelised. Meanwhile, wash and dry the carrot tops thoroughly, then roughly chop and add to a salad bowl. When the carrots are done, remove them from the oven and allow to cool. Toss the carrots with the carrot tops, then add ½ sliced avocado and a handful of toasted pepitas (pumpkin seeds). Season with salt and dress with 2 tablespoons olive oil, a good crack of black pepper and the juice of 1 lemon.

Serves 4 as a side

WOODY HERBS

Woody herbs are robust and generally have thick, inedible stems and small, intensely flavoured leaves. The leaves are rich in aromatic oils and you can often smell them on your skin long after handling them.

Woody herbs can be added to meals towards the end of cooking to lift flavour, or in the early stages of a slow-cooked dish to create complexity. Use them fresh or dried, but remember that home-dried herbs lose some of their potency, so increase the quantity. Conversely, it seems that commercially dried herbs have an unnatural intensity so use them sparingly.

We are fascinated by the medicinal qualities of herbs and use them to make home remedies, such as teas and tinctures, to soothe what ails us (see opposite).

Woody herbs can be stored fresh or dried. To keep their leaves fresh, wrap them in a slightly damp tea towel (you don't want too much moisture) and store in a bag in the fridge for up to 2 weeks.

WASTE TIP

Drying woody herbs will allow you to store them and preserve their flavour. This is an especially good skill for gardeners who might have a rosemary bush that is in need of an unmerciful prune. We use two techniques: air drying and oven drying.

There is something beautifully old-fashioned about having bunches of herbs hanging to dry in your kitchen. To air dry, we tie a bunch of herbs with kitchen string and hang them upside down in a well-ventilated area away from direct sunlight for 2–4 days or until completely dry. Once dry, strip the leaves from the stems and keep in an airtight container or jar.

To dry herbs more quickly, spread them on a baking tray and place in a preheated 140°C (275°F/Gas mark 1) oven for about 15 minutes or until completely dry. Set aside to cool, then strip the leaves and keep in an airtight container or jar.

VARIETIES

ROSEMARY

The needle-like leaves of rosemary are heady in fragrance and flavour, with pine and floral notes. A classic match with lamb, of course, but we also love rosemary with everything from pears to chocolate. Pumpkin (squash) and potatoes, as well as tomatoes, mushrooms and rhubarb, are great pairings too. Rosemary is stimulating and is said to be good for headaches; it was traditionally used to prevent colds.

SAGE

This strong herb is not to everyone's liking, but those who love it *really* love it. When fresh, it is light and a little citrusy. When drier, it becomes musky and bitter. Use sage with other strong flavours for balance. We like it with bacon, pumpkin (squash), strong cheeses such as blue cheese, caramelised onions and cooked apple. Sage has a drying effect for a wet cough, and is calming on nerves. It can also improve memory.

THYME

Thyme is one of the most classic herbs. Adding it to a stew as it cooks for hours will add fragrance and warmth. Thyme's bitter sweetness goes well with onion, white beans, olives, tomato, apple, pear and citrus. It is energising and is said to settle the stomach and intestines.

OREGANO

To us, oregano smells like pizza! Or perhaps pizza should always smell a little like oregano. Oregano has a similar flavour profile to thyme – it pairs with the same foods – but is stronger, plus it has good antibacterial properties. Make a tea for a sore throat or add to a bath to ease cramps.

BAY

Having bay in the kitchen is essential. It has a slightly eucalypt scent, and when added to stocks or slow-cooked dishes it adds a complexity that can't be matched. Bay goes very well with red meat, apple and lemon. Infuse custard, ice cream, jams or marmalade with a leaf or add it to your pickles, as we do. Bay-leaf tea can calm indigestion and reduce headaches.

LAVENDER

Not often thought of as a herb, but it certainly is. Lavender has a sweet earthiness that can add the most delicate fragrance to baked goods. A touch of lavender with baked apple or rhubarb is amazing. Add a lavender flower to a small jar of sugar and leave for a week. Use the perfumed sugar to sprinkle on shortbread or add a little to earl grey tea. Lavender is famous for its calming properties.

HEALING HERBAL TEA

To make a simple herbal tea, put about 2 tablespoons woody herbs (or you can use soft herbs) and 2 cups (500 ml) water in a saucepan over low heat and bring to a simmer. Add honey to taste, then remove from the heat and allow the flavours to infuse for 10 minutes. Strain and serve warm or chilled. Experiment with different flavour combinations.

FLAVOURED HERB VINEGAR

What to do with that last sprig of thyme or rosemary? Make a flavoured vinegar – simply add 3 tablespoons dried herbs or a few sprigs of fresh herbs to a clean jar and cover with 1 cup (250 ml) vinegar. We usually use white wine vinegar because it's a good all-rounder, but woody herbs also go nicely with red wine vinegar and apple cider vinegar. Seal the jar and leave for a few weeks. Taste, and if it's full of flavour, strain the herbs and return the vinegar to the jar. Otherwise, leave for a couple more weeks if you would like a herbier-tasting vinegar. It will keep for 2 years.

HERBY SALT

We make herby salts with excess herbs. It's very easy to do and they are a lovely thing to have on the table. First, be sure your herbs are completely dry as any moisture in the herbs can cause mould to grow. Use pure salt, nothing with added iodine or anti-caking agents – the ingredient list on the packet should only read salt. Use 1 tablespoon crushed, chopped or blitzed dried herbs per 100 g (3½ oz) salt. If you have them, add 1 teaspoon dried chilli flakes or dried lemon zest (page 204). Combine well, then store in an airtight container. They will last forever but the flavour will be best within 6 months.

DRIED BEANS

Beans are the dried edible seeds of the legume family, also known as pulses. While you can eat all types of beans in their fresh form, most commonly they are available as dried produce. Legume plants fix nitrogen in the soil, and if used as a rotation crop on farms, they greatly reduce reliance on nitrate fertilisers and support low-impact sustainable agricultural practices. We don't want to get ahead of ourselves, but there's no doubt legumes will increasingly become an environmentally efficient and nutritious way to feed our communities.

Most of the beans we commonly know are imported varieties, but there are a few Australian-grown alternatives. Adzuki beans are red-skinned with a nutty flavour and are sweeter than many other beans. They go very well with brown rice, and are a good alternative to red kidney beans. Broad (fava) beans are widely available fresh in spring or dried all year round. They have a distinctly mealy taste and are very filling. Mash or sauté them or add to stews. Navy or haricot beans are mild-tasting and slightly creamy. They are used in classic baked bean recipes, but we also use them whenever a white bean is called for.

Cooked dried beans have a very mild, nutty and perhaps faintly mushroom flavour. For this reason, they take seasoning and other flavours very well. Combine beans with carbohydrates, such as rice, potatoes, couscous and bread, and their high protein content will be better absorbed by the body, making them a good meat-free option.

Because pulses are versatile and nutritious, you will find them everywhere in this book. Buying dried beans is always going to be the most economical and sustainable choice; what you pay for a can of beans will get you double the amount of dried. And if you go to a bulk-supply shop you can skip the packaging.

GO WITH ...

Dried beans go with so many other ingredients. In French cooking, beans soak up all the fatty goodness of pork in a cassoulet. In Mexican cuisine, dried beans and rice make a complete meal. So, turn to the flavours and spices that will complement the meal you are making. A few surefire ingredients that go with dried beans include onions, leeks, leafy greens, parsley, coriander (cilantro), sage, carrots, parsnips, parmesan and, of course, bacon.

STORAGE AND PREPARATION

Store pulses in an airtight, preferably glass, container in a cool, dark spot, and add a dried bay leaf to prevent weevils. Stored this way, dried beans will keep for years.

The great pulse-eating cultures, such as India and the Middle East, take their time preparing and cooking beans, sometimes soaking them for 48 hours with many changes of water. We can all learn a lot from this kind of care. The better attention you give pulses, the better the results. Pulses need to be soaked to reduce the anti-nutrients that can upset stomachs and make it difficult for us to absorb their nutrients. To soak, cover the amount of beans you are cooking with three times the volume of water and leave at room temperature overnight. If you want to soak them for 48 hours, go right ahead.

As a general rule, the quantity of dried beans doubles or even triples after soaking. Once soaked, discard the soaking water. Add your beans to a large saucepan, cover again with three times the amount of water and bring to the boil. Do not add salt to the cooking water, as this will toughen the skins. Depending on the bean, simmer for 1–2 hours, until tender. Drain, then store in an airtight container in the fridge for up to 3 days.

THE BEST BAKED BEANS

The trick with this recipe is to resist adding anything extra! The flavour here comes from the slow-cooking. We eat these baked beans for breakfast, lunch and dinner.

Soak 200 g (7 oz) dried beans of your choice (we like navy, adzuki or red kidney beans) in plenty of cold water overnight. The next day, drain and rinse the beans well, then place in a large saucepan and cover with plenty of cold water. Bring to the boil, then reduce the heat to low and simmer for about 1 hour or until the beans are soft. Be sure to check that the water hasn't evaporated during cooking. Drain and rinse the cooked beans under cold water. (If using canned beans, drain and rinse 2 x 400 g/ 14 oz cans at this point.) Preheat the oven to 160°C (315°F/Gas mark 2–3). Melt 2 tablespoons butter in a saucepan over medium heat and sauté 1 diced onion until soft and translucent. Add a chopped

bacon rasher, if you like, and sauté until cooked through. Add 1 teaspoon each of smoked paprika and freshly cracked black pepper, then add the drained beans and 400 g (14 oz) canned tomatoes (or 400 ml/14 fl oz of the passata on page 247) and stir until everything is combined. Transfer to a baking dish and cover with foil. Bake for 45 minutes. Uncover the beans, add 1 tablespoon honey or maple syrup, ½ teaspoon salt and ½ cup (125 ml) stock or water if it's looking dry, and bake for a further 30–40 minutes. Season with more salt and pepper. Left-over beans will keep in an airtight container in the fridge for up to 5 days.

Serves 4 with leftovers

MEXICAN-STYLE BEANS AND REFRIED BEANS

We like to serve these beans as part of our Taco Tuesdays (page 97).

Soak 1 cup (200 g) adzuki, black or red kidney beans in plenty of cold water overnight. The next day, drain and rinse the beans well, then place in a large saucepan and cover with plenty of cold water. Bring to the boil, then reduce the heat to low and simmer for about 1 hour or until the beans are soft. Drain and rinse under cold water. Meanwhile, heat 2 tablespoons vegetable oil in a saucepan over medium heat and sauté 1 chopped onion and 4 chopped garlic cloves for 4–5 minutes. Add ½ teaspoon each of ground cumin, coriander, dried oregano, chilli flakes, salt and pepper and stir through. Add the cooked beans and ½ cup (125 ml) stock or water. Cook for about 5 minutes or until everything is combined and only slightly saucy. Serve with tortillas or hard-shell tacos and the rest of your Taco Tuesday condiments.

Serves 4 as part of a shared meal

TO MAKE REFRIED BEANS

These are just your left-over beans mashed. Place cooked beans and a little oil in a saucepan and add enough water or stock to make the beans a little saucy. Cook over medium heat until simmering and the beans have absorbed some of the liquid. Reduce the heat and mash the beans with a potato masher or fork and continue to cook until paste-like.

PEARS

Pears are related to apples, but are less acidic and have a distinct floral creaminess. There is a sweet, sabulous quality to cooked and raw pears that adds both texture and flavour to dishes.

While there are over 3000 varieties of pear, William Bartlett, Bosc and packham pears seem to dominate supermarket shelves. All are often sold unripe, so we begin the week by using firm pears in salads. To ripen pears, either leave them in the fruit bowl with other fruits where they will slowly ripen, or put them in a brown paper bag on your bench. Once they are perfectly ripe, store them in the fridge to stop them over-ripening. Once ripe, we roast or poach them, and when they're finally over-ripe we make chutney, pear butter or a crumble.

Pears are an excellent source of fibre and are effective at keeping your digestive tract in good working order. They are also high in vitamins A and C, making them a healthy staple in winter kitchens.

GO WITH ...

The pear's subtle flavour warms up with spices, such as clove, cinnamon, star anise, nutmeg, ginger and allspice. The more buttery notes in a pear make it a good companion to lemon, orange, yoghurt, nuts and bitter greens, as well as cheeses such as goat's, blue and parmesan.

WASTE TIP

Rescue your mushy old pears and make pear butter (see opposite) or a quick pear chutney. The chutney is delicious with a roast, a bitey cheddar or poached eggs. Follow the apple chutney recipe on page 145, but swap the spices and flavourings for 1 tablespoon chopped rosemary or thyme, the zest and juice of 1 lemon and plenty of freshly cracked black pepper.

Honey caramel roasted pears

ROASTING PEARS

This is one of the most beautiful ways to cook pears – it makes them velvety and taste of caramel. We've included a sweet version to serve with ice cream, cakes, porridge, muesli and yoghurt, plus a savoury version to add to a cheese plate, a leafy salad with parmesan and nuts, or to serve as a side with meats. Roasting firmer pears will take a little longer, which means the pieces maintain their shape and add a little texture. If your pears are very ripe, don't cook them for as long or, better yet, make the pear butter opposite.

HONEY CARAMEL ROASTED PEARS

In this recipe a thick, glossy, buttery caramel forms under the pears, which makes them extra delicious.

Preheat the oven to 180°C (350°F/Gas mark 4). Halve 3–4 pears, cut out the cores and cut the pear halves into long wedges. Place the pear in a small baking dish so they fit snugly, and stir through 2 tablespoons orange butter (page 203) (or 2 tablespoons butter and the zest of 1 orange), 1 tablespoon honey, maple syrup or brown sugar and ½ teaspoon grated nutmeg, ground cinnamon or ground ginger so the pears are evenly coated. Bake for 25 minutes, shaking the dish every now and then, until a caramel has formed on the bottom of the dish and the pear is soft and golden.

SAVOURY-ROASTED PEARS

Preheat the oven to 180°C (350°F/Gas mark 4). Halve 3–4 pears, cut out the cores and cut the pear halves into long wedges. Place the pear on a baking tray, making sure the pieces have some room to move. Drizzle over 1 tablespoon apple cider vinegar and 2 tablespoons olive oil, then sprinkle with ½ teaspoon salt and 1 tablespoon raw sugar. Bake for 20–30 minutes, shaking the pan every now and then, until the pear is golden around the edges and soft in the centre but still holding its shape.

PEAR BUTTER

When there's a few mushy pears in the fruit bowl, make this pear butter. Fruit butters like this one don't actually have any butter in them; they are more of a fruit spread with the consistency of butter. They are lower in sugar than jams, which means they won't last as long, but a jar or two in the fridge is lovely spread on toast, banana bread, pancakes and scones. This is a cheat's version, which ignores straining and uses the whole fruit. It won't win you a preserving prize as it's far too rustic, but it's full of flavour and makes a delicious winter breakfast or afternoon tea.

Place 300–400 g (10½–14 oz) chopped ripe pear in a saucepan with the zest and juice of 1 orange, ½ cup (125 ml) water and a sprig of thyme or rosemary. Simmer over low heat for up to 20 minutes or until the pear is very soft and falling apart. Add 1 tablespoon honey and 1–2 tablespoons brown sugar and simmer over medium heat until the mixture thickens. You can leave it chunky and rustic or blitz with a hand-held blender to a smooth purée. Pour into a clean jar and use within 10 days.

Makes 1 cup (310 g)

BANANAS

Bananas are the world's very first fruit – although ancient bananas, with their large hard seeds and bitter flesh, were very different from the soft, sweet bananas we eat today.

There are more than 500 varieties of bananas in the world, but in Australia the two most popular varieties are cavendish and lady finger. The banana industry has reports of poor environmental and labour standards, but if you choose organic or wax-tipped 'eco' varieties, they are much more likely to be harvested in more sustainable conditions. Because bananas are inexpensive and available all year round, they often get purchased and then left in the fruit bowl until the fruit flies arrive. For this reason, they are one of the most wasted foods. Whatever bananas you buy, try not to forget about them – and if they do go black we have plenty of recipes for turning them into something delicious.

The fruit itself is high in potassium and magnesium, and an excellent source of fibre. The skin, however, is not delicious and sadly destined for the compost bin. Some things are just not meant to be eaten.

Store bananas in the fruit bowl. Once ripe, they can go in the fridge; their skins will go brown but the fruit will be fine. To freeze, peel and chop bananas into small rounds and then store in the freezer. Don't freeze them in their skins!

GO WITH …

The sweetness of banana works well with deep, nutty, earthy flavours and warm spices. Coffee, nuts, chocolate, caramel, coconut, brown sugar, maple syrup, cinnamon, ginger, cloves, coriander (cilantro), bourbon, whiskey and rum all pair wonderfully with banana.

USE IT ALL

Everyone knows how to make banana bread and banana smoothies. For something different, try the black banana jam, quick banana chutney, banana whip and homemade dried banana chips, opposite.

QUICK BANANA AND COCONUT CHUTNEY

This fast-cooking chutney is a great condiment to serve with curries, grilled fish, rice and lentils, and tastes wonderful with a bitey cheddar on rye. Try it with the curried vegetable pocket pies on page 216 or the dal on page 135.

Heat 3 tablespoons vegetable oil in a saucepan over medium heat. Add 1 finely chopped onion and 1 teaspoon salt and sauté for 4–5 minutes, until the onion is soft and sweet. Add 1 tablespoon grated ginger, ½ teaspoon ground turmeric, 1 teaspoon mustard seeds, 1 teaspoon cumin seeds, 1 teaspoon chilli flakes and a pinch of cayenne pepper. Sauté until fragrant, then add up to 2 cups (400–500 g) roughly chopped over-ripe banana, 100 ml (3½ fl oz) apple cider vinegar or white wine vinegar and 2 tablespoons caster (superfine) sugar. Simmer over medium heat, stirring often, for 5–8 minutes, until the chutney starts to thicken. Add ½ cup (45 g) desiccated coconut and mix well. Taste, and add more salt or chilli if needed. Simmer for another minute or two until the chutney is thick and glossy, then allow to cool and store in a jar or airtight container in the fridge for up to 1 month. It tastes even better after a few days!

Makes 1 x 400 ml (14 fl oz) jar

BANANA WHIP: THE QUICKEST ICE CREAM EVER

This takes 5 minutes to make, uses up all the bananas in your freezer and tastes just as good as ice cream. The riper the banana, the tastier the whip!

Break up 4 frozen bananas and place them in a food processor with ½ teaspoon ground cinnamon, 1 teaspoon vanilla extract and a squeeze of lemon juice. Whiz until the banana forms a smooth paste – if the texture feels too crumbly, add 1–2 tablespoons cream or yoghurt, or if you want it sweeter add 1–2 tablespoons brown sugar, then whiz again. For an adults' version, add 1–2 tablespoons rum. Serve.

Serves 4–6

BANANA CHIPS

Eat these banana chips as a snack or make a trail mix with equal amounts banana chips, cashews, toasted seeds and dried coconut shavings.

Preheat the oven to 100°C (210°F/Gas mark ½). Slice up your banana and place in a bowl with a squeeze of lemon juice. Toss gently. Place the banana slices on a baking sheet and bake for about 1½ hours, then turn the chips over and bake for another 1½ hours or until crisp and golden. Store in an airtight container for 2 weeks.

BLACK BANANA JAM

Just when you think your bananas are destined for the bin, make this jam: it tastes of caramel and makes French toast and crêpes even more delicious.

Mash 3–4 over-ripe bananas and place in a saucepan with the zest and juice of 1 lemon or orange, a splash of vanilla extract, a pinch of ground cinnamon and ⅓ cup (60 g) brown sugar. Pour in 100 ml (3½ fl oz) water or apple juice and combine well. Place over low heat and stir to dissolve the sugar. Increase the heat to medium and cook down for 10–15 minutes, until the mixture is thick and glossy brown. Spoon into a clean jar and store in the fridge for up to 3 weeks.

Makes about 320 g (11½ oz)

GINGER

Ginger has a spicy, warm and lemony flavour. It is closely related to turmeric, cardamom and galangal and, depending on the freshness of the ginger you buy, you can smell the traces of these relatives. Because ginger lends itself to so many cuisines and is used in both sweet and savoury dishes, it is an indispensable ingredient.

For as long as ginger has been used for culinary purposes, it has also been used medicinally. It is one of the few home remedies for colds and nausea that continue to be made in kitchens. Ginger has trace amounts of iron, magnesium, potassium and vitamin C. It is the compound gingerol that is anti-inflammatory and anti-microbial, with properties that support immune health and can help with acute discomforts, such as sore throats.

Ginger is available all year round and there are two harvest times. In late summer to early autumn, young tender ginger is available. This is a soft buttery colour with blushing pink spots on the skin that you don't need to peel. Its flavour is more delicate and less spicy. Eat it fresh and grate into stir-fries and salads.

More readily available is fully mature ginger, which is harvested in autumn and winter when the plant dies back. This ginger is a light-beige colour and looks more knobbly. The higher oil content in mature ginger means that it is warmer and spicier. It has a thin, papery skin that we rarely remove, but if the ginger is old it can become tough. We use mature ginger for cooking and baking. Store young ginger in the fridge and mature ginger on the kitchen bench.

GOES WITH ...

Ginger goes with so many ingredients that this list could be inexhaustible, but we use it a lot with pumpkin (squash), sweet potato, carrots, green beans, bok choy, cabbage and chilli. When it comes to fruit, we like to pair ginger with apple, pear, all types of citrus, rhubarb and dried fruit.

USE IT ALL

Don't let the last knob of ginger go mouldy in the fridge! Either grate or slice it, then freeze it for up to 6 months, or try pickling it or adding it to kitchen scrap paste (see opposite).

QUICK PICKLED GINGER

Always keep a jar of this in the fridge. The best thing about it is that you can keep adding ginger to it. So all the knobbly ends that usually go wrinkly and mouldy in the fridge can be thinly sliced and just popped in the jar. Finely dice the pickled ginger for stir-fries and dipping sauces, or mince and serve with oysters. Toss through a noodle salad and use the brine as your dressing, or add to the Vietnamese salad on page 96.

Finely slice 200 g (7 oz) washed and dried ginger (there is no need to peel it if you do this). Place the slices in a bowl and cover with 1 tablespoon salt, mixing through with your hands. Leave to stand for 1 hour, then strain away the water, lay the ginger on a tea towel and wring out all the excess salt and moisture. Place the ginger in a clean jar, making sure you separate the slices as you go. Make a brine by combining 1 cup (250 ml) rice wine vinegar and ¼ cup (55 g) caster (superfine) sugar in a saucepan over low heat. Stir to dissolve the sugar and bring to a simmer. Pour the brine over the ginger, making sure it is completely submerged. Allow to cool and then store in the fridge forever!

Makes 200 g (7 oz)

GINGER COOKIES

You only need a bowl, a fork and a spoon to make these super-gingery cookies. They are perfect with a cuppa.

Using a fork, whisk ¾ cup (185 g) softened butter and 1 cup (185 g) lightly packed brown sugar together in a bowl. Add 4–5 tablespoons grated ginger, 1 beaten egg and the zest of 1 lemon and set aside. In another bowl, sift together 2¼ cups (335 g) plain (all-purpose) flour and 1 teaspoon baking powder. Fold the butter mixture into the flour mixture until incorporated. Pull the dough together, cover and rest in the fridge for 1 hour. Preheat the oven to 180°C (350°F/Gas mark 4). Place tablespoon-sized balls on a lined baking tray, then press down lightly and sprinkle with flaked sea salt. Bake for 15 minutes or until cooked through, then set aside on a wire rack to cool.

Makes 30

SPICY KITCHEN SCRAP PASTE

This is an excellent waste-warrior recipe that uses up that last little bit of ginger to make a delicious spice paste. It's amazing in laksas, broths and stir-fries, as a marinade for fish, and stirred through yoghurt to baste grilled chicken thighs. You'll only need a very small amount to get a good punch of flavour. Save up your scraps in a container in the fridge until you have enough to make this.

You need 200 g (7 oz) kitchen scraps to make this paste: ginger, garlic, onion, spring onions (scallions), chillies, carrot, celery, coriander (cilantro) leaves and stems all work well. Blitz your ingredients in a food processor with 2 teaspoons salt to make a paste. Transfer to a clean jar or container and store in the fridge for up to 1 month.

Makes about 200 g (7 oz)

USE IT ALL LOAF

Makes 1 loaf

This tea loaf recipe is a staple at the Cornersmith cafe and in our kitchens at home. We love it because you can throw in any grated fruits or vegetables, any nuts, seeds or choc chips and any spices you need to use up and it always works. Avoid very over-ripe fruit as it will make the loaf too wet.

We eat this for breakfast, pop it into lunchboxes and serve it with tea in the afternoon.

150 g (1 cup) self-raising flour
¼ teaspoon bicarbonate of soda
   (baking soda)
¼ teaspoon salt
1 teaspoon ground spice
   cinnamon
   ginger
   nutmeg
   allspice

2 eggs
½ cup (110 g) caster (superfine)
   or raw sugar
150 ml (5 fl oz) sunflower or
   good-quality vegetable oil
300 g (10½ oz) grated fruit
   or vegetables
   apple
   pear
   carrot
   pumpkin (squash)
   beetroot (beets)
   zucchini (courgette)

75 g (2½ oz) pantry strays,
   plus extra to top
   choc chips
   dried fruits
   nuts
   seeds
   or a combination

Preheat the oven to 180°C (350°F/Gas mark 4). Line the base of a 23 cm (9 inch) loaf (bar) tin with baking paper.

Whisk the flour, bicarbonate of soda, salt and ground spice in a large bowl.

Using electric beaters, beat the eggs and sugar until pale, thick and frothy. Slowly add the oil and continue to beat for a few more minutes until smooth and well combined. Add the grated fruit or vegetables and stir to combine.

Fold the wet mixture into the dry mix, adding your choice of pantry strays. Pour the batter into the prepared tin and scatter a few extra nuts or seeds over the top.

Bake for 50–60 minutes or until a skewer inserted in the centre of the loaf comes out clean. Leave to cool a little before turning out of the tin onto a wire rack to cool.

This loaf will last, well wrapped, for up to 1 week.

COMBINATIONS WE LIKE

Try any of the following combinations:

- Pumpkin (squash), apple, ground ginger and pepitas (pumpkin seeds)
- Beetroot (beet), pear, allspice and choc chip
- Zucchini (courgette), apple and hazelnut.

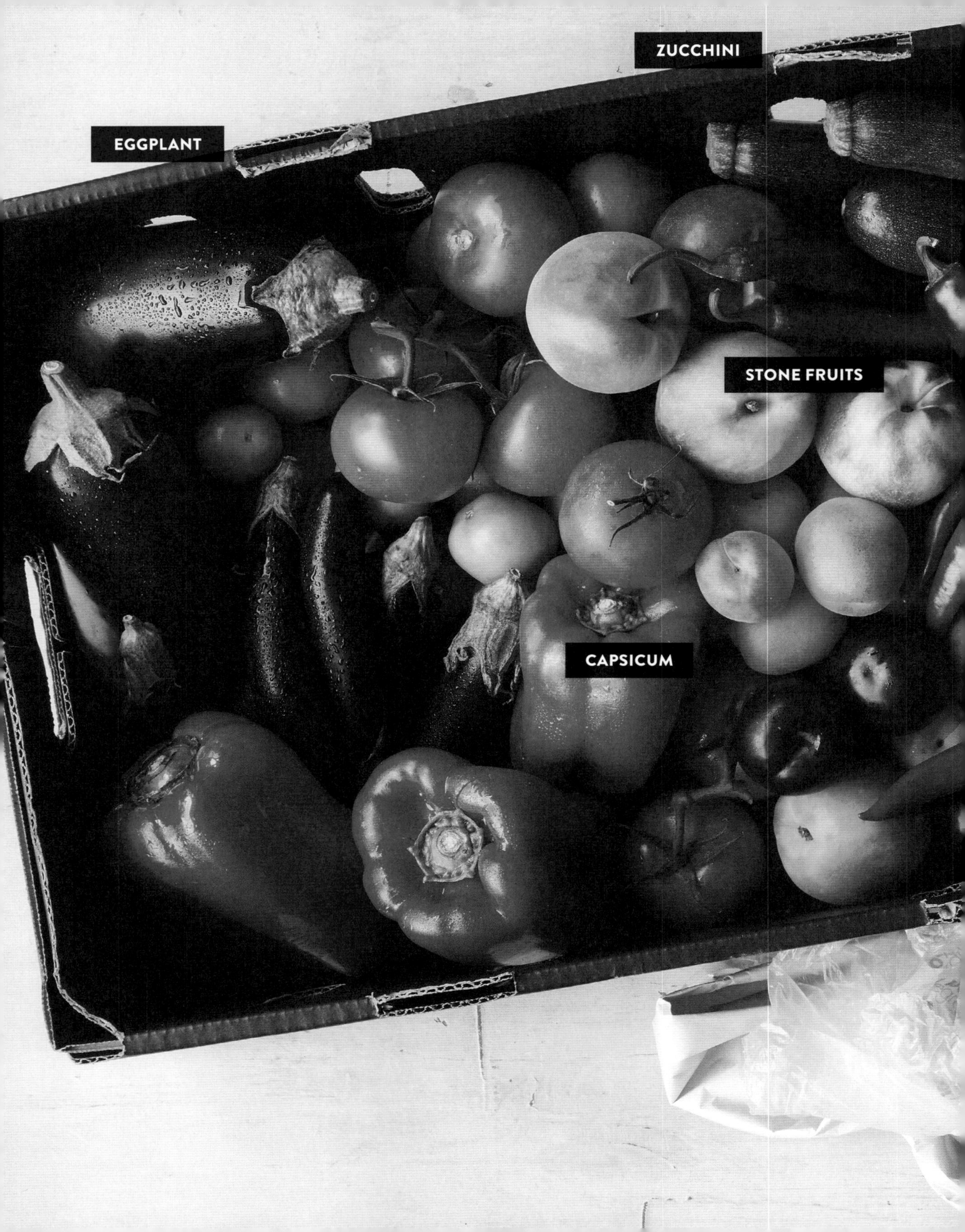
ZUCCHINI
EGGPLANT
STONE FRUITS
CAPSICUM

SHOPPING BASKET 8

Cooking in summer seems simpler, with an abundance of ingredients whose flavours come together easily. Now is the time for tomatoes and stone fruits to be eaten fresh at every meal. For preservers, this is the season to get busy in the kitchen, making passata, hot sauces and summer-fruit jams. The recipes in this basket have been feeding our friends and families for many summers. They honour an old-world philosophy in the kitchen where nothing is wasted: wrinkly vegetables, stale bread and over-ripe fruits are loved for their potential, and not thrown away because of their imperfections.

TOMATOES

BASIL

CHILLI

MINCE

FROM THIS BASKET ...

MEALS

Zucchini, mince and bread kofta (page 251)

Summer harvest lasagne (page 254)

Stir-fried chilli eggplant (page 259)

Less-meat mince for burgers (page 267)

French toast (page 269)

SIDES

Simple tomato salad (page 248)

Tomato rice (page 249)

Zucchini mash (page 251)

Simple zucchini salad (page 251)

Ratatouille (page 252)

Harissa-roasted eggplant (page 259)

Basil pesto (page 263)

Spiced mince (page 265)

Panzanella (page 270)

Simple peach salad (page 273)

Grilled peaches with honey and salt (page 273)

SNACKS, SWEETS & DRINKS

Basil ice cream (page 263)

Basil-infused booze (page 263)

Croutons (page 269)

Crackers from old bread (page 269)

Plum and honey ice blocks (page 273)

Cornersmith muffins (page 276)

QUICK PRESERVING IDEAS

All-purpose roasted tomato sauce (page 247)

Quick tomato ketchup (page 249)

Roasted wrinkly vegetable pickle (page 256)

Roasted capsicum harissa (page 258)

Indian eggplant kasundi (page 259)

Easy sambal (page 261)

Make your own chilli flakes (page 261)

Homemade jam (page 274)

NOTHING GOES TO WASTE

Slow-roasted wrinkly tomatoes (page 248)

Semi-dried tomatoes (page 248)

Fermented chilli paste (page 261)

Breadcrumbs (page 269)

TOMATOES

Tomatoes have travelled far from their South American origins to become so central to cooking the world over that consumers demand they are available year round. While we can buy insipid tomatoes in the dark of winter, they have been grown in hothouses, picked green and sprayed to ripen off the vine. They look like a tomato, but do they really taste like a tomato?

The real tomato season runs from late spring to early autumn, peaking in the summer months. This is when tomatoes are sun-ripened and burst with a sweet acidic flavour that does nothing to put an end to the confusion of whether they are a fruit or a vegetable (for the record, they are a fruit). At the very beginning of the season, unripe green tomatoes are available. Their flavour is more sour and a bit leafy, and they are great for pickling.

The taste of a ripe summer tomato is something to savour. During the season, our home and work kitchens get busy as we make enough passata, canned tomatoes and ketchup to keep us well stocked throughout the rest of the year.

For those less inclined to preserve, tomato season means eating as many tasty tomatoes as you can every day – we suggest you buy them by the bucket and include them in every meal. You can also cook tomatoes down and use them as you would passata. Of course, buying canned tomatoes is a convenience few will give up. Choose locally processed tomatoes free from additives and avoid those with added seasoning. They don't taste very nice, and it's easy to add your own basil.

Tomatoes are rich in vitamins A and C, as well as potassium. They are also high in the antioxidant lycopene, which may protect the skin from ultraviolet rays (not that a tomato sandwich at the beach is a replacement for sunscreen).

Keep ripe tomatoes at room temperature for a few days. Once ripe, store them in the fridge for a few more days and start thinking about making passata.

GO WITH ...

Tomatoes can vary from tart to sugar-sweet depending on the season and growing conditions. A ripe tomato is also a little salty and possesses the elusive umami; that is, for all a tomato's sweetness, they also have a savoury complexity that lingers. Fresh tomatoes pair so well with basil that together they are practically a meal. They also go with hard cheeses, olives, cucumber, salad greens and olive oil, as well as garlic and ginger. Combine tomatoes with other fruits, such as cherries, peaches and strawberries, for instant show-off salads. The combination of cooked tomatoes, eggplant (aubergine) and capsicum (pepper) can never go wrong. Cooked tomatoes also love every kind of meat and seafood. In short, tomatoes play well with others.

USE IT ALL

The quick tomato ketchup on page 249 is our handy tip for using up a couple of very soft and wrinkly tomatoes. It only takes 15 minutes to make and tastes so much better than supermarket versions.

ALL-PURPOSE ROASTED TOMATO SAUCE

Makes 4–6 cups (1–1.5 litres)

Also referred to as passata (once it has been blended smooth), this rich and flavoursome tomato sauce is put to use in pastas, stews and soups or on pizza bases. The tomatoes are roasted to intensify their flavour and this sauce can be eaten as is – rustic and chunky – or blitzed in a food processor. If you have a mouli, use it now! It removes the skins and seeds from your sauce, which can be bitter, and transforms your roasted tomatoes into a traditional Italian-style passata. This sauce freezes really well or, if you're a preserver, bottle it and follow the instructions below to make it safe to store in the pantry.

2 kg (5 lb 8 oz) ripe tomatoes, halved
1 onion, cut into wedges
½ head garlic, separated into unpeeled cloves
100 ml (3½ fl oz) olive oil
2 teaspoons salt
1 teaspoon freshly cracked black pepper
Handful of torn basil leaves (optional)

Preheat the oven to 180°C (350°F/Gas mark 4).

Place the tomato halves, cut-side up, on two baking trays, along with the onion wedges and garlic cloves. Drizzle the olive oil over the top and season with the salt and pepper, then mix well with your hands. Roast for up to 45 minutes, or until the tomatoes are blistered and the onion is starting to soften and brown. Remove the trays from the oven and set aside to cool for 15 minutes.

Tip everything into a bowl and, once cool enough to handle, squeeze the garlic out of their skins and mix through the tomato and onion, breaking everything up with a fork. Add the basil leaves if you want some extra flavour.

You can serve the sauce as is, tossed through hot pasta, or blitz in a food processor for a smooth consistency, or run the mixture through a mouli. If you want your passata to be thicker, slowly simmer it in a saucepan over low heat until it reaches your desired consistency. For pizza sauce, reduce the sauce even further until thick and rich.

The sauce will last for 4–5 days in the fridge or up to 3 months in the freezer.

To preserve your passata, follow the instructions on page 278 to sterilise jars or bottles. Using a funnel, fill the hot jars up to the thread with the hot passata (reheat it if necessary). Wipe the rim with a clean cloth and seal. Heat-process (see page 278) the jars for 1 hour and then store in a cool, dark place for up to 1 year.

HOW TO USE

- Stir through pasta with olives or capers, lots of fresh basil and shavings of the salted ricotta on page 37 or parmesan
- Add 2 cups (500 ml) passata to 2 cups (500 ml) stock and you have the base of a minestrone soup (page 189)
- Use in the baked bean recipe on page 233
- Use in the lentil stew on page 137
- Make the tomato soup on page 191.

SLOW-ROASTED WRINKLY TOMATOES

During tomato season, we make sure we have a container of these in the fridge at all times! It's an excellent way of cooking tomatoes that need to be used up. Slow-roasting tomatoes hides all their blemishes, concentrates their flavour and means you have an excellent accompaniment on stand-by for eggs, toasties and pasta, and as a side with pies, rice dishes or grilled meats. Alternatively, try making the tarte tatin on page 209 using slow-roasted tomatoes instead of blood oranges. It makes a simple yet impressive-looking tart, which can be served with a green salad for lunch or dinner.

Preheat the oven to 120°C (235°F/Gas mark ½). Place halved or quartered tomatoes (cherry tomatoes can stay whole) in a bowl and lightly drizzle with olive oil, salt and cracked black pepper. If you like your tomatoes sweet, add 1 teaspoon caster (superfine) sugar as well. Spread the tomatoes out on a baking tray, making sure they have plenty of space around them. Slowly roast for 2–3 hours, until the tomatoes are rich in colour and deep in flavour.

Store in an airtight container in the fridge for up to 1 week.

SEMI-DRIED TOMATOES

You can also follow the above method to make semi-dried tomatoes.

Once the tomato has slow-roasted for 2–3 hours, reduce the temperature to 80°C (175°F/Gas mark ¼) and continue roasting for another few hours until they are almost dried, but still have a plumpness to them. Once cooled, you can store semi-dried tomatoes in a jar and cover them with olive oil or left-over pickling brine (or a combination of both), adding a few basil stems or a whole chilli to the jar for some more flavour. They will last for a few weeks in the fridge. Keep in mind that the drier your tomatoes are, the longer they will last.

SIMPLE TOMATO SALAD

If you think you can't make impressive salads, then try this and enjoy all the compliments. The key is to let the ingredients marinate together at room temperature for at least 15 minutes before serving. This salad is also wonderful with green tomatoes, or try a mix of both red and green.

Thinly slice 3–4 ripe tomatoes into rounds and layer on a plate or in a shallow bowl. Add a minced garlic clove or two if you want a punch of flavour, 1½ tablespoons good-quality vinegar, such as apple cider, sherry or red wine, 1½ tablespoons olive oil, ½ teaspoon salt and cracked black pepper and a pinch of caster (superfine) sugar. Set aside at room temperature for at least 15 minutes before drizzling over a little more olive oil and serving. You can also top the salad with fresh herbs, sliced olives or crispy capers, or thin slices of bocconcini or buffalo mozzarella and a generous handful of basil leaves.

Serves 4 as a side

TOMATO RICE

This is a good recipe to make when provisions are low and there are only tomatoes and rice in the house. It's simple, tasty and fills everyone up with little effort. Serve with a fried egg and condiments, grilled fish, roast vegetables or as part of a Mexican feast. Tomato rice is made in households around the world, so change the flavours depending on what you're serving it with. Indian or Malaysian spices work well, as do Spanish flavours, plenty of fresh herbs and lemon.

Preheat the oven to 180°C (350°F/Gas mark 4). Roughly chop 2 large or 3 medium-sized tomatoes (you can also use canned tomatoes if you don't have fresh), 1 small onion and 2 garlic cloves. Blitz in a food processor until puréed. You will need 2 cups (500 ml) of purée, so add another tomato if you need more liquid.

Heat 3 tablespoons olive oil in a flameproof casserole dish over medium heat and add 1¼ cups (250 g) white rice, ½ teaspoon each of salt and cracked black pepper, 2 teaspoons lemon zest, ½ teaspoon optional chilli flakes and ⅓ cup (20 g) chopped coriander (cilantro). Lightly toast the rice until it starts to crackle, then add the tomato purée and 1 cup (250 ml) vegetable stock or water with a little extra salt, and stir. Bring the mixture to a simmer, then cover and place in the oven for 15 minutes. Remove the dish from the oven and stir the rice. Taste to see if the rice is cooked and check the seasoning. Add more salt and pepper or chilli if needed, then re-cover and cook for a further 5 minutes. Remove from the oven, fluff up the rice with a fork and serve.

If you want to add Spanish flavours or are serving the rice as part of a Mexican-style feast, add ½ teaspoon each of ground cumin and sweet or smoked paprika when you add the lemon zest.

Serves 4–6

QUICK TOMATO KETCHUP

This is a quick ketchup that we make at home when there's a few extra wrinkly tomatoes lying around and we can't bear watching the children eat store-bought ketchup any more.

In a saucepan over medium–low heat, place 2 cups (400 g) roughly chopped tomatoes, 2 tablespoons apple cider vinegar, 2 tablespoons brown sugar, 1 grated garlic clove, 1 teaspoon salt, ½ teaspoon paprika, ½ teaspoon ground cumin and 2 cloves. Stir to dissolve the sugar and salt, then simmer for 15–20 minutes or until the sauce is thick and the tomatoes are pulpy. Allow to cool, then blitz with a hand-held blender or in a food processor. Store in the fridge for up to 1 week.

Makes 1 cup (250 ml)

EGGPLANT, ZUCCHINI AND CAPSICUM

These are the stars of the summer harvest. Eggplant (aubergine) and capsicum (pepper) both belong to the genus *Solanum*, while zucchini (courgette) is a summer melon. What all three have in common, other than the fact they are fruits and not vegetables, is their slightly bitter flavour that transforms into sweet lusciousness when cooked. In summer, they are staple ingredients in the kitchen and their versatility makes them inexhaustible.

Eggplant, zucchini and capsicum are all thin-skinned and should be stored in the same way: unwashed and whole in a paper bag in the fridge, keeping the bag open to allow air to circulate. Stored correctly, they should stay fresh for 10 days.

EGGPLANT (AUBERGINE)

Native to southern Asia where they still grow wild, eggplants have been cultivated in China and India for thousands of years. The spongy mild flesh soaks up oils and sauces when cooked, transforming the eggplant's texture into a hearty richness that is somewhat meaty. Eggplant is high in fibre and, like any deeply coloured fruits and vegetables, it is also high in antioxidants. Avoid disappointment and don't eat raw eggplant.

ZUCCHINI (COURGETTE)

The zucchini's ancestor originates in Mesoamerica, but the zucchini we know today was developed in Italy in the 19th century. It has since become a classic ingredient in Italian cooking.

When selecting zucchini, smaller is better, as larger zucchini are more watery and have less taste. Zucchini is particularly high in vitamins A and B and potassium.

CAPSICUM (PEPPER)

Native to South America, the capsicum belongs to the family that also includes chillies. Available in a gradient colour spectrum from green through to red, each colour has a different flavour, with green being the most bitter and grassy, and yellow, red and orange being sweeter and fruitier.

GO WITH ...

Raw zucchini and capsicum are mildly bitter and fresh-tasting, and can be thrown into salads or paired with leafy greens or soft herbs. As mentioned above, raw eggplant should be avoided. When cooked, all three become sweeter and more mellow with a sumptuous texture. Cook them slowly with woody herbs to complement their warmth, or pair with strong flavours such as cumin, paprika, ground coriander, black pepper, garlic, ginger and olives.

USE IT ALL

Our wrinkly vegetable pickle recipe on page 256 will put a stop to any of these vegetables ending up in the compost.

ZUCCHINI MASH

This dish is perfect for using up zucchini (courgettes) that have seen better days. Eat this as a side to koftas, sausages or fish, in pasta or on pizza, or on toast with an egg for lunch.

Start by slicing 500 g (1 lb 2 oz) zucchini into 1 cm (½ inch) thick rounds. In a heavy-based saucepan, heat ⅓ cup (80 ml) olive oil or 75 g (2½ oz) butter over medium heat. Add 2 crushed garlic cloves and stir for a few seconds, taking care not to burn the garlic. Add the zucchini, ½ teaspoon fennel seeds, ½ teaspoon chilli flakes (optional) and ½ teaspoon each salt and cracked black pepper. Reduce the heat to low, then cover and gently cook for 20 minutes. Remove the lid and cook for a further 10–15 minutes to reduce the liquid. During this time, the zucchini will collapse and become a mash all on their own. Taste and add a good squeeze of lemon juice and an extra pinch of salt, if you like.

Serves 2 as a side

ZUCCHINI, MINCE AND BREAD KOFTA

Reducing your meat intake while not forgoing flavour is much easier than you might think. These koftas use very little mince, but there is so much flavour you won't miss it at all.

Grate 2 zucchini (courgettes), then sprinkle with ¼ teaspoon salt and set aside. Tear 1 cup stale bread or old bread crusts into 3 cm (1¼ inch) pieces and soak in ⅓ cup (80 ml) milk or stock and set aside. In a bowl, place 300 g (10½ oz) lamb mince, 2 minced garlic cloves, ½ cup (15 g) chopped herbs such as parsley, dill or basil and ¼ teaspoon each of salt and cracked black pepper. Mix well to combine, then gently squeeze the liquid from the bread and add the bread to the mince mixture. Squeeze as much moisture as you can from the zucchini and then stir through the mixture. Form into 40 g (1½ oz) oval-shaped kofta or meatballs, then set aside in the fridge for 20 minutes. Heat 100 ml (3½ fl oz) vegetable oil in a frying pan over medium heat and fry the koftas or meatballs in batches until golden. Drain on paper towel and serve with flatbreads (page 199) and the simple tomato salad on page 248.

Makes about 16

SIMPLE ZUCCHINI SALAD

This is the salad Alex makes when she's asked to bring a salad. Quick to prepare, pretty and fresh, it is an excellent alternative to a basic green salad. Make sure you use a mandoline or vegetable peeler to make the thin zucchini (courgette) ribbons; they look much more impressive!

Combine ¼ cup (35 g) currants and a good splash of apple cider vinegar in a small bowl and set aside. Very thinly slice, mandoline or ribbon using a vegetable peeler 3 zucchini and gently place in a flattish dish. Sprinkle with a few generous pinches of salt and cracked black pepper, a squeeze of lemon juice and a pinch of chilli flakes. Add 2 handfuls of basil leaves plus the soaked currants and gently mix. Taste, and add more salt and pepper if needed, then drizzle with good-quality olive oil and the currant-soaked apple cider vinegar. Lightly mix and serve immediately. For a heartier version, add toasted nuts of your choice and dollops of ricotta or feta.

Serves 4 as a side salad

RATATOUILLE

Makes 1.3 kg (3 lb)

This dish is an excellent way to use up summer vegetables, especially those that have sat in the crisper for too long. The low and slow cooking time disguises any blemishes and wrinkles and turns tired vegetables into a harmony of summer flavours.

Serve this ratatouille with polenta and goat's cheese or with the tomato rice on page 249. It also makes a great base for baked eggs (see page 21) or as a side with any grilled meats, fish or roast chicken.

We often find that kids don't like eggplants, but if you purée the ratatouille in a food processor it turns into a cleverly disguised vegetarian sauce to use in a pasta bake or lasagne (see page 254).

1–1.5 kg (2 lb 4 oz–3 lb 5 oz)
    mix of eggplants (aubergines),
    red capsicums (peppers) and
    zucchini (courgettes)
Salt
½ cup (125 ml) olive oil
1 onion, thinly sliced
3 garlic cloves, minced
½ teaspoon freshly cracked
    black pepper
A few bay leaves, a sprig of thyme
    or left-over basil stems
2 ripe tomatoes or 400 g (14 oz)
    canned tomatoes

If you're using eggplants, cut them into 3–4 cm (1¼–1½ inch) chunks, then place in a bowl and sprinkle with salt, using 1 teaspoon of salt per eggplant. Mix well and set aside. Thinly slice the capsicum and cut the zucchini into thin rounds.

Heat the olive oil in a flameproof casserole dish over medium heat and sauté the onion and capsicum for 20 minutes until soft and sweet. Add the minced garlic, ½ teaspoon salt, the pepper and herbs and sauté for another minute.

Tip the eggplant in a tea towel and give it a good scrunch to remove the salt and liquid, then add to the dish and sauté for 5–7 minutes. Add the zucchini and tomato, mix well, then cover. Reduce the heat to the lowest setting and gently cook for 30 minutes.

Remove the lid and give everything a good stir. It's up to you when you want to stop cooking the ratatouille: 30 minutes will give you a light, fresh summer stew, while another 30 minutes or more will result in a rich colour and deep flavour as the vegetables start to fall apart and meld into each other. A final 15–30 minutes of cooking, uncovered, will thicken the ratatouille, which works well if you're looking to use it as a pasta sauce or lasagne filling.

Before turning off the heat, taste and stir through more salt and pepper if needed.

SUMMER HARVEST LASAGNE

Serves 4–6

FOUNDATION RECIPE

This lasagne is gobbled up every time it hits the table and it appears the kids haven't cottoned on to the fact that it's full of their most-hated vegetables: eggplants (aubergines) and zucchini (courgettes). Make this a day or two after you've made a big batch of the ratatouille on page 252. Most of the work is done, so all you need to do is assemble and cook. We make a seasonal version of this lasagne depending on what produce is around. See below for some ideas.

Olive oil
3 cups (750 g) ratatouille
   (page 252)
1 quantity cheese sauce (page 100)
6 large lasagne sheets
¼ cup (25 g) grated parmesan
Salad of your choice, to serve

Preheat the oven to 180°C (350°F/Gas mark 4). Lightly oil a 20 cm (8 inch) square baking dish.

Place the ratatouille in a food processor and blitz to suit who you are feeding. A complete purée disguises all the vegetables and creates a smooth and decadent lasagne, while a chunkier vegetable mixture will give you a hearty, more rustic-looking lasagne.

Make the cheese sauce, then layer lasagne sheets, ratatouille and cheese sauce until the dish is full and all the elements are used up. Finish with a layer of cheese sauce and a little grated parmesan.

Bake in the oven following the lasagne packet instructions and serve with a green salad, the simple zucchini salad on page 251 or the panzanella salad on page 270 if you're feeding more people.

COMBINATIONS WE LIKE

Replace the ratatouille with the same amount of the following sauces for excellent meat-free lasagne ideas:

- Mushroom bolognese (page 152)
- Pumpkin and sage sauce (page 220)
- A mix of slow-roasted wrinkly tomatoes (page 248) and passata (page 247).

ROASTED WRINKLY VEGETABLE PICKLE

Makes 1 x 500 ml (17 fl oz) jar

Make this recipe! This antipasto-style pickle is the most delicious way to rescue very tired-looking vegetables. By roasting, then covering the ingredients in a light vinegar brine and oil, you end up with preserved vegetables, a little like those you find at Italian delicatessens. This pickle will last for a few weeks in the fridge if you don't eat it all in one go. We eat it on toast with ricotta or curd, stirred through pasta or a panzanella salad (page 270), served on a cheese board or pizzas, in burgers and toasties or as a side at a barbecue. Just don't tell your friends that it's actually pickled compost!

500 g (1 lb 2 oz) wrinkly vegetables
 eggplants (aubergines)
 capsicums (peppers)
 zucchini (courgettes)
 fennel
 cauliflower
 onions
 chillies
3 tablespoons olive or vegetable oil, plus an extra ⅓ cup (80 ml) to seal your jar or container
1 teaspoon salt
1 cup (250 ml) white wine vinegar
⅓ cup (75 g) caster (superfine) sugar
Flavourings of your choice (choose two or three)
 2 sliced garlic cloves
 a little lemon peel or zest
 a little orange peel or zest
 1 rosemary sprig
 1 teaspoon peppercorns
 1 oregano sprig
 1 teaspoon chilli flakes
 1 teaspoon fennel seeds
 1 teaspoon coriander seeds
 1 teaspoon cumin seeds

Preheat the oven to 180°C (350°F/Gas mark 4).

Chop your vegetables into good-sized wedges, then place on a baking tray and drizzle over the olive or vegetable oil and half the salt. Mix well with your hands to combine, then spread out the vegetables in an even layer so they have room to char a little at the edges. Roast for 20–30 minutes, until cooked and starting to brown, but not falling apart.

While your vegetables are roasting, make a brine by combining the vinegar, ½ cup (125 ml) water, the sugar and remaining salt in a saucepan over low heat. Stir to dissolve the sugar and salt, then bring to the boil. Once boiling, remove from the heat.

Place your chosen flavourings in a clean jar or airtight container, then pack in your roasted vegetables and pour over the hot brine, making sure the vegetables are completely covered. Cover the surface with the extra oil, then seal and store in the fridge for up to 3 weeks. Allow to sit at least overnight before eating, but it will taste even better after 3–4 days.

COMBINATIONS WE LIKE

- Cauliflower, turmeric, cumin and coriander seeds
- Fennel, orange zest, chilli and fennel seeds
- Onion, woody herbs, lemon and garlic
- Eggplant (aubergine), zucchini (courgette), chilli, garlic and oregano.

ROASTED CAPSICUM HARISSA

An iconic and indispensable condiment in kitchens across North Africa and the Middle East, harissa has a similar status to hummus.

Preheat the oven to 200°C (400°F/Gas mark 6). Quarter 500 g (1 lb 2 oz) capsicums (peppers) and chop a small brown or red onion into wedges. Place on a baking tray and drizzle over 50 ml (1¾ fl oz) olive oil, along with ½ teaspoon salt. Mix well, then spread out on the tray and roast for 30 minutes. Allow to cool.

Thinly slice 20–50 g (¾–1¾ oz) red chillies (depending on how hot your chillies are – if they are powerful, remove the seeds and go easy; you can always add more later). Roughly chop 2 garlic cloves. Transfer the chilli and garlic to a food processor and add the capsicum and onion, 1 teaspoon ground cumin, 1 teaspoon caraway seeds, ½ teaspoon smoked paprika and salt, a pinch of cayenne pepper and 3 tablespoons apple cider vinegar or left-over pickling brine. Purée to a smooth consistency, then taste and add more salt, chilli or cayenne pepper if needed. If the harissa still looks a little dry, add a splash more vinegar and a little oil and purée again. Spoon into a clean jar or airtight container, cover with oil and seal. It will keep in the fridge for up to 3 weeks.

Makes 1 x 400 ml (14 fl oz) jar

IDEAS FOR HARISSA

This vibrant spicy sauce is so versatile! Once you've tried all the ideas listed here, add a tablespoon or two to yoghurt along with a squeeze of lime for a spicy dressing, or brush it over grilled corn with plenty of butter. It's also a nice condiment with an omelette or fried eggs.

ON PIZZA
Dollop a few teaspoons of harissa onto the potato and sausage pizza on page 139 before cooking.

IN TOMATO RICE
For a spicy version of the tomato rice on page 249, add 2 tablespoons harissa to the puréed tomatoes before adding the rice.

AS A CONDIMENT
Add 3 tablespoons harissa and a good pinch of salt to ⅓ cup (90 g) mayo or ketchup for a condiment with a kick to have with barbecued corn, burgers, koftas, fritters or wedges.

FOR ROASTING VEG
Coat diced veggies (carrots, pumpkin/squash, cauliflower, sweet potato, etc.) in a little oil and mix through a few tablespoons of harissa and a pinch of salt before roasting.

MAKE A MARINADE
Combine ½ cup (125 g) natural yoghurt, ⅓ cup harissa, the juice of 1 lime, ½ teaspoon salt and 1 minced garlic clove and use as a marinade for fish, chicken or lamb.

IN HUMMUS
Stir 2 tablespoons through a batch of hummus (page 200–1) for a spicy kick.

WITH GREEN VEGETABLES
Add a dash of olive oil, a little salt and 1 tablespoon harissa to steamed broccoli or charred green beans.

INDIAN EGGPLANT KASUNDI

This is our all-time favourite Cornersmith relish. We serve this with poached eggs, curries, rice dishes, grilled vegetables and meats. It gets better over time so if you can, let it sit for a week before you eat it.

Preheat the oven to 200°C (400°F/Gas mark 6). Prick 500 g (1 lb 2 oz) eggplants (aubergines) all over with a fork, then rub them with vegetable oil. Place on a baking tray, then roast in the oven for 20–30 minutes or until the eggplants are tender. While they are roasting, thinly slice 1 large onion. Heat 2 tablespoons vegetable oil in a frying pan over medium heat and sauté the onion for 8–10 minutes until soft and sweet, then add ½ teaspoon ground coriander, 1 teaspoon ground cumin, ½ teaspoon ground turmeric, ½ teaspoon chilli flakes, 1 teaspoon salt, 2 minced garlic cloves and 30 g (1 oz) grated ginger. Sauté for 1–2 minutes until fragrant. Roughly chop the roasted eggplants, skins and all, and add them to the pan with ¾ cup (185 ml) red or white wine vinegar and ⅓ cup (75 g) caster (superfine) sugar. Cook for 15–20 minutes, until thick and glossy, then transfer to a clean jar while hot. Store in the fridge for up to 3 months or follow the sterilising and heat-processing instructions on page 278 for longer storage.

Makes 1 x 500 ml (17 fl oz) jar

STIR-FRIED CHILLI EGGPLANT

This is a fiery dish somewhere between a curry and a stir-fry. It is best to use the smaller Lebanese eggplants (aubergines) for this, but larger eggplants cut into strips also work well.

In a food processor, place 1 small roughly chopped onion, 8 garlic cloves, 4 roughly chopped green chillies, 3 cm (1¼ inch) piece chopped fresh turmeric or 1 teaspoon ground turmeric, 3 cm (1¼ inch) piece chopped ginger and ½ teaspoon salt and blend to a paste. Heat 160 ml (5¼ fl oz) vegetable oil in a heavy-based frying pan over medium heat. Add the spice paste and sauté for 2 minutes. Meanwhile, slice 500 g (1 lb 2 oz) Lebanese eggplants in half lengthways. Add the eggplant to the spice paste and stir for 3 minutes. Add 3 tablespoons lemon juice and 1 tablespoon brown sugar, then reduce the heat to low, partially cover and cook for 20 minutes or until the eggplant is very soft. Season to taste, and serve with rice and natural yoghurt.

Serves 2–3

HARISSA-ROASTED EGGPLANT

Smother eggplants (aubergines) in harissa to make this bold side.

Preheat the oven to 180°C (350°F/Gas mark 4). Quarter 2 eggplants and cut lengthways into 6 wedges. Place in a mixing bowl and stir through 3 tablespoons harissa and 3 tablespoons olive oil. Mix well to ensure the eggplant is well coated. Spread the eggplant out on a baking tray and roast for 30 minutes or until soft inside and starting to brown. Allow to cool. Combine ⅓ cup (90 g) natural yoghurt, the zest and juice of ½ lemon, 1 minced garlic clove and ¼ teaspoon sumac in a small bowl. Place the eggplant on a serving plate, drizzle over the yoghurt dressing and top with soft herbs.

Serves 4 as a side

CHILLI

There would be considerably less heat in the kitchen if it weren't for yet another ingredient hailing from Central America – the chilli.

The fiery relative of capsicums (peppers), a chilli's heat comes from the chemical compound capsaicin, found in the membrane which holds the seeds. This heat varies with variety and growing conditions: the drier the climate, the less water in the chilli, the more intense the heat. Chilli intensity is usually measured on the Scoville Scale, which rates the burning sensation that's produced by eating a chilli. At the very bottom of the scale are capsicums, with no capsaicin. Moving up the scale are jalapeños which are relatively sweet and mild, small bird's eye chillies, and then all the way to the hellfire of a Carolina reaper – a chilli we have not, and never will, try. The long green and red chillies that are most often found at the market usually have a mid-level heat (though this is very subjective as one person's hot chilli is another person's baby food). Green chillies are not fully ripened and have a milder intensity, while red chillies are fully ripe and at their maximum intensity. They can be swapped according to your tolerance.

While chillies are rich sources of vitamins B, C and K, they tend to be eaten in such small quantities that they don't make much of a nutritional contribution to our diets. The capsaicin that gives chilli its heat is used in topical medicines as a pain relief, which may have the same properties when eaten.

Store fresh chillies in an airtight container in the fridge for 2–3 weeks. Keep in mind that the thinner the skin of the chilli, the shorter its shelf life. Because chillies have such a short season, drying them is an essential practice, especially in Mexico where they are used year round. Make your own chilli flakes by following the steps described opposite.

GOES WITH ...

Get past the heat of a chilli and you will discover complex flavours that range from green and fruity to deep and smoky. Fresh or dried, even a small amount of chilli will add depth and an unexpected balance of flavour to many dishes. The fire of chillies and the acid of tomatoes can become as explosive a combination as you want. A little chilli and a lot of tomato adds an edge to passata (page 247) or tomato ketchup (page 249), while adding a lot of chilli to tomatoes will make a simple salsa that can have you crying lava tears, in the best possible way. Chilli brings the missing heat to its cousin the capsicum. It also gives bite to silky eggplant, counters the bitterness of olives and, combined with garlic and olive oil, becomes a pasta sauce unto itself. Chilli and chocolate is an earthy combination that's used in savoury Mexican mole sauces; try adding a pinch of chilli powder to chocolate desserts when you feel like living dangerously.

USE IT ALL

If you have a glut of chillies in your garden, follow any of the preserving recipes in this book for year-round heat. And if you only have one or two chillies left, pop them in a small jar, cover with your favourite vinegar, let them infuse for a few weeks and use for salad dressings with a kick.

EASY SAMBAL

We love this recipe because it's so simple and flavoursome, and you can use up all the bits in the fridge. Grated ginger would also work well here, as would fresh coriander (cilantro), lime or lemon zest and a little lemongrass.

Place 1 roughly chopped tomato, 4–8 chopped chillies of your choice (depending on how hot you like it), 3 peeled garlic cloves and a few shallots (or ¼–½ onion) in a food processor and briefly blitz until everything is roughly chopped. Heat 2 tablespoons vegetable or sunflower oil in a frying pan over medium heat and add the chilli mixture, along with 2 tablespoons brown sugar, ½ teaspoon salt and 1 tablespoon red wine vinegar. Cook, stirring often, for about 15 minutes, until the sambal is rich and thick. Spoon into a clean jar or airtight container and store in the fridge for a few weeks.

Makes about ½ cup

MAKE YOUR OWN CHILLI FLAKES

Drying chillies is the best way to preserve any excess, especially if you have a prolific chilli bush. When the season is at its height, we fill the oven and dehydrator with chillies and make our own chilli flakes and chilli powder to use for the rest of the year.

If you have a dehydrator, pop whole chillies in overnight and dehydrate following the manufacturer's instructions.

If you're drying chillies in the oven, cut them in half lengthways, then spread out on a baking tray or a wire rack. If you have a fan-forced oven, press the chilli between two wire racks, then put the racks on a baking tray to stop the chilli moving around. A low and slow oven set to around 60°C (140°F/ Gas mark ¼) will maintain the colour of the chilli, but it can take up to 6 hours or so to dehydrate. If you want to speed up the process, increase the heat to about 110°C (230°F/Gas mark ½) and leave the oven door slightly ajar to get some air in there. Keep an eye on the chillies so they don't burn, and dehydrate for 1–3 hours depending on the size of the chillies. You need them to be completely dry and brittle before turning into flakes. Allow to cool completely,

then either break them up with your hands (wearing gloves!) or blitz them in a coffee or spice grinder into flakes or powder. Store in airtight containers or jars for up to 12 months. You can also add equal parts chilli and salt to make a delicious spicy seasoning. Feel free to add extra flavours, such as crushed fennel seeds, dried orange or lemon powder (see page 204) or dried herbs.

FERMENTED CHILLI PASTE

Fermented chilli pastes and sauces have a vibrancy and complexity that goes well beyond their heat. They need a bit more care in the fermenting process, but it is well worth the effort.

In a food processor, place 200 g (7 oz) roughly chopped long red chillies, 3 chopped garlic cloves, 3 cm (1¼ inch) piece chopped ginger, ¼ teaspoon salt and ¼ teaspoon caster (superfine) sugar. Pulse until you have a thick paste with a little texture. Transfer to a clean 300 ml (10½ fl oz) jar, top with 1 tablespoon water and seal with a lid (see page 278 for further instructions on fermenting). Leave at room temperature for 3–7 days, opening the jar every second day to let out any carbon dioxide building up inside. Once it tastes spicy and mildly sour, store it in the fridge where it will keep for up to 6 months.

Makes 1 x 200 ml (7 fl oz) jar

BASIL

Basil's sweet clove perfume fills a room on a warm day, and its heady flavour makes a good cook out of anyone. Its seasonal availability should be respected; buying a sad and expensive bunch of basil in winter is something to be avoided.

Basil's ability to easily cross-breed and voyage over boundaries has resulted in many cultivars, with scents ranging from cinnamon and lemon to the liquorice notes of Thai basil. Seek out difference when you can and try to grow some of the harder-to-come-by varieties of this much-loved herb.

Basil is very high in vitamin K and magnesium, and its essential oils are known to have anti-inflammatory properties as well as reducing blood sugar.

The less you cook basil the better. Don't add basil at the beginning of any cooking process. Keep things as fresh as possible and you will retain basil's complex flavour. Tear basil or chop it with a sharp knife so as not to bruise the leaves.

Notoriously hard to keep fresh, basil will go some distance if you store it carefully. The preferred method is to snip the ends off the stalks and keep it in a glass of water, like you would flowers. Place a plastic bag loosely over the bunch, keep it on the kitchen bench and it will last up to 1 week. Another method is to wrap it in a damp tea towel, then place it in a plastic bag in the fridge where it will keep for up to 4 days.

GOES WITH ...

Depending on the company it keeps, basil can be spicy or grassy in flavour. The pairing of basil and tomato is more like a good marriage: complementary and reliable but passionate. Tomato's acidity is balanced by the warmth of basil. Red meat brings out basil's clove and anise flavour. Paired with egg and chicken, basil tastes fresh – together they make the best chicken and basil mayonnaise sandwich. Basil goes well with creamy textures, whether that's soft nuts, such as pine nuts and walnuts, or cheese. Basil is also an essential addition to dishes made with eggplant (aubergine), zucchini (courgette) and capsicum (pepper), as they all come into season together.

USE IT ALL

We make a herbaceous basil and black pepper syrup when we have basil stems left over from making salad or pesto. Follow the mango skin syrup recipe on page 85, adding a tablespoon of black peppercorns when simmering. Drizzle over fruit salad, mango or grilled nectarines, use as a cocktail syrup or add to sparkling water on a booze-free day.

BASIL PESTO

This book is full of pestos, but how can we write about basil without including the classic pesto Genovese. The word pesto means 'to pound' and refers to the preferred method of using a mortar and pestle to make pesto. This recipe is based on the great doyenne of Italian cooking Marcella Hazan's pesto, which uses a food processor (and if she gives you permission to use a food processor then, truly, it is allowed).

Wash and thoroughly dry the leaves of 1 bunch of basil. Place the basil in a food processor with ½ teaspoon salt, 2 crushed garlic cloves, 3 tablespoons pine nuts and 160 ml (5¼ fl oz) olive oil. Blend together until combined and smooth in texture. Scrape the pesto into a bowl and stir through 40 g (1½ oz) finely grated parmesan cheese. Use the pesto as a pasta sauce, served over roasted vegetables or as a dip.

Makes 1 cup (200 g)

BASIL ICE CREAM

This ice cream treads a fine line between fresh and decadent – it is somehow both at once – plus it is super easy to make if you have an ice-cream machine. We make this recipe by hand, which takes a little longer, but it is worth the effort. Serve a scoop in a fancy glass after dinner.

Place 300 g (10½ oz) caster (superfine) sugar and the picked leaves of 1 large bunch of basil in a food processor and blitz until you have a fragrant coarse mixture. Add 250 g (9 oz) mascarpone and 4 cups (1 litre) natural yoghurt and mix on low speed. Scrape the mixture into an 8 cup (2 litre) plastic container and freeze for 1 hour. Remove the container from the freezer and thoroughly stir the ice cream. Return it to the freezer and repeat this process every hour for 6 hours until the ice cream sets. Once finished, leave the ice cream to freeze for at least 5 hours.

Makes 4 cups (1 litre)

BASIL-INFUSED BOOZE

Infusing alcohol is Alex's favourite party trick. It looks and tastes impressive but only takes a few minutes, and is an excellent way to use up excess herbs, citrus peels and ripe fruits. In summer, this basil-infused vodka makes a fresh herbaceous cocktail or it can be drizzled over fruits for a grown-up dessert. We drink it over ice with a little soda on hot summer nights. The softness of the basil leaves means you should only infuse them for 2–3 days. This recipe also works really well with mint.

Place 1 bunch basil, including stems and leaves (or use whatever you have left over), ¼ cup (55 g) caster (superfine) sugar and 2 cups (500 ml) vodka in a clean jar. Cover and leave on the bench for 2–3 days, gently swirling the jar now and again to dissolve the sugar. Taste as you go and feel free to add more sugar if you like it a little sweeter. When you're happy with the basil flavour, strain the vodka, then compost your basil or muddle it straight into a cocktail!

Makes 2 cups (500 ml)

MINCE

Economical, versatile and convenient, minced (ground) meat is the base for a lot of family favourites. In a sustainable kitchen and in a future where we are all looking to reduce our meat consumption, mince might be the easiest place to start.

Mince itself is a solution to using up the cuts of the animal that are either too tough or too small to be eaten alone. These lesser cuts can account for up to 40 per cent of an animal, and mincing them changes their texture and makes it possible to enjoy the flavour. By combining mince with vegetables or using it wisely to season otherwise vegetarian meals, you can make 1 kg (2 lb 4 oz) mince stretch over many meals. When buying any meat, pay attention to where it has come from. Try to buy pasture-raised meats from reputable butchers or markets when you can, and know that huge trays of mince at very low prices come with environmental and labour costs that are not reflected at the checkout.

Mince has a very short shelf life due to its large surface area. When mince is fresh, it has a red surface, so to extend its shelf life and make it appear more fresh than it actually is, some producers and retailers add sulphates, which prolongs that red surface colour. This is illegal but widespread. Buy your mince from a butcher so you can be sure it is additive free, and try to avoid supermarket trays of mince, as they just create more packaging in the world. If you do buy them, make sure there is no excess liquid around the meat as this indicates that the meat has not been kept at a cold-enough temperature. If you can, make the mince you buy last over a few meals.

Mince should be kept in the bottom of the fridge for up to 2 days. If you want to keep it for longer, put it in a zip-lock bag, flatten the meat out evenly and store in the freezer for up to 3 months. Thaw in the fridge overnight.

Here, we include recipes for making 'reduced-meat' koftas and hamburgers, and an excellent spiced mince that can be used as a condiment on anything from flatbreads to baked potatoes, and in pasta, wraps and rice dishes to add meaty flavours without making it the main event.

MINCE AS A CONDIMENT

Using meat – whether it's red meat, poultry or seafood – as a seasoning or condiment is not new, but it just might be the future of meat eating. Most traditional styles of cooking use meat alongside grains, legumes and vegetables to enhance flavour, and never as the main event. As we try and reduce our meat consumption, we increase vegetable-based ingredients and a world of possibilities opens up. Savour meat for its rich flavour, and make a little go a long way.

SPICED MINCE

This recipe takes inspiration from the Lebanese spiced lamb that is traditionally sprinkled over hummus. Full of flavour, this spiced mince is used as a condiment, adding a kick of spice, salt and fat to dishes. We like to sprinkle it over potato pizzas (page 139), stuff it into flatbreads with slaw (page 124) or use it as a layer in lasagne.

In a large bowl, place 400 g (14 oz) minced lamb, 3 minced garlic cloves, 1 teaspoon salt, 1 teaspoon ground cumin, 1 teaspoon dried thyme, ½ teaspoon cracked black pepper and a pinch of cayenne, if you like. Using your hands, mix everything together until thoroughly combined.

Heat a frying pan with 1 tablespoon olive or vegetable oil over medium–high heat. Add half the mince mixture and cook, stirring often, until brown, even charring at the edges (keep the heat high to avoid the meat stewing). Remove the first batch of mince, add another tablespoon of oil to the pan along with the remaining mince and cook in the same way. Combine both batches of mince in the hot frying pan and drizzle over 1 tablespoon honey and 1 tablespoon freshly squeezed lemon juice. Taste and balance the flavours and serve straight away or allow to cool and store in an airtight container in the fridge for 3–4 days.

Makes 1 cup

BEEF MINCE VARIATION

Replace the cumin with smoked paprika and use on bean nachos, baked potatoes and pasta with tomato sauce.

PORK MINCE VARIATION

Replace the cumin and dried thyme with 1 tablespoon freshly grated ginger, and replace the lemon juice with soy sauce. Use in the satay salad bowl on page 76, the lettuce cups on page 63 or the fried rice on page 159.

HOW TO USE MINCE AS A CONDIMENT

HUMMUS

To make hummus more of a centrepiece, use the recipe on page 200–1 and top with 200 g (7 oz) of the spiced mince and fresh herbs. Serve with flatbread and salad.

PIZZAS

Sprinkle 150 g (5½ oz) of the spiced mince over one of the potato pizzas on page 139 as soon as it comes out of the oven.

ON BRAISED OR CHARRED VEGETABLES

Serve 100–200 g (3½–7 oz) spiced mince over the slow-cooked tired green beans on page 167, the zucchini mash on page 251 or the harissa-roasted eggplant on page 259 to make a complete meal.

WRAPS

Top a salad wrap with pickles and 50 g (1¾ oz) spiced mince and pop in a lunchbox.

RICE DISHES

Add 200 g (7 oz) spiced mince to the tomato rice on page 249 or the pilaf on page 161.

LESS-MEAT MINCE FOR BURGERS

Makes 4–5 burger patties

You never really outgrow burgers. As a kid, they're your favourite food; as an adult they are pure nostalgia. Burgers are a symbol of good times: eating in the back garden; road trips; special treats. They are well loved in both our houses, and coming up with a recipe that was going to reduce the amount of meat we are eating and convince the kids was a challenge. In this recipe we keep it very simple: a small amount of mince, brown lentils (because we are sneaky), and seasoning that doesn't get carried away. You could use more aromatic herbs if you want a more sophisticated burger, or enjoy its simplicity and let the condiments do the talking.

1 onion, roughly chopped
3 garlic cloves, roughly chopped
1 handful torn parsley leaves
1 teaspoon salt
½ teaspoon freshly cracked
    black pepper
1½ teaspoons smoked paprika
1 teaspoon dried thyme or oregano
200 g (7 oz) canned or cooked
    brown lentils
300 g (10½ oz) minced (ground)
    meat of your choice
1 tablespoon Worcestershire sauce
½ cup (30 g) fresh breadcrumbs
    (or use the breadcrumb recipe
    on page 269)
Vegetable oil, for cooking

Place the onion, garlic, parsley, salt, pepper, paprika and dried herbs in a food processor and blitz until finely chopped. Add the lentils and blitz again until roughly combined – don't let it turn into a paste!

Tip the mixture into a bowl, then add the mince, Worcestershire sauce and breadcrumbs. Using your hands, mix together until combined. Form the mixture into 4 equal-sized burger patties and refrigerate for 30 minutes to 1 hour.

Heat a little vegetable oil in a frying pan over medium heat or heat a barbecue flat plate to medium and cook the burgers for 5 minutes on each side.

Serve on soft buns with pickles, chutney, mayonnaise, chilli jam, tomato sauce, leafy greens, slices of tomato, cheese … the works!

WHAT TO DO WITH LEFT-OVER BREAD

Whether it's the ends of a sliced loaf, some stale sourdough or the last hunk of a baguette, bread is one of the most wasted foods in households. However, ingenuity can turn a dry piece of bread into a salad or sauce or pudding. The chewiness and dryness of days-old bread is exactly what you need to soak up milk and eggs for French toast, or to hold its own under a generous slosh of olive oil in panzanella (page 270). Collect the odd ends and freeze them for when they will come in handy. There is no excuse to throw stale bread away.

BREADCRUMBS

Save the ends of your bread and store them in the freezer. Once you have enough, make this breadcrumb mix (although you can, of course, halve the recipe, or double or triple it). Use it to crumb vegetables and meat or the fish cakes on page 53. You can also use it to bind meatballs, burgers or sprinkle it on top of pasta.

Preheat the oven to 110°C (225°F/Gas mark ½) for 15 minutes. Blitz 250 g (9 oz) bread slices into rough breadcrumbs in a food processor, then spread out on a baking tray and dry in the oven for 30–60 minutes, depending on how large the breadcrumbs are. Keep checking to ensure that they don't burn! Allow to cool, then blitz again until you reach your preferred breadcrumb consistency. Transfer to a bowl and mix in 1 tablespoon smoked paprika, 1 tablespoon dried oregano, 1 teaspoon mustard powder, 1 teaspoon salt and 1 teaspoon cracked black pepper. Store in a glass jar in the freezer (don't worry, it won't become solid) for up to 6 months.

Makes about 2 cups (120 g)

CROUTONS

Another way to use up stale bread is to turn it into crispy fried croutons for salads, soups and snacks.

Preheat the oven to 180°C (350°F/Gas mark 4). Heat 3 tablespoons vegetable oil in a frying pan over medium–high heat. Add 3 minced garlic cloves and cook, stirring, for a few seconds, making sure the garlic doesn't burn. Throw in 1–2 cups (50–100 g) bread chunks and a good sprinkling of salt, then stir well to coat the bread in the garlicky salty oil. Once the bread is starting to crisp, transfer to a baking tray and bake for 3–5 minutes, until crisp but not hard. Allow to cool completely, then store in an airtight jar or container for 3 days.

Makes 1–2 cups (50–100 g)

CRACKERS FROM OLD BREAD

Transform inedible stale bread into the best crackers for cheese and dips.

Preheat the oven to 130°C (235°F/Gas mark ½). Combine 2 tablespoons olive oil, 1 teaspoon salt and 2 teaspoons dried herbs, such as rosemary, in a bowl. Dab 2–3 stale bread slices with the oil mixture and place on a baking tray. Dry in the oven for 30–40 minutes, until the bread is crisp. Store in an airtight container for 3 days.

FRENCH TOAST

What English speakers call French toast, the French call *pain perdu* (lost bread). This sounds quite melancholic, as if the last hunk of bread is going to be orphaned unless someone rescues it by soaking it in eggs and milk. You must use stale bread for French toast as fresh bread will fall apart when soaked.

Cut a hunk of stale bread into 4 slices about 1.5–3 cm (⅝–1¼ inch) thick. In a large bowl, whisk 3 tablespoons full-cream (whole) milk and 2 eggs, adding a pinch of ground cinnamon if you like. Soak the bread slices, one at a time, for about 1 minute, turning the slices over now and again. Melt 1 tablespoon butter in a frying pan over medium heat and fry for 2 minutes on each side or until the bread is golden brown. Serve with a drizzle of honey or jam, maple syrup or the orange zest butter on page 203.

Makes 4

PANZANELLA

Serves 4–6

Accompanied by a few glasses of wine on a hot night, this classic Italian salad is filling enough to be a meal on its own, or serve it alongside lasagne to keep the children happy. The stale bread soaks up the dressing so that every mouthful is full of flavour.

8 tomatoes, quartered
1 small red onion, very finely chopped
½ teaspoon caster (superfine) sugar
1 teaspoon salt, plus extra to serve
2 capsicums (peppers), halved
120 ml (4 fl oz) olive oil, plus extra for drizzling
2 tablespoons red wine vinegar
1 garlic clove, minced
200–300 g (7–10½ oz) stale bread torn into 5 cm (2 inch) pieces (focaccia, sourdough or a crusty white Italian loaf work best)
1 tablespoon capers, drained and rinsed, chopped
1 bunch basil, leaves picked and torn
Freshly cracked black pepper

Preheat the oven to 180°C (350°F/Gas mark 4).

Combine the tomato and onion in a bowl and sprinkle over the sugar and half the salt. Set aside at room temperature.

Place the capsicum on a baking tray, skin side up, and drizzle over 2 tablespoons of the olive oil. Roast for 30–45 minutes until soft and blistered, then remove from the oven and allow to cool. Remove the skin, slice the capsicum into strips and set aside.

In a small bowl, combine the red wine vinegar, garlic and remaining olive oil and salt and toss through the bread.

Strain the tomato and onion very well, then place in a large salad bowl. Add all the remaining ingredients and toss gently to combine. Drizzle with a little extra olive oil, season with salt and pepper and serve immediately.

STONE FRUITS

Peaches and nectarines, plums and apricots ...
we wait all year for stone fruit's fleeting season,
and when it arrives we celebrate. While all stone
fruits have distinct flavours, we tend to buy peaches,
nectarines, plums and apricots because they can
be used interchangeably in recipes. Stone fruits
can be either clingstone or freestone. Clingstone
means that the flesh doesn't easily come away from
the stone, and these fruits are often preferred by
preservers as the fruit tends to be sweeter and more
tender, making them perfect for jam. But, if you've
ever prepared 10 kg (22 lb) of apricots for bottling,
you will know the sweet relief of a freestone fruit.
If you are at the markets, you can ask the seller what
kind you are buying, otherwise it is a gamble – but
delicious either way.

Stone fruits have significant amounts of vitamins
A and C and potassium. Ripe stone fruits are fragrant
and will yield when you give them a light squeeze.
They are often sold a little under-ripe, so keep them
in the fruit bowl at room temperature until ripe. You
can speed up this process by placing stone fruits in
a paper bag, out of direct sunlight for a day or two.
Keep ripe fruit in the fridge for up to 1 week.

GO WITH ...

While we swap peaches for apricots willy nilly in
recipes, we do pair different stone fruits with different
flavours. Here is a guide.

PEACHES AND NECTARINES

The differences between peaches and nectarines are
subtle but detectable. Peaches are fuzzy and blushing
with notes of almond, while nectarines have a smooth
skin like a sunset and can be almost tropical in flavour.
Both go very well with cream, yoghurt and ice cream,
along with other summer fruits, such as mangoes and
cherries. Combined with tomatoes, the traces of wine
in peaches and nectarines seem coaxed out; in baking
and jam-making, pair them with fresh flavours like
lime, lemon, basil, mint and cardamom.

PLUMS

Deep in flavour, earthy and a little boozy when fully
ripe, plums are one of the more dramatic stone fruits.
They pair well with intense flavours, such as black
pepper, cardamom, cinnamon, red wine, ginger and
chocolate. Like all stone fruits, plums love dairy –
stewed plums on ice cream is a simple treat.

APRICOTS

When properly ripe, apricots are creamy, with hints
of almond and lavender. Don't eat apricots until they
are soft and all their sugars have developed, otherwise
their flesh is floury. Apricots go well with cherries
and other stone fruits, along with a little splash of
rosewater or brandy. They also pair well with savoury
food, such as chicken, pork or onions. Dried apricots
go particularly well with both hard and soft cheeses.

USE IT ALL

Never throw bruised, over-ripe fruit in the bin.
Try the homemade jam on page 274.

PLUM AND HONEY ICE BLOCKS

We've been making these ice blocks since the kids were small, and we still make them every summer for old time's sake. Plums make a great colour, but these ice blocks are also delicious with peaches, nectarines or even mangoes.

Roughly chop 500–600 g (1 lb 2 oz–1 lb 5 oz) ripe plums and discard the stones. Place the fruit in a saucepan with 3 tablespoons water and ¼ cup (90 g) honey. Cover and simmer over medium–low heat for 10 minutes or until the fruit starts to collapse. Remove the lid, mash the fruit with a fork, then simmer for another 10 minutes. Set aside to cool slightly, then blitz the mixture using a hand-held blender to make a smooth purée. Set aside to completely cool.

Combine ½ cup (125 g) natural yoghurt with 1 tablespoon brown sugar. Either stir the fruit purée into the yoghurt before spooning into 6–8 ice-block moulds, or layer the yoghurt and fruit purée into the moulds. Freeze overnight and serve.

Makes 6–8 ice blocks

SIMPLE PEACH SALAD

Some of the finest salads have the fewest ingredients. In this salad, it is the technique of grilling peaches to give them a sweet smokiness that brings a lot of flavour. Tarragon and rocket are fragrant and just bitter enough to balance things out beautifully.

Combine 1 bunch large-leaf rocket or 3–4 cups (150–200 g) rocket leaves, ½ bunch tarragon leaves and 4 peach halves grilled with honey, salt and chilli (see recipe opposite) and cut into wedges. Dress with your best-quality olive oil, salt and cracked black pepper and a generous drizzle of balsamic vinegar.

Serves 3–4 as a side

GRILLED PEACHES WITH HONEY AND SALT

Serve these grilled peaches with grilled meats or in a simple salad.

Halve 2–3 firm but ripe peaches and discard the stones. Place the peach halves in a bowl and drizzle with a little olive oil, making sure all sides are lightly coated in the oil. Heat a griddle pan or barbecue grill plate to medium, then grill the peach halves, cut side down, for 3 minutes or until slightly tender, with black grill-marks. Turn the peach halves over and grill for another 3–4 minutes, then, using tongs to hold the peach halves, grill the sides for 1–2 minutes or until juicy and tender but not falling apart. Transfer to a plate and immediately drizzle with honey, salt and chilli flakes.

For a sweet version, add honey, a little butter and ground cinnamon to the hot grilled peaches and serve with yoghurt for breakfast.

HOMEMADE JAM

Makes about 2 cups (640 g)

Few things beat homemade apricot jam on toast with lots of butter. Alex makes this once every few weeks during stone-fruit season, when apricots or peaches are cheap or they're getting a bit too soft in the fruit bowl. You can, of course, use any stone fruit that you have to hand, and feel free to swap out the orange for any other citrus that you have. We serve this jam on French toast for breakfast and use it in the scrolls on page 146.

This simple recipe doesn't require sterilised jars – it's fridge jam, made to be eaten right away. It will keep for up to 1 month in a clean jar or container in the fridge.

1 kg (2 lb 4 oz) pitted stone fruit
  apricots
  plums
  nectarines
  peaches
  cherries
Citrus zest and juice
  1 orange
  1 lemon
  1 lime
Spices and herbs
  grated ginger
  ground cinnamon
  ground cardamom
  rosemary leaves
  thyme
1 cup (230 g) caster (superfine)
  sugar

Place the fruit in a wide saucepan and add the citrus zest and juice, 1 teaspoon ground spices or 1–2 tablespoons chopped herbs along with ½ cup (125 ml) water. Simmer over very low heat for 15–20 minutes, until the fruit is soft and collapsed. If it's looking too pulpy, add an extra 3 tablespoons water, along with the sugar.

Stir to dissolve the sugar, then bring to a simmer and cook, stirring occasionally, for 15–25 minutes until thick and glossy. Allow the jam to cool for 5–10 minutes before carefully spooning into clean jars. Wipe the rims clean with clean paper towel and seal immediately. Store in the fridge for up to 1 month.

COMBINATIONS WE LIKE

- Plum, lemon and ginger
- Apricot, orange and ground cardamom
- Nectarine and lime
- Peach, lemon and rosemary.

CORNERSMITH MUFFINS

Makes 12

Baking muffins kind of just happens to you as a parent. One day you find yourself obsessed with snacks. Enter the muffin. Even if you aren't a baker, they are the baked good that can be whipped up quickly and easily. As for what goes in a muffin, may we suggest that you avoid getting too earthy. Use the fruits or vegetables that are everyone's favourite and finish off the more delicious pantry strays, such as coconut, chocolate chips, ground spices, seeds and nuts. Stick to what you know is delicious and these muffins will always be the answer to lunchbox and snack dilemmas.

380 g (13½ oz) self-raising flour
1 cup (230 g) caster (superfine)
  sugar
1 egg
150 ml (5 fl oz) flavourless oil, such
  as vegetable or sunflower oil
1 cup (250 ml) full-cream (whole)
  milk
200 g (7 oz) chopped fruit
  or squeezed and dried grated
  vegetables
  apples
  pears
  stone fruit
  berries
  zucchini (courgette)
  pumpkin (squash)
100 g (3½ oz) pantry strays
  nuts
  seeds
  coconut flakes
  chocolate chips
  sultanas (golden raisins)

Preheat the oven to 180°C (350°F/Gas mark 4). Whisk the flour and sugar in a bowl and set aside. In a separate bowl, beat the egg, then slowly whisk in the oil. Gradually add the milk, whisking as you go.

Make a well in the centre of the flour mixture and slowly incorporate the wet mixture. Gently stir in your choice of fruit or vegetables and pantry strays.

Divide the batter among 12 greased holes of a standard muffin tin (or line the holes with paper cases) and bake for 20–25 minutes or until a skewer inserted into one of the muffins comes out clean.

COMBINATIONS WE LIKE

- Nectarine and coconut
- Plum and almond
- Cherry and chocolate chip
- Raspberry and grated apple
- Zucchini (courgette) and sultana (golden raisin).

STERILISING PRESERVING JARS OR BOTTLES

To sterilise jars or bottles, give them a wash in hot soapy water and a good rinse, then place upright in a baking dish in a cold oven. Heat the oven to 110°C (225°F/Gas mark ½) and, once it has reached temperature, leave the jars in the oven for 10–15 minutes, or until completely dry, then remove them carefully. For hot packing, pour the hot mixture straight into the hot jars; for cold packing, let the jars cool before adding your pickles or preserves. To sterilise the lids, place them in a large saucepan of boiling water for 5 minutes, then drain and dry with clean paper towels, or leave them on a wire rack to air dry. Make sure they are completely dry before using.

HEAT PROCESSING

This process uses heat to stop the growth of bacteria, removes oxygen from the jar and seals the lid, making your preserves safe to store in the pantry rather than the fridge. Get the biggest pan you have, such as a stockpot, and put it on the stovetop. Lay a folded tea towel in the bottom of the pan, then sit your filled, lidded jars on the tea towel. Make sure your lids aren't on too tight! Roughly match the water temperature to the temperature of the jars (to help prevent breakages from thermal shock), then pour in enough water to cover the jars, either completely or at least until three-quarters submerged. Bring to the boil over medium heat. The heat-processing times are given in the recipes and start from boiling point. Carefully remove the hot jars from the water using preserving clamps or a very thick cloth. Line your jars up on the benchtop and let them sit overnight. As they cool, a vacuum will form inside each jar and suck down the lid, sealing them securely. In the morning, the lids should be concave, meaning they are sealed. These jars can be safely stored in the pantry for up to 2 years. If you have concerns about the seal of any of your jars (sometimes a couple of jars fail to seal correctly), store them in the fridge and use their contents within a few weeks.

FERMENTATION

Lacto-fermentation is the method of fermentation used in this book to make sauerkraut, kimchi, brine pickles and hot sauce. During lacto-fermentation, lactobacillus bacteria present on the surface of fruit and vegetables convert carbohydrates into lactic acid. This lactic acid not only preserves produce, but it also gives fermented food its distinct sour flavour. For successful lacto-fermentation all you need are clean jars, the produce you want to ferment, pure salt (that is, salt with no additives), and water if you are making a brine. During the fermentation process, you need to store your jar/s out of direct sunlight and where you will remember to check on it. Fermentation will begin immediately but the flavour of fermented foods takes some time to develop. We recommend between 2 days and 2 weeks, depending on the weather (food will ferment more quickly in warmer months), and how punchy you like things to taste. Try your ferments after a few days and see what you think. One of the by-products of fermentation is carbon dioxide and this will build up in a sealed jar. Release the carbon dioxide by opening the jar/s every few days. Once you are happy with the flavour of your ferments, pop them in the refrigerator and they will last a few months.

ACKNOWLEDGEMENTS

This book began in our homes, cooking for our children and trying to answer that eternal question: what's for dinner? So, thank you to Maeve and Max, Felix and Zelda for inspiring a lifetime of breakfasts, lunches, dinners and endless snacks. This book is part of your collective histories and something we hope you will carry into your futures. Knowing how to feed yourself well is one of the best life skills we can give you.

We would both like to thank our mothers, Lizzie and Margie, for instilling in us the importance of sitting around the dinner table, sharing food and making memories. This book is a mish-mash of all the meals you've made for us over the years.

We are also indebted to the community of chefs, teachers, preservers and students we have spent time with at Cornersmith. We thank you all for making us more thoughtful cooks in our homes and at work, and many of these recipes have been inspired by your talents. We are particularly grateful to our friend and colleague, Greer Rochford, who has generously shared her recipes, expertise and time in the making of this book. And a big thank you to Clare Barnes, James Grant and Maddy Dobbins. And to William Fraser for a careful eye and being a grammar taskmaster at the last minute.

This book would never have made it out of our chaotic heads without the hardworking team of super women at Murdoch Books: Jane Morrow, Virginia Birch, Megan Pigott, Lucy Heaver and Kirby Armstrong. Thank you for making sense of this insane jigsaw puzzle, championing our ideas and reining us in when needed. We loved working on this book with you.

To photographer Cath Muscat and stylist Vanessa Austin, we will never forget the two-week bubble we spent with you making this book. You made all the hard work a joy and we laughed every day.

And finally, a giant high-five to each other. We wrote this book while working fulltime, raising children and homeschooling during a pandemic. WE DID IT!

INDEX

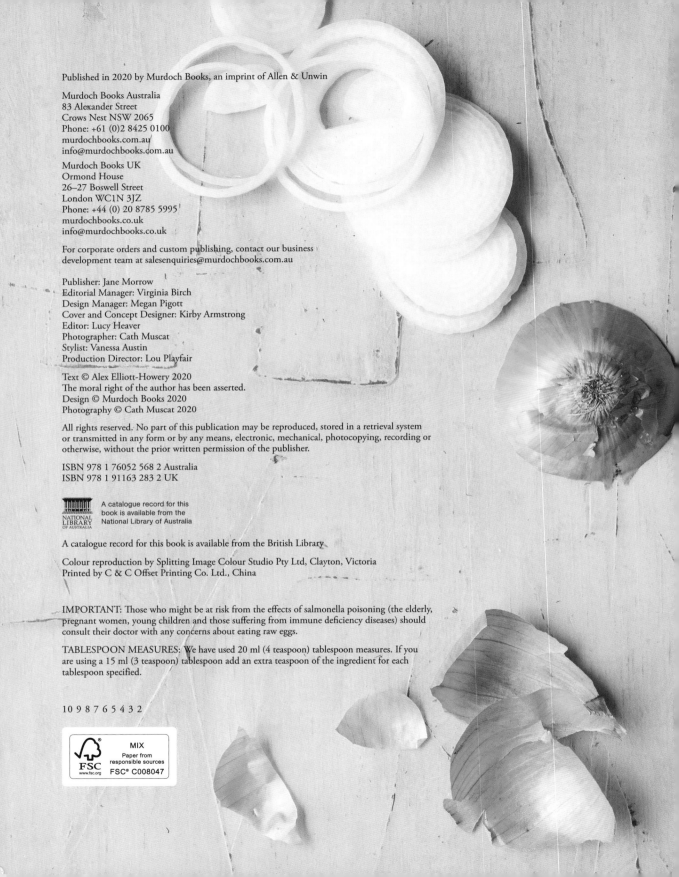

Published in 2020 by Murdoch Books, an imprint of Allen & Unwin

Murdoch Books Australia
83 Alexander Street
Crows Nest NSW 2065
Phone: +61 (0)2 8425 0100
murdochbooks.com.au
info@murdochbooks.com.au

Murdoch Books UK
Ormond House
26–27 Boswell Street
London WC1N 3JZ
Phone: +44 (0) 20 8785 5995
murdochbooks.co.uk
info@murdochbooks.co.uk

For corporate orders and custom publishing, contact our business
development team at salesenquiries@murdochbooks.com.au

Publisher: Jane Morrow
Editorial Manager: Virginia Birch
Design Manager: Megan Pigott
Cover and Concept Designer: Kirby Armstrong
Editor: Lucy Heaver
Photographer: Cath Muscat
Stylist: Vanessa Austin
Production Director: Lou Playfair

ISBN 978 1 76052 568 2 Australia
ISBN 978 1 91163 283 2 UK

A catalogue record for this
book is available from the
National Library of Australia

A catalogue record for this book is available from the British Library

Colour reproduction by Splitting Image Colour Studio Pty Ltd, Clayton, Victoria
Printed by C & C Offset Printing Co. Ltd., China

IMPORTANT: Those who might be at risk from the effects of salmonella poisoning (the elderly,
pregnant women, young children and those suffering from immune deficiency diseases) should
consult their doctor with any concerns about eating raw eggs.

TABLESPOON MEASURES: We have used 20 ml (4 teaspoon) tablespoon measures. If you
are using a 15 ml (3 teaspoon) tablespoon add an extra teaspoon of the ingredient for each
tablespoon specified.

10 9 8 7 6 5 4 3 2

MIX
Paper from
responsible sources
FSC® C008047